PAUL D. BARCHITTA

MARKET ME

How to Market Your Idea ... Your Brand ... and Yourself!

iUniverse

MARKET ME
HOW TO MARKET YOUR IDEA … YOUR BRAND … AND YOURSELF!

iUniverse books may be ordered through booksellers or by contacting:

iUniverse
1663 Liberty Drive
Bloomington, IN 47403
www.iuniverse.com
1-800-Authors (1-800-288-4677)

ISBN: 978-1-5320-7458-5 (sc)
ISBN: 978-1-5320-7532-2 (hc)
ISBN: 978-1-5320-7459-2 (e)

Library of Congress Control Number: 2019942701

Print information available on the last page.

iUniverse rev. date: 06/13/2019

Contents

Dedication

L ife is about doing something with the opportunities that you
have been given. This book is dedicated to my brother Michael
Christopher Barchitta who never had the chances or opportunities
in his life that were given to me.

This one is for you Bro!

About the Author

P aul D. Barchitta is a Tenured Professor in the Maritime Transportation/Business Department at the United States Merchant Marine Academy, located in Kings Point, NY. The U.S. Merchant Marine Academy is one of five Federal Service Academies including, West Point (Army), Annapolis (Navy), Air Force, Coast Guard, and Merchant Marine.

Prior to accepting this appointment, he was as a tenured faculty member for The City University of New York (CUNY) at Queensborough Community College. He has been a Professor at the following institutions in their respective Marketing/Business Administration Departments; SUNY College@ Old Westbury, Nassau Community College, Stockton College, Brooklyn College, LaGuardia Community College, Parsons School of Design, Wagner College, and St. John's University. He has also traveled to Taiwan on behalf of the American Education and Cultural Foundation to teach Marketing and Management.

He has a Post-Graduate, Advanced Certificate (30 Credits above an MBA) from a Doctoral program at NYU, in Corporate Training & Development. He has an M.B.A. in Marketing, and a B.S. in Finance from St. John's University.

He has over twenty five years of sales experience in the Medical Device and Healthcare/Hospital industry. He has been a Field Sales

Trainer and has sold a wide variety of medical products. Some of the product lines that he has sold are surgical stockings and lymphedema pumps that are prescribed for patients suffering from vascular disease, deep vein thrombosis equipment that prevents blood clots in patients during and post-surgery. Other lines have included general surgical instruments, spinal instruments, endoscopic, and laparoscopic instruments that are used in the operating room during surgery. Patient controlled anesthesia pumps that regulate the amount of pain medication that a patient receives after surgery, and syringe pumps that are used to deliver small, precise doses of medication to premature infants. He has been a President's Club Winner for sales quota achievement for three major, global, medical device manufacturer's including Johnson and Johnson's Surgical Instrument Division, Smith's Medical's Infusion Division, and Beiersdorf-Jobst's Vascular Division.

He is the author of *A Salesman Walks Into A Classroom...The Art of Sales Meets The Science of Selling*.

Introduction

I asked a professor for some career advice one day, career advice about becoming a professor. He said, "You are interested in this racket, I mean profession?" That perked my interest. How could a racket be a profession? When you love what you do and it does not feel like work, you have found your passion, your racket.

By my mid-twenties the light went off in my head that I wanted to teach at the university level. Being a college professor seemed like a cool job. I remember the day of illumination. I was giving a sales presentation (lecture) to a group of medical students at a medical school. This was common practice in the medical device industry, to indoctrinate young doctors on the features and benefits of your products that can help them treat their patients. It was a three hour sales presentation on vascular disease, effecting the circulation of the blood in your legs. There was some anatomy and physiology content along with my products being the solution to these described vascular disorders. It was more than a sales presentation, it was a lecture at a major university, in a lecture hall as the backdrop for my presentation. That was it. The light went off. That was the day I found my calling. Teaching at the university level. There was only one problem. Other than my day as a guest lecturer, I had no formal teaching experience or teacher training, let alone any credentials qualifying me for this occupation. I took the necessary credentialing steps and went back to graduate school to pursue my career as a professor. By the time I was ready to graduate I solicited the one hundred and fifteen colleges and universities in the New York Metropolitan area about my availability to teach at their institutions.

My angle was to teach sales classes in their respective business departments. Who was more qualified to teach classes in sales than a salesperson? Ask a marketing professor when was the last time they sold anything? Silence was a common response. I got hired to teach at two institutions a week after I completed graduate school. As a matter of fact I cashed my first check as a professor before completing my graduate degree, filling in as a substitute professor. I have not looked back since then. That was in 1996. The part-time, adjunct professor sales classes led to full time teaching, and I have been a full time tenured professor at TWO major universities in this country since the beginning of the new millennium. It has been a cool job!

The sales classes led to teaching other Marketing electives including the basic, introductory Marketing course taught at every academic institution of higher education in this country, known as Marketing 101.

While contemplating the idea about the writing of a book, a few thoughts went through my head. I had already published a book on sales, so what is next? It was an easy decision. I love Marketing! I am Marketing! I love to observe what I refer to as "Brilliant Marketing", whether it is an innovative commercial on television, a catchy jingle on the radio, a billboard that catches your eye, or the way that a salesperson conducts a sales presentation. I salute "Brilliant Marketing" and make notations about it throughout this book. What constitutes "Brilliant Marketing?" To quote the professor who explained why the profession is a racket, when he was asked what is the most effective form of Marketing his response was, "The one that works!" Brilliant Marketing is the one that works!

The umbrella of Marketing is so vast and so misunderstood that it needs an explanation. I need to chronicle Marketing from my perspective, from my point of view. That is the goal of this book, to explain the basic core concepts of what Marketing is and what it is not. To emphasize the importance of Marketing in your overall business strategy and to debunk the myth that all Marketing is deceptive, misleading and unethical.

There are a myriad Marketing topics addressed in this book that can serve as a blueprint for success from defining who is your customer, when and why they adopt your innovation, to the decision making process that the customer goes through. Who gets involved in the purchasing decision, what data is collected to help make the decision, and how to fight the stigma associated with unethical marketing practices are all discussed. Why taking a snapshot of your product offerings, why new products are the lifeblood of an organization, and the importance of developing a brand are examined as well.

Dissecting the methods of how products are promoted, from why advertising is a mentality to the effectiveness of the relationship that a salesperson can have with a customer to techniques that are devised to give the customer an incentive to buy the product now are reviewed. How to spin and manipulate a message, the utilization of Social Media, and how the distribution of products has evolved along with the importance of developing a global vision is argued.

My strength in the classroom is my ability to connect the Theory of Marketing with the practical aspects of Marketing in the real world. That is what my classroom lectures are all about. Marketing is such a broad topic that it is impossible to devote a justifiable amount of classroom lecture time to cover all of the aspects of Marketing, even in a Marketing 101 course. While designing my Marketing 101 course I scoured the dozens of marketing textbooks used at universities throughout this country and came up with a course curriculum and syllabus that addresses the basic foundation and building blocks that anchor a Marketing Strategy. For a topic to make it into my lectures there must be real world applications, content and theory that is not only described in a Marketing textbook but followed through, referenced and practiced every day in the real world. This book is a compilation of my Marketing 101 lectures supplemented with some of my real world Marketing adventures. Enjoy!

Marketing Is Awareness

On the first day of a Marketing 101 class I pose a few questions to my students. Why are you taking this course? What do you think this class is all about? What is your perception of Marketing? How would you define Marketing? I am amazed at the responses, some say advertising, commercials, and selling but no one ever responds with, "Marketing is Awareness!" I ask them to have an open mind and give me the opportunity over the next few months to change their perceptions of what they think Marketing is all about. On the last day of every class it is common for students to say, "I had no idea of what Marketing is all about." That is what I am asking you to do as you read this book, to place your previous preconceptions about Marketing to the side and look at Marketing through a different prism or different lens and with a different perspective.

If I was asked to define Marketing with one word and only one word I would use the word Awareness. Every product starts out as an idea in someone's head, the idea is brought to a drawing board, and the process of the Product Life Cycle begins. At this point the idea is still a secret, yet nobody knows about it. You can convert the idea into a product, but the "market", which is out there in the real world, has no idea that this is the greatest idea since sliced bread. This idea can be conceived in a basement, garage, an attic, or a sophisticated new product development laboratory. It does not matter, it is still a secret and the "market" needs to know about this fantastic invention or innovation. How do you do this? How do you let the world know about this gadget, widget or discovery? How do you make the "market" aware of this gadget, widget or discovery? That is the core of what Marketing is all about. Raising awareness. There are multiple formats that can get your message out there, and that is what Marketing is all about. Finding the right "Mix" to get the message out to a targeted audience who might have an interest in your next gadget, widget or discovery, is the fundamental purpose of this book. To expose the reader to the various methods, techniques and theories that will convert your invention, innovation or idea into a success.

The marketing department of a company is exploding with growth and opportunity. There was a time when the marketing department was not as significant as it is today, marketing was more of an afterthought. Marketing departments were diminutive, marketing budgets were scant. Companies were bottom line focused on manufacturing and finance. Oh, has that changed! Today, it is common to replace organizations with that type of strategy and direction with a strategy and direction that leads with a slant toward marketing.

SECTION 1

The Marketing Environment: Be Aware Of What Surrounds You

This section provides an overview of the Marketing Ecosystem

Chapter 1

The Four P's of Marketing

Marketing Mix

The "Marketing Mix", commonly referred to as the, "4 P's" of Marketing is where it all begins. Edmund James McCarthy was a Marketing professor and author. McCarthy proposed the theory of the "4 P's" Marketing Mix in his 1960 book, Basic Marketing: A Managerial Approach, which has been one of the major textbook publications utilized in marketing courses at universities since its publication. Not only has McCarthy's theory been studied at the university level for more than fifty years, corporations have implemented his theory and woven it into their overall Marketing strategy for decades. The Marketing Mix paradigm, in its famous version of the "4 P's", went all the way through the evolution of marketing theory being the object of discussion both in academic literature and managerial practice. It's a fact that the "4P's" is a milestone of marketing theory. McCarthy's Marketing Mix has been widely adopted through time by managers and academics, becoming a key element of marketing theory and practice (Dominici, 2009).[1]

---

[1] Dominici, G., (2009). From Marketing Mix to E-Marketing Mix: A Literature Overview and Classification. International Journal of Business and Management, 4(9) p.17-24.

Most marketing textbooks introduce the concept of the "Marketing Mix", at the end of chapter one and sometimes in chapter two. I do not agree with that. Once marketing has been defined as "Awareness", the next topic to discuss is the "Marketing Mix". It has to. It has to be discussed because everything in marketing starts with the "Marketing Mix". Everything in marketing somehow always brings you back to the "Marketing Mix". Every element of marketing is somehow a derivative, or component of the "Marketing Mix".

My first eye opening exposure, or the raising of my awareness of what the Marketing Mix was, occurred between my junior and senior year of college. I was a Finance major on the other side of the business spectrum with finance and accounting on one side and sales and marketing on the other. Marketing as a career, was nowhere on my radar. I had to take a Marketing 101 course to fill a graduation requirement. The professor was relentless about the concept of the 4 P's of marketing and beat it daily into our heads. I never got it out of my head. Product, Price, Promotion and Place.

When I run into people and they ask me, "What do you do for a living?" I respond with, "I am a Professor." The next question I always get is, "What do you teach?" I say, "I am a Marketing Professor." A common retort is, "Oh, I remember that class, the 4 P's of Marketing."

The "Marketing Mix" is the combination, or "mix" if you will, of all of the components that entail the marketing of a product. The four "P's" include Product, Price, Promotion and Place, (McCarthy, 1960).[2]

A Product is what you offer to the marketplace. Price is what you have to give up, or sacrifice to obtain or acquire the product. Promotion means how you alert, or get the word out about your product to the market. Place is defined as where and how do you obtain the product.

---

[2] McCarthy, E.J. (1960). Basic Marketing: A Managerial Approach. Irwin Publishing.

Is there an order to the "4 P's", is one more important than the other? That is what the "mix" is all about. Discovering what IS the correct "Marketing Mix" for your products is the challenge. The "4 P's" can be juggled, shifted, emphasized and deemphasized.

Product is the most inflexible of the "4 P's." Making product modifications and product improvements cannot be done at the snap of a finger. Altering manufacturing specifications cannot be done overnight. Price is the most flexible of the "4 P's" and you can snap your fingers and adjust your price on the spot. Changing the direction of your promotion and place strategies can be accomplished but fall somewhere between the strains associated with making a change to your product and the ease of dropping your price on the spot.

While there can be some variability among the importance of the "4 P's", if I was asked, "If you had one advantage in the marketplace over your competitors, meaning if you could have a competitive advantage at one "P", which one would you choose?"

It is a "Hands-Down" response. Give me the first "P" Product all day every day. When you have product advantages over your competition you have a substantial advantage over the competitive offering. When you have product advantages the first "P" leads the way, drives the bus, and can pave the way towards success. I say this from being on every side of the competitive selling spectrum. The other three "P's" follow suit when your competitive advantage begins with your product.

I have been through the ringer of the "Marketing Mix" where my competitive advantage was not the first "P" product and I would trade that advantage over any of the other "P's."

This does follow the traditional model of the "Marketing Mix" that was put in place in the early 1960s. Build the great product, the market will come to you. Exclusive distribution, where there were one or two retailers in a geographical area was the order of the day. Hunting and searching for the celebrated solution to your problem (product) was the norm. There is nothing wrong with that belief, strategy or practice, it worked. Today other factors have entered the conversation. There was an initial, huge gap between product and the other "3 P's", regardless of the significance or the order of the importance of the other "3 P's."

Today that gap has been closed. Competitive offerings or alternatives have flooded the marketplace and have closed the gap between product and the other "3 P's." Customers have choice. You are not the only game in town. While exclusive distribution still exists, the paradigm has been shifted to intensive distribution. Intensive distribution means as many outlets and avenues where a customer can solve their problem (product) as possible. This has opened the door for other elements of the "mix" to elevate their position and close the gap between product and the other "3 P's."

Price is now a factor. The question of "How Much" now has to be considered because the customer does have choice. It might not be an exact match, but the competitive advantage can be close enough to raise the curiosity of the customer to see what their alternatives are. Have you ever looked at a product and the first question that you ask is, "How much?" as opposed to, "What can this product do to help solve my problem?" That is a price question and the flooding of the market with competitive alternatives has contributed to the closing of the gap between product and price.

Promotion, or the vehicle in which you deliver your message, has now emerged as a major factor in the marketing of your product. In the previous model, word of mouth was the primary form of promotion. If you had a superior solution (product) to a customer's problem, eventually the word would get out and around about your product and ultimately the customer would end up at your doorstep. What proves to me that the gap between product and promotion has been narrowed are industries and occupations that never relied on promotion as part of their strategy have now joined the promotion game. Doctors and lawyers hardly ever advertised their services. If you were the best doctor or lawyer in town, the word got out that you were the best, and you would have a line of patients or clients out the door. In fact, in the previous model if you did engage in any form of promotion it was looked upon as a negative. If you were a doctor or lawyer that utilized promotion there was a stigma associated with this, that you were soliciting business. You were not good enough to generate enough business through word of mouth, so you needed to revert to promotion. Today the promotion of a healthcare or law practice has become an integral part of the success of that practice. The same goes for hospitals and universities. Today it is fashionable for these institutions to tout that they have the best nurses in town or that they are ranked as a top academic institution.

Place represented the most significant gap away from Product. In the traditional model Place was necessary but not significant. If the customer wanted the product they would search and find their solution (product). Place was the outlet where the product was purchased. This "P" has grown in importance in the new model more than any other of the "3 P's." Place has grown so much that in many marketing textbooks the word "Place" has been replaced by the word "Distribution."

The optimal situation is when you have competitive advantages in all of the "4 P's." I am not saying that this is rare, but I am saying that is difficult to achieve this position in the marketplace. An example would be a fast-food franchise that displays on their marquee that they have "billions" served. Any time that you have mass produced and sold over a billion units of a product you have "Product" advantages. When the price point of your product can be advertised as a "dollar menu" you are going to attract a noteworthy audience giving you "Price" advantages. When your tag line or slogan, "I'm loving it!" rolls off your tongue and is embedded into your memory you develop "Promotion" advantages. When you have retail outlets in every community in this country, and thousands of retail outlets globally, in close to one hundred countries, you have conquered the fourth "P" Place as well. This is how you become one of the most profitable franchises in American history, by having competitive advantages in all of the "4 P's."

What if you do not have all of these advantages? Most companies and most products do not. This has contributed to the development of the other "3 P's." Some have an advantage in only one "P", some have two, some perhaps three. The gap has closed between the first "P" product and the other elements of the "Marketing Mix." Companies have had to concede their deficiencies and weaknesses and focused on the development of their strengths which can be one, two or possibly three of the "4 P's."

Examples and permutations of the advantages and disadvantages of the "4 P's" are numerous. You can truly innovate a great product, but if it is priced too high or priced out of the market, where the substitute for this innovation is more cost effective, the innovation will not sell. Great product poor price!

As stated earlier it is all about awareness, you can have a superior product, but if the market is not aware of its superiority it will not sell. Great product poor promotion!

Customers are looking for convenience and availability, so the great product with limited or exclusive distribution can fall victim to a lesser competitor who has superior distribution (place). Great product poor place!

The flip side of all of this is true as well. What is the mission statement of mass merchandising? Great price, promotion, selection, availability, and distribution. Dollar stores are flooding the marketplace. Odd lot and off-price discount retailers are in abundance and are flourishing. Great price but poor product!

An example of great promotion but poor product is a movie trailer. A few clips from a movie can be spliced together, whether it is an action flick or comedy. With an aggressive advertising and promotional campaign a movie that is not filled with action or is not very funny can be cloaked in a shroud of promotion that can generate sales at the box office. Great promotion poor product!

There was a time when distribution was specialized. This type of distribution outlet sold this type of product and another distribution outlet sold a different type of product. Cross-distribution, where there are no boundaries for distribution rules the day. This strategy can overcome product deficiencies and can become profitable. Great place poor product!

Chapter 2

Who is Your Customer?

Demographics

Who is your customer? What an elementary question. Of course you need to know who your customer is. Sounds simple? Mistakes are made every day by marketers who fail to identify who their customer really is. Demography is the study of the vital statistics of a population. Demographics paint a picture of your average, every day typical customer. Demographics helps marketers answer questions of who to target with their promotional efforts.

You want the picture to be as clear as possible, black and white, with no gray area. A crystal clear portrait of your typical customer, not a fuzzy, cloudy or abstract portrait. Fuzzy, cloudy and abstract opens the door for mistakes.

Think of demographic variables as the paint for the canvas. The more complex the product, or the more niche of a market, the more variables (colors) that are needed. The more general the market, the less variables (colors) that are necessary.

Painting the picture of the everyday customer in other countries and cultures is not the same as the portrait in this country. We have the freedom of choice in this country. The domestic market here is huge and diverse. In other global markets customers think and act the same way based on their culture and purchase behavior. This makes it easier to paint the picture when the market is more homogeneous, the domestic market in this country could not be more heterogeneous.

DEMOGRAPHICS

Paints a Picture

Who Is Your Customer

Demographic Variables:

DEMOGRAPHIC VARIABLE	TYPE
AGE	PRIMARY
GENDER	PRIMARY
INCOME	SECONDARY
EDUCATION	SECONDARY
OCCUPATION	SECONDARY
ETHNICITY	SECONDARY
RACE	SECONDARY
RELIGION	SECONDARY
LOCATION	SECONDARY
GEOGRAPHICAL SHIFTS	SECONDARY
MARITAL STATUS	SECONDARY
HOUSEHOLD SIZE	SECONDARY

These are only a few of the demographic variables that are needed to paint the picture. Some demographic variables are primary variables and are used frequently, some are secondary variables and are not as prevalent. Age and gender are strong demographic variables and conjoint variables because how old you are and what gender you are plays a significant role in what products you need. Gender used to be an easy one to figure out. You were either male or female. There are male oriented products that are promoted to males and female oriented products that are promoted to females. With today's societal changes with regard to sexual orientation the picture has become complicated. A perfect example of a picture that was once black and white is now abstract.

Age

The basic fundamentals in marketing include two components: a customer and their ability to pay for a product. If you have no customer you have no market, if the customer does not have the wherewithal to purchase your product you have no sale. Why baby boomers are such an attractive market to target is that they meet both criteria, they fit the formula, they are the solution to the theorem. Baby boomers are the largest segment of the population, and they have the most disposable and discretionary income. Sure there are a lot of millennials out there, and they are a force to be reckoned with, but they do not have the money that the baby boomers have.

You hear all of this buzz about the baby boomers, the baby boomers this and the baby boomers that. Why all of the fuss? If you were to graph all of the potential customers in this country by age, from if you were born today to the age of one hundred, and you wanted to plot where is the largest segment of the market?

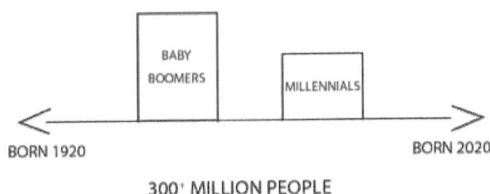

BORN 1920   BORN 2020

300' MILLION PEOPLE

Baby boomers, born between the early 1940s and mid 1960s represent the largest market of potential customers by age. There are more baby boomers than any other segment of the population. The second factor that separates the baby boomers from any other segment is their ability to pay for a product. This is what delineates the millennials, who are the second largest segment of the population, from the baby boomers. The average sixty year old baby boomer has more disposable and discretionary income than the average millennial. Baby boomers have been tabbed as the most successful generation. Millennials, for the most part are the children of the baby boomers, and the current slacker lifestyle that is commonplace among millennials, has to be placed at the feet of the baby boomers.

There is a back story behind the power that the baby boomers have in the marketplace. It goes back to the principles of supply and demand. Before World War Two, the birth rate, the amount of babies being born was growing at a slow rate. After the war men returned home, it was a happy time in this country. What do you think happened BOOM, babies, babies, and more babies. The demand for baby related products such as diapers, baby powder, baby shampoo, baby oil, strollers, playpens, baby food and ALL baby related products went through the roof. Again, think of age as a strong demographic variable. How old you are has a direct relationship to the products that you need. If you were in the baby business at this time you made a fortune.

What I find extremely interesting is that this spike in the demand for products has followed the baby boomers throughout their life. By the late 1950s and early 1960s baby boomers were pre-teens. What product was popular with pre-teens during this era? Bicycles. Are bicycles as popular today with pre-teens, no video games are. If you were marketing bikes during this time frame you were able to capitalize on the spike in demand for this product.

What is a big change in your life as you turn sixteen or seventeen years old? The ability to drive a car. It is no coincidence that the hey-day of the American muscle car reached its peak in the mid to late 1960s when baby boomers began to drive.

World events such as the earlier war that was mentioned can have an impact on demographics and product decisions. By the mid-1960s the Vietnam War was a reality. With a draft that was enacted, one way to avoid going to Vietnam, or at least to get to the bottom of the draft list, was to enroll in college. Baby boomers were college age at this time. What was the end result? College campuses swelled with admissions. Most community colleges in this country were founded during this time to meet the demand of customers (students). If you were marketing any college related products, such as textbooks, you enjoyed this spike in demand for your product.

Let's fast forward to the early 2000s where the first baby boomers started to turn fifty. What is going on in your life as you start your second fifty years of life? What products start to become important to you? You wake up on your fiftieth birthday and you look in the mirror and you start to notice a few things. You do not look as good as you once did. You do not feel as good as you once did. Retirement, while still down the road, is staring you in the face. The reflection in the mirror might not be as favorable as you like. What can you do? Make some lifestyle changes. You want to look younger, so any products that make you look younger such as plastic surgery might become an option.

Remember the formula, the amount of potential customers and their ability to pay for a product. At fifty you might have the money for plastic surgery that you may not have had a few years ago. Plastic surgery has, no pun intended, boomed, since the baby boomers started to turn fifty. The fitness craze has caught the eye of the baby boomers. Anything fitness related from gym memberships, exercise equipment, vitamins and supplements that can make you look and feel younger is on the radar of baby boomers. Retirement investments including mutual funds, hedge funds, and retirement homes have all enjoyed a boost in their popularity due to the fact that the baby boomers see retirement as their next stage in life.

What is the next product vertical that is awaiting the baby boomers and their influx of demand based on their age and position in the family life cycle? Anything that is healthcare related from pharmaceuticals, medical equipment, estate planning, assisted living facilities, fifty-five and over retirement communities, long-term care insurance and yes again diapers! Pharmaceutical companies (Big Pharma) have always been profitable, but they are waiting with their arms wide open as the baby boomers approach the pill popping stage of their life. What I mean by that is that the advances that have been made by the pharmaceutical and medical device industry have no question prolonged the life of consumers. Today it is normal for consumers in an advanced age demographic to wake up and take two pills for this, three pills for that, and four pills for whatever ailment that they have contracted over their lifespan. The cash register between baby boomers and Big Pharma is about to explode! What is left after this stage for the baby boomers, similar to the Product Life Cycle, decline and death? Someone once said that the only guarantee in life is death and taxes. That is not true. Taxes can be avoided but death is inevitable. The funeral business has had a long history of being a profitable enterprise, wait until the largest section of our population, the baby boomers begin their demise. The demand for caskets, head stones, cremation services, and insurance for final expenses will grow exponentially. Is it not funny that the demand for diapers went through the roof when the baby boomers were born and will again go through the roof when the baby boomers complete their life cycle! The point that I am trying to hammer home regarding the baby boomer analogy is that it is not only how old you are that can dictate what products become important to you it is what is going on in your life as well.

We are living longer and while you can prepare the best that you can for retirement it just seems that you can never have enough money. People are not only living longer, they are working longer. Years ago it was almost unheard of for someone to work past the age of seventy. Today that is not the case. Beside the fact that they have to work there is a trend of working beyond seventy for other reasons. You spend so much of your life going to work that your body and mind are conditioned to work. Once your working life is over there is a sentiment that you need to stay active both mentally and physically. Why quit your career, especially if it is something that you enjoy doing.

When you hear the grouping of consumers by age with a dash in between two numbers is an example of demographic segmentation by age. You hear a lot about the 18-25 year old demographic, why is this age group so important to marketers? During this stage of life you begin to make product decisions on your own. In the earlier age demographic you were at the mercy of your parents, they bought the brand of toothpaste that they wanted, the brand of jeans that they could afford, and the same goes for toilet paper and other household products. During the 18-25 demographic, if you vacate your parent's abode you begin to make brand decisions on your own. You inaugurate the Brand Intensity process and begin to make your own decisions about what products you prefer. Brand Awareness and Brand Insistence can begin to set into the mindset of the customer during this age demographic. Once Brand Insistence is realized by a young customer, marketers can have a customer for life. There was a time when this age demographic (18-25) was out of the family household and on their own, the recent demographic shift of millennials remaining at home has pushed the age number way past the age of twenty-five and closer to the age of thirty!

Gender

Even products that were black and white decisions, where the picture of who the customer is, has become cloudy and fuzzy. There was a time when there were male oriented products, that men purchased and female oriented products that females purchased. Men went to the pharmacy to purchase condoms, and there was a time when there was some trepidation and embarrassment of a male stepping up to the counter and saying, "Where are the condoms?" Females went to the pharmacy to purchase feminine hygiene products. Today it is common for men to do the shopping and asking, "Where are the tampons, and women stepping up to the counter and inquiring do you have this brand of condoms?" Oh my how things have changed!

Income

Income can impact what products are appealing to the consumer. So can education level. Nurses (occupation) need products that accountants (occupation) do not need. Ethnicity can impact decisions based on food, hair, and skin care products. Race is a variable that certainly is evolving. Bi-racial and multi-racial customers are growing in leaps and bounds. Multiculturalism has to be factored into demographic decisions. Religion can impact clothing and food product decisions.

Location

Location, or where you live is a demographic variable, and can impact product decisions. Where are the customers located? Customers who live in the urban sections of a city have product needs that differ from customers with suburban addresses, and have different needs from customers in rural zip codes.

Markets

A market has many definitions. Think back one hundred years. When a customer would walk into a village and pick out the groceries for the day's family meal. Fast forward to where we are today when the groceries for today's family meal can be purchased and delivered to your doorstep ordered off of a device that fits in your hands. Think about a market that buys and sells pieces of companies and used to be located on a street named after a wall. That market has been turned on its ear where again today those transactions can be completed utilizing a device that fits in your hands. No need to physically be on that street to be a player in the market!

I have a different interpretation of a market from a demographic perspective. A market starts out as a settlement. Someone settles in an area. Drive through any area of this country and you will see a sign that tells you when the village was founded and settled. It can be hundreds of years ago. Over time the population started to grow. The settlement became a village which developed into a town and swelled to a city evolving into a metropolis sprouting the concept of the megalopolis.

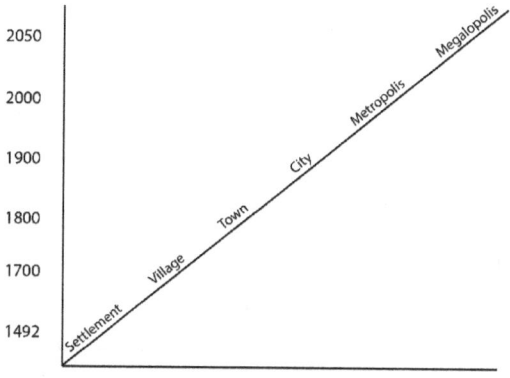

How do you chop up or dissect this vast domestic market? You can chop it into fifty states, but that is too broad. A popular way to segment the market is by county. There are over three thousand counties in this country, and you just segregated the market from fifty pieces to over three thousand pieces. To drill down to the smallest most infinitesimal pieces of a market would be by zip code. There are over forty-two thousand zip codes in this country. That's a lot of tiny pieces of a market.

A rule of thumb is to focus on the top thirty to forty markets. What are the top thirty or forty cities in this country? Where are the lines drawn that separate the markets? Using the top three markets in this country as an example, New York City, Los Angeles and Chicago. Do you look at these markets as a whole or do you slice the markets into smaller pieces that would include the five boroughs of New York, plus Long Island to the east, northern New Jersey to the west, and southern Connecticut to the north, east Los Angeles and west Los Angeles, or the north side of Chicago compared to the south side of Chicago? Do you include bedroom communities which are residential suburbs colonized by individuals who commute to the city to make a living?

Components of the Promotional Mix including Advertising and Personal Selling rely on this model. What is the budget for Advertising? Are there resources to flood thirty markets with an advertising campaign? Or are there resources to blanket two hundred markets with your message? Most forms of Advertising conform to this belief. Television likes to look at the top thirty markets. So does radio. Ratings drive advertising dollars. Who is watching what and listening to whom in the thirty prime markets is imperative. How many salespeople are deployed? If you focus on the top thirty markets you need at least thirty salespeople, maybe a few more to place more than one salesperson in the larger market. If you chop the market into two hundred pieces you need two hundred salespeople.

Below are the Top Thirty Television Markets listed by their 2018-2019 Nielsen ranking. The point is that you need to plot the markets and make a decision on which markets to penetrate and which markets to place on the back burner. Developing a marketing footprint in the top markets is a no brainer, of course you want to market your product there. The dilemma arises when you get to the bottom of the list and even look beyond the Top Thirty Markets to the Top Fifty markets and have to make a decision where to allocate precious marketing resources.

MARKET	RANK
NEW YORK	1
LOS ANGELES	2
CHICAGO	3
PHILADELPHIA	4
DALLAS	5
WASHINGTON, DC	6
HOUSTON	7
SAN FRANCISCO	8
BOSTON	9
ATLANTA	10
TAMPA	11
PHOENIX	12
SEATLLE	13
DETROIT	14
MINNEAPOLIS	15
MIAMI	16
DENVER	17
ORLANDO	18
CLEVELAND	19
SACRAMENTO	20
ST. LOUIS	21
PORTLAND	22

CHARLOTTE	23
PITTSBURGH	24
RALEIGH	25
BALTIMORE	26
NASHVILLE	27
INDIANAPOLIS	28
SAN DIEGO	29
SALT LAKE CITY	30

https://en.wikipedia.org/wiki/List_of_television_stations_in_North_America_by_media_market[3]

Geographical Segmentation

Geographical shifts in the population are also demographic variables. Population migrates to where the job opportunities are. Population means consumers. Migration follows the money. More than one hundred years ago there was a massive movement of people from Europe to the United States. Where did they settle? Harbors in the North East became a popular destination. Why and how did New York City become the center of the universe?

New York harbor was the deepest allowing for the bigger ships to land in New York. The bigger ships carried two things, products and people! Jobs became available and the North East began to explode with opportunity. As the country became more industrialized this growth spread from the North East to the Midwest. This became known as the "Rust Belt". States within the rust belt net include New York, Pennsylvania, West Virginia, Ohio, Indiana, Michigan, Illinois, Iowa and Wisconsin.

---

[3] Top 30 Designated Market Areas (DMAs) listed by the 2018-19 Nielsen ranks. https://en.wikipedia.org/wiki/List_of_television_stations_in_North_America_by_media_market

The loss of manufacturing jobs has shifted migration south. Cost of living and favorable climates are also contributing factors. The "Sun Belt" comprises of states including North Carolina, South Carolina, Georgia, Florida, Alabama, Louisiana, Mississippi, Arkansas, Texas, Oklahoma, New Mexico, Arizona, Nevada, and California. The point is that if you have a limited advertising budget you should advertise in the Sun Belt compared to the Rust Belt.

Traditional Household

The 1950s were a golden era for our society. Demographics were so simple then. The average American household was consistent, husband (male) and wife (female), on average two and a half kids, a dog and a white picket fence. Boy has that changed! Talk about going from a black and white portrait to something today that is more of a mosaic! Marketing and advertising primarily targeted the housewife, who was home all day. Soap Opera's dominated the airwaves with in-programming (during the broadcast) messages about household products.

Let's start with marital status as a demographic variable. I remember being in the first grade in the early 1970s. Just about all of my classmates were from families that were together, mother and father. By the time I got to high school in the early 1980s half of my friends were from split families, mother and father not together. This rise in divorce and single parent households changed the American family forever. The typical American household was fractured. The rise of dual income families, latch-key children, who arrived home after school to find an empty house became the norm. This led to single parent households, which has bred a culture today of parents of children who never get married, nor have any desire to get married, with the residual effect being today's new demographic market, the single parent. Where regardless of gender the single parent performs the functions of both the mother and the father of the child.

What is "Tradition?" If you were to ask me I would define Tradition as something that takes a long time to establish, should be respected and never should be questioned. Back in the day when a man made the decision to get married it was customary for him to ask for the permission of the woman's father, for his daughters hand in marriage. Did I do that? Of course I did! Did I think twice about it? Of course not, it was Tradition! Recently a jewelry store chain ran a television commercial where a young man was asking for permission to marry a woman. He opened the jewelry box, smiled at the engagement ring, and looked across from him and did not ask the woman's father for his permission, he asked the woman's pre-teen son for his permission to marry his mother. Oh my how things have changed! Brilliant Marketing!

Another demographic phenomenon is the rise of Millennials, customers in their twenties, many of whom, who are still living with their parents. Some graduate from college only to be saddled with massive student loan debt and no promising career opportunities and others who never finish or even go to college who are still living off of their parent's dole in their basement.

Age and marital status has changed as well. A generation ago it was common to get married in your early twenties. As a matter of fact, if you were a single woman at the age of thirty, there was a stigma or label placed on you, "As to what is wrong with you, you are not married yet?" Today that is not the case. The current generation of Millennials are the bi-product of the 1970s generation brought up with divorce being commonplace. This has fostered a society against getting married at such an early, immature age. Millennials are not rushing to get married and maybe that is a residual effect of the split and single family trend, they are more selfish, and maybe they do not want the responsibility and cost associated with raising a family.

A fact of life and nature is that women do have biological clocks that are ticking. Years ago, having a baby after the age of thirty-five presented an immense risk to both the mother and the child. Today the advancements made in pharmaceutical and medical technology have spawned the concept of giving birth at a much more advanced age, slowing down and prolonging the biological clock for females.

Starting a family at an advanced age does have advantages, you are more mature at forty compared to when you were twenty and you should be in a better financial position. However there are some drawbacks. The longer the age gap between parent and child the chance of a wider generation gap. Chasing a two year old around at twenty is easier than chasing a two year old around at forty, you simply have more energy. Dropping off your child at kindergarten in your late forties is different than dropping off your child at kindergarten in your mid-twenties. As your child advances through school you do not want to be mistaken for their grandmother at their college graduation. Forget about growing old watching YOUR grandchildren grow-up, the later you start a family, the later YOUR children will start their family.

The family life cycle is a relatively new phenomenon moving away from the traditional family model. It is a time line where you start out single, then can get married, start a family, get divorced, be single with children, married without children, divorced with children, divorced without children, remarried and start a new family etc... It splinters the traditional family into demographic segments that can create a niche for certain products.

Demographic Conclusions

Sorry for all of this confusion but you can see how the picture of the typical consumer has changed in the last generation. Marketers make errors by painting the picture and leaning on the finished portrait as if it was written in stone. Today's portraits are more fluid and less static and should not be written in stone, but written in sand. Meaning that the picture of today's customer is evolving, morphing and changing as we speak. Today's customer might not be yesterday's customer and who knows what the profile of the customer will look like tomorrow.

Chapter 3

Think Like The Customer

Diffusion Of Innovation

The importance of new products cannot be underestimated. The only thing that you can count on in business is that things will change. The way that you do business today is not the way that you did business yesterday. The way that you do business tomorrow is not the way you do business today. Innovation cannot be ignored and must be embraced.

Adopting the innovation, as profound as it might be, does not happen overnight. I think about the music industry. Yes, there have been songs that the first time that you hear them they become instant hits, but most hit songs take some time to catch on, they need to marinate, they need to grow on you before they are accepted (adopted) as a hit. The same mentality can be applied to many products. When they are introduced to the market a few consumers adopt the innovation and the audience needs to build. That is the ultimate definition of marketing, how to raise the awareness of the market that this innovation can truly be ground breaking. Marketers need to know where their product is in this continuum. Marketers need to read the market correctly to gain a thorough understanding of which stage their product is in. Marketers need to know how much of the market is ahead of you and how much of the market is in the rear view mirror. An underestimation of where your product is throughout this continuum can be a gaffe that can stall the launch and development of the product.

Several marketing scholars have come up with a model that goes by multiple monikers including The Consumer Adoption Process, The Spread of New Products and The Diffusion of Innovation (Robertson, 1967).[4] They all refer to the same graph that moves a product from innovators, early adopters, early majority, late majority, and laggards.

Diffusion of Innovation

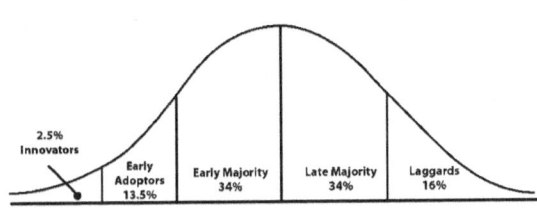

Innovators represent 2.5% of the market and are the first group to adopt the innovation. There is a notion that the innovators are a special group, they crave the idea of being first to adopt the new innovation, to be able to boast that they are the first to have it on their block. Innovators wait in line to be the first to snatch up the new smart phone, video game or motion picture the minute that it becomes available. I am not saying that I disagree with this notion, but if you have the time to wait in line for any of the new product introductions then maybe you should reevaluate what you are doing with your life. I look at the innovators from a different angle. Who was the first person on the block to purchase an automobile? Who was the first person on the block with a television in their living room? It was the rich person, the consumer who could afford the new innovation,

---

[4] Robertson, T., (1967). The process of innovation and the diffusion of innovation. Journal of Marketing. 31(1) p.14-19.

not a consumer who desires new products, it was the consumer who had the cash! When you analyze the graph identifying that your product is in the innovation stage, what is encouraging is that 97.5% of the total market is available to you. Raising awareness and gaining acceptance becomes the strategy. There is skepticism about the new innovation and the mere fact that customers are resistant to change can slow the process of moving to the next stage.

Early adopters make up 13.5% of the market and embrace fresh innovations prematurely but cautiously.

Early majority signifies 34% of the market are more methodical yet they adopt the fresh innovation before the everyday customer.

Late majority counts for 34% of the market, are more cynical, and only adopt the innovation after a preponderance of customers have consumed the product.

Laggards add up to 16% of the market and are your most old-fashioned customers and do not welcome or embrace change and innovation. Laggards often only adopt the innovation once the product has been accepted and has become the established standard. Laggards are often overlooked which can be a mistake, they are still customers, they are just slow customers.

Consumer Decision Making Process

As a marketer you need to be able to think like the customer, reverse the roles and get inside the head of the customer and answer the question, of "Why" do customers buy products? It is the essence of what Consumer Behavior is all about.

Want Versus Need

I have had this argument for years with both marketing academics and corporate marketing executives. I ask the question, "Why do customers buy products, because they want them or they need them?" It is the Want versus Need debate. The overwhelming consensus from both the academic and corporate side is that customers buy products because they want them. When I argue with the academics, many of whom are colleagues, when they get on their soap box about marketing creating the want, I counter their argument with, "When was the last time that you sold something?" Crickets, silence, and a blank stare, because many of them have never sold a product in their life! Marketing creates an illusion, a desire, a fantasy, with advertisements filled with hyperbolic statements that convince and persuade the consumer to purchase a product. I am not saying that this is not the case, but if you ask me why consumers buy products it is because they need the product. When you need something in life you have a problem. Focusing on solving a consumer's problem with your product as the solution is becoming more of a popular strategy.

My support for the need versus the want is rooted in my experiences as a salesperson. As a salesperson you need as much help as you can get to convince the customer to purchase your product. At one point in my career I thought that I had the deck stacked in my favor. I was selling hand held surgical instruments to surgeons in the hospital. In accordance with the spectrum of price on one side versus quality on the other end of the spectrum, usually your product offering is on one side versus the other. This was not the case. My surgical instruments were the top of the line with regards to quality. It was a well-known market fact. If a poor quality surgical instrument breaks during a surgical procedure it can cause complications during the procedure. The sales pitch to the surgeon was, "Dr. X have you ever had a colleague break a surgical instrument during surgery?" You never asked if "they" broke an instrument during a surgical procedure because you might be challenging their expertise and skill in the operating room. But planting the seed in their head does work. My next pitch is to place the highest quality surgical instrument in their hand, and they can immediate see the quality of the product.

Quality does drive the price of a product up. Yes, I was selling a high-end product, which was sold at a premium price. Here was more support for my product being the choice of the customer. I was selling for the largest healthcare company on the planet, with incredible brand recognition, where when you knocked on a customer's door and they said who are you? The brand name of the company would open the door and give you access to the audience that you need.

This company had so much brand recognition and could literally sell thousands of products to this customer. Since the hospital purchased so many of the company's products, if they purchased more volume this can impact the overall price of all products purchased by the hospital. The end result was that I was able to offer the top of the line product, at a reduced competitive price, from the global leader in the medical device market, combined with my ability as a salesperson, and was consistently greeted with the response at the end of my sales presentation, with a resounding NO! I would come back to my office at the end of the day almost banging my head against the wall. Why? There was no need. The customer did not have a problem that I could help solve with my product being their solution. Of course you are selling products as a salesperson, but what you are truly selling is a solution to the customer's problem. No need, no problem, no sale!

Need Recognition

Something needs to trigger a stimulus in the mind of the customer where the light goes off in the customer's head and they recognize that they need a product. A terrific example is the gas light in your car. Everyone knows that you need gas in your car yet how many people do not recognize that they need gas until the gas light goes on alerting them that they need gasoline?

A need can exist but can be masked or hidden. Part of today's consultative selling approach is to help the customer to uncover the need and help solve the customer's problem.

Information Search

Information search is a fancy word for shopping. Has the way consumers shop for products changed? Are you kidding? In this step shopping means how do you begin to assemble a list of possible purchase alternatives?

Evaluation Of Alternatives

Today's market is clouded and crowded with an overabundance of product choices, substitutes and alternatives. There was a time when a consumer walked in to purchase a product and you had two choices, the cheap one or the expensive one. Which one do you want the cheap one or expensive one? It was quick, it was simple, and a lot of thought did not go into the decision. So which one do you want the cheap one or the expense one?

The myriad of alternatives causes the customer to have to sift through each alternative and narrow down the selection to a handful of choices. The clouding of judgment occurs because in the past while there may have been only one cheap alternative and one expensive alternative today there might be several cheap choices and several expensive choices not to mention the alternatives that fall in the middle of the price versus quality spectrum who are not the cheapest substitute or most expensive alternative but right in the middle with a little of each!

Purchase

All of the preliminary homework has been completed and now it is time to make the decision to purchase. Marketers and salespeople do not understand why this hurdle is so brutal to overcome. This is where you are asking the customer for a commitment, a partnership between the product and the customer, where the marketer is reaching into the customer's pocket and taking their money. Customer's like their money and are reluctant to part with it. Marketers need to overwhelm the customer with the reassurance that making the decision to spend their money on this solution to their problem (product) is the shrewdest decision they have made in a long time.

Post-Purchase Behavior

There are parallels between the Consumer Decision Making Process and the Steps in the Selling Process. In previous marketing and selling models the final step in each process was for the customer to make the decision to purchase the product, and in the selling model for the salesperson to close the sale. Today's models extend the process beyond purchase and close to include Post-Purchase Behavior and following up after the sale. This moves away from the transaction approach which has no interest in what happens after the decision to purchase or following-up after the close of the sale. This strategy is aligned with the relationship marketing and selling approach which is attempting to have a customer for life, not just a customer for today!

Cognitive Dissonance is defined as an uncomfortable feeling after a purchase is made. The consumer needs to mentally justify the decision and here is where the doubt can set in after the purchase is made. Consumers never blame themselves for the questionable purchase decision, the initial blame is always placed on the salesperson who convinced, coerced or persuaded the customer to part with their cash and purchase the product. It is imperative for marketers to be able to measure levels of cognitive dissonance. A marketer's goal is almost a zero tolerance policy where I want low levels of cognitive dissonance.

I do not want you to feel bad after you purchase a product. I do not want you waking up the next day saying, "What was I thinking?"

I want the customer to wake up the next day and scream from the rafters about the stupendous decision they made to purchase the product.

Consumer Decision Making Process

Buying Center

The decision making unit of an organization is known as the Buying Center. The Buying Center includes all of the individuals and units that play a role in the purchase decision making process. This group includes the actual users of the product, those who make the buying decision, those who influence the buying decision, those who do the actual buying, and those who control the buying information. The Buying Center includes all members of the organization who play any of the roles in the purchase decision process.

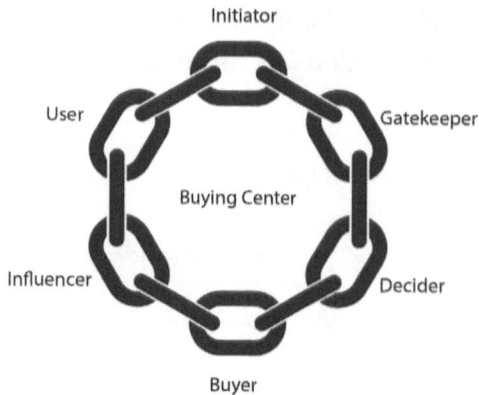

Initiator

An initiator is the first employee in an organization who recognizes a need for a product, brings it to the attention of the organization, and is requesting that action to solve the problem be initiated.

Users

The user is the employee who will actually use the product in their daily activity at work. The user is possibly the only employee who actually puts their hands on the product. Users can help design the product specifications and detail why a specific product is needed. A user can also be the initiator.

Influencers

Influencers can stipulate the criteria that is used to evaluate alternatives. Influencers have the technical expertise to separate the features and benefits of the product alternatives that are being considered. They can be users of the product as well, but typically have more of a voice (influence) in the purchase decision.

Buyers

The buyer's role in the buying center is to negotiate the terms of the purchase. The buyer also is the buying center member who facilitates the transaction, and actually places the order for the product.

Deciders

The decider has the ceremonial status within the buying center to choose and endorse the vendor. The decider is the most difficult member of the buying center to make a sales presentation to, because they are important high level executives in the organization's hierarchy.

Gatekeepers

The gatekeeper controls the flow of information to other members of the buying center. Purchasing agents often have authority to prevent salespeople from seeing users and deciders. Purchasing agents can view their gatekeeping role as the foundation of their power. Other gatekeepers can include technical personnel and personal secretaries. A secretary can act as a gatekeeper by deciding which vendors obtain an appointment with a buyer. Too often salespeople discount the power that the gatekeeper can have. They can wrongly assume that they do not have any power or influence on the decision to purchase a product. This is the furthest thing from the truth. The gatekeeper plays a major role in the buying center.

I learned about the power of the gatekeeper a long time ago. When I made the decision to shift my career from full time selling to full time university teaching I had one problem. I had no teaching experience with no formal teacher training in my background. When I was an undergrad student teaching was nowhere on my radar as a possible career track, I majored in business, specifically Finance. Once the light went off in my head about the career shift I need to build credentials to get me in the door as a professor. This started with going back to graduate school to get an MBA in Marketing. Once that was completed I started to apply to every university in the New York City metropolitan area. There are one hundred and fifteen colleges and universities within this geography. This included the entire spectrum of academic institutions from the Ivy League all the way down to the community college level. Yes, I sent out one hundred and fifteen resumes with the associated follow-up. I did not care who or where the institution was I needed to build a teaching resume. I did receive a couple of part-time adjunct professor assignments and I was on my way. I also scoured all publications on a weekly basis where professor opportunities were advertised.

I came across an advertisement from a top tier academic institution in the newspaper. The first thing I said to myself was, "I will never get hired there, and I have limited part-time teaching experience." One of the first rules of marketing yourself is never sell yourself short, you never know what can happen.

I submit my resume the old fashioned way by snail mail. Two weeks went by and I did not receive any kind of response, no phone call, or letter in the mail acknowledging the receipt of my resume. I just figured they are not considering my application. I did not let it end there. I was not satisfied with that result. I decided to print out another copy of my resume and hand deliver it to the institution. The institution was one of the five Federal service academies. I arrive on the campus with only the name of the department head and the building where his office was. This is a military base, very official, yes sir no sir workplace environment.

I locate the building and I walked my resume up to the department head's office. Who was there to greet me? His secretary, the gatekeeper. Talk about the text book, poster child of a secretary (gatekeeper), an older woman, the grandmotherly type. I said, "I am here to follow-up on the professor vacancy that was advertised, and I brought another copy of my resume, is Captain "X" available?" She gave the textbook gatekeeper reply, "Oh, he is very busy but I will make sure that he gets it." She looks down at my resume and noted where I live and said, "Young man you live far away and you drove all the way out here to submit your resume?" I live only thirty-eight miles away but on the other side of New York City and it can take more than one and a half hours on a good day to get there. I did not go out of my way to drop off the resume, I was making a sales call on a hospital close to the institution. I said to her, "Yes, I drove all the way out here to hand deliver my resume."

Another two weeks go by with no response. I did not let this discourage me. I decided to go back to follow-up only now I knew where I was going and I remembered the gatekeeper's name. I walked in and she said, "I remember you, you are the young man who lives far away, did you drive all the way out here again?" It was the same story as the last time, I was making another sales call at the same hospital but I said to her, "Yes, I drove all the way out here to follow-up on the professor opening." She said the magic words, "I was just in his office and he is not that busy right now, come with me!" We walk in together and she introduces me to Captain "X", very intimidating, in a military uniform, and I introduced myself to him. I said, "My name is Paul Barchitta and I very interested in the professor opportunity." He rolled his eyes and said, "Do you know how many applications I have received?" He pulls out a stack of about two hundred resumes. Where was my application? At the top of the pile? No all the way at the bottom, he would have sifted through all of the applications and found someone who was more qualified. I knew it was at the bottom because I spotted the blue binder that I submitted. He pulls it out from the bottom of the pile, looked at it, and said, "This is you?" I said, "Yes, that is my application and I would love the opportunity to teach here." He takes my resume and places it on the top of the pile! A few days later I received a call to come in for an interview. I got the job and stayed there for three plus years until I received a full time professor opportunity at a nearby university. I stayed there for twelve years and became a tenured professor at the other university. The phone rang one day and it was his office calling saying they had an opening and would I like to come back on a full time basis? I went back to the top tier institution and became a tenured professor there as well and have been there for eight years. This does not happen without the respect and recognition that I gave to the gatekeeper. I owe a lot to that gatekeeper! NEVER sell yourself short!

The buying center can vary from company to company and there can be multiple buying centers within an organization. It comes down to what is the problem that the company trying to solve with the purchase of a product acting as the solution to the problem. The buying center is not a formal department and does not show up on an organizational chart. It is more of a group of employees who get together to resolve an issue that the company is having. The more structured the organization, the more structured the buying center. It is often organized by a committee format. With a chairperson and associated committee members who all play a different role in the buying center. The chairperson can be the decider, but the chairperson can also be the buyer or influencer. That is the problem, this is a fluid and dynamic group of customers, and a salesperson needs to ascertain who is in what role in the buying center. In one buying center the user can have more of a voice in the decision than another. In another buying center the buyer is really making the decision regardless of what the user says. A buying center can include noticeable departments that can be common between different companies but their role and their degree of influence can vary from company to company.

What can extend the sales cycle is the commitment by the buying center to convene as a group and make a decision as to which product are they going to select. The problem is that all of the members of the buying center have THEIR regular job to do. They are busy, so carving out time for the buying center to get together can be a challenge. Some buying centers choose to meet on a specific day of the month, for this example the first Thursday of the month or the last Wednesday of the month. If they cannot come to a decision, the committee does not meet again until the next month and this can frustrate the salesperson. It comes down to a sense of urgency. How urgent is it that the buying center comes to a conclusion? Product alternatives need to be considered, possible product trials and evaluations have to take place. You as the salesperson may not be the only vendor that the customer is considering, kicking the can down the road when it comes to choosing a vendor.

Other pitfalls that salespeople face when dealing with the buying center is finding out who is really making the decision to purchase the product? Everyone has an ego and it is fashionable for a member of the buying center to say to a salesperson when it is just the two of them that, "I am very important in this company." This may be true, but maybe not as true as the customer thinks for this purchase decision. Who do you believe? Trust no one, assume that every member of the buying center has some influence on the purchasing decision. A tip to determine who is really calling the shots is to observe the buying center when you are in front of them as a committee. Where does the chairperson sit? At the end of the table, in the middle of the table? Observe how other members of the buying center defer to each other. This can be a signal as to who in the buying center regardless of their job title can have more influence over the group than others. A salesperson needs to have a champion in the room. A champion is a member of the buying center who will standup and exert their influence on the group. Again, a champion can be the user, influencer, or buyer. A champion sells the salesperson's product in front of the buying center when the salesperson leaves the room and only buying center members remain.

An issue that is out of the control of the salesperson is the political atmosphere among buying center co-workers. There can be conflicting political agendas and determining a consensus among buying center members is not as easy as it sounds. What if one member is in favor of one vendor for whatever reason, but another buying center member sides with a different vendor just too intentionally disagree with the other member? This is common and can impede the success of the salesperson.

The balance of power can shift from buying center to buying center. An example of how the same job title can have different roles in the buying center is a hospital. In some hospitals surgeons have the power to make the decision on what products to use, while in others nurses make product decisions. Still in others supply center managers can make the decision or buyers and hospital administrators can exert their influence. This can be different in another hospital that literally can be across the street. You can sell the same product for the same price to the same customer yet the individual pulling the trigger on the sale can vary from customer to customer.

Life is about lessons. The lessons that you learn from decisions that you make that can impact your life. I learned this lesson about the Buying Center. When referring to the sales cycle, I ask my students how long is too long of a sales cycle? Is five years too long? Of course it is! When I reminisce about the most significant sale of my life it brings me back to the importance of respecting the Buying Center.

Why did it take five years? Let's start with this. For the first four years of the journey I could not get anyone in the Buying Center to give me the time of day for one reason. Need! They did not need my equipment. They were happy with their current vendor and my solicitations fell on deaf ears. In year five things started to change. The champion, who was at the heart of the stonewalling, was out on medical leave. It was a serious situation where the majority of the Buying Center members seriously doubted if the champion would ever return to work. The champion was the Chief of Orthopedic surgery at the hospital. This opened the door for new products that needed to be considered by the hospital. The Buying Center chain was fractured and I was given an opportunity. My product was evaluated by the hospital and a year later the hospital came to the conclusion to purchase my medical device. Other members within the Buying Center became champions of my cause. The nursing department wanted the device because of the ease of use and patient satisfaction compared to the competitor. The supply department became a champion due to the service and dependability that I could provide compared to the competitor. The purchasing department became a champion because I could save the hospital money compared to what my competitor was charging the hospital.

It was the largest sale that I ever made in my sales career. I will never forget the day that I received the Purchase Order closing the sale. It was on my thirtieth birthday! What a present! Turning thirty can be traumatic, you start to look in the mirror and evaluate what you have done with your life. I thought that birthday was traumatic until I turned forty. After turning fifty it is not traumatic anymore, it is a matter of survival and discovering that your body parts just don't work the way they used to.

Every salesperson who is worth their salt not only calculates, but spends their commission before it is received. Commission on this deal and most deals is realized when the product is shipped from our warehouse to the loading dock of the hospital. This occurred on a Friday. What a great birthday! I will never and have never forgotten it.

Monday morning rolls around, and I get a phone call. It was a voicemail from the champion who the week before not only recovered, but returned to work after almost a year of being away from the hospital. All the voicemail said was that I needed to be in the office of the Chief of Orthopedic surgery immediately. I listened to the message. It sounded so cryptic. The Chief of Orthopedic surgery was out of the Buying Center because of the illness. I ignored this member of the Buying Center because he was out of the Buying Center, out of the loop.

41

I arrived at the office, thinking the worst. If the order does not get shipped from my warehouse to the hospital, the deal is canceled and I just spent the weekend celebrating the best sale of my life. It was the end of March, not too warm in New York City, however I started to sweat about the consequences. I started to perspire through my suit! I approached the office with a sheepish look. Like walking on egg shells. I stuck my head only through the door of the office. The Chief of Orthopedic surgery is sitting at his desk with his feet up. Body language is a vital part of the sales process. How does your customer greet you when you walk into their office? This was the farthest thing from a warm welcome. He pointed his finger at me and said, "Sit the 'profanity' down." Every other word was profanity. Use your imagination! He starts the conversation by stating who he is in the Buying Center. He said, "I am the Chief of Orthopedic surgery at this hospital. I have been using your competitor for over twenty years and have not had one issue with their device. We are not switching to your device!"

My perspiration was starting to turn to tears. The biggest sale of my life was going down the tubes. Goodbye commission, goodbye to my birthday celebration. The Chief of Orthopedic surgery says to me, "Who helped you get in the door here, who helped you process this order?" Every third word was laced with profanity. I had to make a decision, do I take all of the blame? Do I fall on the sword or do I try to save my skin and reveal the members of the Buying Center who helped me out? The Chief was so powerful and intimidating I had no choice. I ratted out everyone in the Buying Center! I said, "Mary in the nursing department, Joe in the supply department, Jane in the purchasing department, Sue in the operating room." Instead of dismissing me and starting his investigation he made me sit there and sweat and squirm. He wrote down every member of the Buying Center who became a champion of mine. He then proceeded to call every member of the Buying Center and chew them out reminding them about HIS position in the Buying Center. Again, every third word was laced with profanity. More perspiration and more tears!

After his explosion of accountability to the members of the Buying Center, I was still just sitting there not knowing what to say or do. He picks up my business card and stares at it. The name and logo of the company was next to my contact information. He puts his finger towards the brand name of the company and says, "Where do I know this name from, with more profanity?" I responded with we are a leader in the Vascular industry. He says, "That's where I know the name from." He picks up his leg that was mangled from the accident and led to his medical leave. He said, "Look at my leg I need to wear surgical stockings for the rest of my life." I said, "You need to wear surgical stockings?" He said, "Yes, every day for the rest of my life." He showed me the brand that he was wearing, they were the cheapest surgical stockings on the market, back to my statement about doctors being the cheapest people on the planet. I said, "I can get you free samples of surgical stockings." He was interested. While the equipment that I was marketing was the Dog of our product line our surgical stockings were the gold standard, the market leader, no question the Star product of our product line. By the next morning I delivered one thousand dollars of surgical stockings. He tried them. He called me a couple of days later. He said, "My legs feel great, does your equipment do the same thing?" It was a stretch, possible misleading the customer, but I blurted out, "Yes, the equipment has the same effect on your circulation that the stockings have." He then says, "Can you keep getting me more free stockings?" I obliged and he agreed to let the deal for my equipment go through. A miracle!

Not only was it the largest sale in my life, it was the largest sale in the history of the company for the product, catapulting me to the top of the sales ranking for the company. I became the number one salesperson in the company, and set records for sales quota achievement, the most consecutive months at number one, and other sales records that have not been broken since.

The normal procedure after an equipment sale is consummated is to take the next step in the process and train the staff on the use of the product and begin an implementation project.

During the process I met with the orthopedic surgeons to educate them on the device. One of them says, "We track the incidence of DVT (Deep Vein Thrombosis) on all of our total hip and total knee replacement patients. What are we going to do now?" I did not know what he was talking about, yet I told him to just keep collecting the data. The orthopedic department would scan a patients legs when they were admitted to the hospital to see if they had DVT (Blood Clot) before they entered the hospital, a preexisting condition. They then would scan the legs during the surgery to see if a blood clot had developed during the surgery. Before the patient was sent home, they would scan the legs one more time to make sure that a blood clot did not develop while the patient was recuperating. All of this was just collected as "raw data". The data was used as documentation to cover the backside of the surgeon and hospital in case something went wrong. It is all about liability. If a patient dies because of a blood clot that was brought on by a surgical procedure, the hospital and surgeon can be sued.

I went home and did not think anything about the, "What do we do now" statement. The light went off in my head, wait a minute there is data here. At the time my company had no clinical proof that our device prevented blood clots in orthopedic surgical patients. In fact our competitor, who I displaced, had mountains of clinical proof (studies), close to fifty published articles in the most popular medical journals from studies conducted at the top teaching hospitals in this country.

A popular name for the Buying Center in a hospital is the New Product Evaluation Committee. A group who meets periodically to determine what new products the hospital should evaluate and possibly purchase. It is common to have each vendor make their presentation in front of the group at once. Here is how the clinical proof was presented by my competitor. The competitor would say, "We have close to fifty clinical studies from major teaching hospitals in the country that were published in the top medical journals." They would then rattle off the names of the hospitals and the names of the journals. Then they would literally dump copies of all of the studies on the table and say, "Ask the next marketer to talk about the clinical studies that they have that prove their device prevents blood clots and DVT!"

Ouch! That ended my presentation. We had no clinical proof that our device can prevent a blood clot. As a matter of fact we even used the competitor's clinical studies in our presentations to say that "A" pump can prevent a blood clot and DVT. That burned me up so much.

I started to think, we had no studies, yet there was raw data available on my competitor's device and now raw data being collected on my device. At the time there were no head to head comparison studies of competitive devices. The research focused on the premise that a pump can and does prevent a blood clot and DVT.

At this point I did not discuss this with anyone. Here was my dilemma. What if the comparative data favored my competitor, who already had a pile of evidence in their favor? That would signal the death knell for me, and the product, not only at this hospital but in hospitals all over the country. How do you think my newfound friend, the Chief of Orthopedic surgery, would have felt that research that was conducted by his department, under his watch, proved that the product that the hospital was using for twenty years WAS the best product and the decision to replace that product was a mistake? It would not have mattered how many free stockings he had received, I would be out the door.

I presented the notion to my regional sales manager. He thought it was a risk but a good idea. Here is why he was a great regional sales manager, he thought that I, not he, or the higher ups in the corporate headquarters should have a big say in this decision. We approached our internal clinical research department. What clinical research department? I just mentioned that we had no studies or proof that our device prevented blood clots and DVT. We did have a clinical research team but they focused on clinical studies on the Star and Cash Cow products, not the Dog.

I get the corporate approval to move forward. Where do I start? I go back to my champion, the Chief. I remember going to that meeting as well, with a different expectation compared to our first meeting after he delivered the cryptic voicemail summoning me to his office to rat out the members of the Buying Center. I asked him what the hospital's plan was regarding the raw data that his department had compiled. It was confirmed that it was a liability issue and part of the hospital's protocol to monitor the patient throughout their visit to the hospital. I mentioned that my company would be interested in "Sponsoring" a clinical research trial at his hospital. He thought about it. When a medical device manufacturer tells a surgeon that they are willing to "Sponsor" something that is code word for something is in it for you. What was in it for the Chief? He could have his name included on a published clinical study. He brought the idea to the research science department of the hospital where there were Attending Physicians on staff who were more scientists than they were doctors. That prompted a meeting between both sides. The Chief asked the scientists how much money they needed to complete the trial. They threw out a figure, on the spot the Chief looks across the table at my Regional Sales Manager and myself and doubles the figure! What were we supposed to say? They thought it was a great idea because half of the data was already collected. They decided to compare the last six months of patients who had total knee or total hip replacement surgery using my competitors device, with the first six months of patients having the same type surgery but were using my device.

The trial begins and I remember experiencing a tremendous amount of anxiety during the six months because what if the data that was collected was not in my favor, what if the sample size did not match, or what if no conclusions could be determined? Data has to be statistically significant in order for conclusions to be drawn.

Demographic variables that were compared were age, length of stay in the hospital measured in days, length of surgery measured in minutes and the incidence of a "New Thromboembolic Event", [5]a blood clot. The number of patients that were compared was statistically significant as was there age.

So what? Where's the "So what" about those demographic variables? I used to say here is the magic behind the numbers. Let's start backwards. If a patient develops a "New Thromboembolic Event" during the surgery that increases the length of the surgery in the Operating Room (OR). Surgeons and staff are evaluated on how long their surgery takes, eating up valuable OR time. The OR is the most important part of a hospital. Why? The OR generates the most amount of revenue for the hospital. It is the restaurant mentality that servers have to live with, turn the tables, get the customers in, and get the customers out. Once a baseline of time is established for a particular surgical procedure, if the surgeon exceeds that baseline, this can become a component of their overall evaluation by the hospital. It can affect their compensation in the form of bonuses that can be paid for efficiency in the OR. What can extend the length of OR time? A complication during surgery. A blood clot is a complication during surgery.

Once a "New Thromboembolic Event" occurs the length of stay in the hospital shoots through the roof. It shoots through the roof because the hospital cannot release the patient until the blood clot is treated

---

[5] Ariosta, F., et al, (1996). Effective Thromboembolic Prophylaxis with Gradient Sequential Compression Pump for Total Hip/Knee Replacement. Cardiovascular Surgery.

which can take several days. The hospital room that the patient resides in is the opposite of the OR. The OR generates revenue while the hospital room loses money for the hospital. It is not like a hotel, if you stay four nights, you pay for four nights. Whether you stay one night in a hospital or fourteen nights in the hospital, the hospital is reimbursed a flat fee regardless of your length of stay. That is why patients are pushed out of the hospital so rapidly today spawning the emergence of the "Ambulatory Surgery" environment that we currently live in.

The data comes in. I am on pins and needles. The data is statistically significant. The data shows an overwhelming amount of evidence in my product's favor. To use the old boxing axiom, it was not a split decision, it was a unanimous decision. Where's the "So what?" How do you turn data into a sales pitch? My pump reduced the amount of "New Thromboembolic Events", meaning that less blood clots were developed on my pump, not only less blood clots, but NO blood clots compared to the competitor. No blood clots led to shorter surgery time, and a shorter length of stay in the hospital, both saving the hospital money. If you can tell a hospital that your product reduces OR time and the length of time that the patient will stay in the hospital, and save the hospital money, you will open some eyes and answer the question of "So what."

The study gets published in a medical journal, the Chief and the team of researchers, get the recognition for the study and the Chief actually became a spokesperson for the company presenting the results of the research at Orthopedic Surgery conferences. How about that for a kick in the backside! The Chief of Orthopedic Surgery, who wanted to hang me by my toes, now became a champion and advocate for the marketing of the medical device! Every salesperson in the country was able to use the results of the study in their sales presentation. Our pitch was something like this, "I know that my competitor has a mountain of research that supports their pump, but this is the only head to head study comparing the two devices." The study became known as the "Barchitta" study among my colleagues. That was what I was most proud of. The fact that I impacted the marketing of a product, not just for my customers, but for hospitals throughout the country.

If you walk through that entire time line, which spanned over six years, from the first four years of rejection, through the year of evaluation by the hospital, to the close of the deal, to the near debacle associated with ignoring the Chief, to the stress associated with the clinical trial, to seeing the study published and distributed to marketers across the country was a worthwhile life lesson regarding the impact and importance of respecting everyone's role in the "Buying Center."

Chapter 4

The Myth and Manipulation of Analytics

Marketing Research

Data is currency. Data is power. Analytics (Data) rule the day. Why? To combat the marketing gaffe of a failed new product launch, analytics act as the safety net when the product fails. Data softens the blow of the disappointment associated with the failure of a product. Data becomes the excuse, the fall guy, the reason why the decision was made to go in that direction was driven by the Marketing Research. There are two directions that a marketer can take when making a decision to do something one way or the other. Following what the marketing research has dug up and recommends is one direction. The other direction is to follow your heart, your gut, your instinct and rely on your experience to lead you to the decision. Leaning on the data saves your job. If you make a mistake and you make the wrong decision you are going to have to answer to someone at a higher pay grade and made accountable and justify your decision. In your defense if you plead, "I followed what the analytics said, look at the results of the Marketing Research we collected." Marketing Research is the crutch and can get you off the hook and possibly justify your existence in the organization and maybe save your job. If your response or defense of your decision is, "I decided to go in that direction because I felt it in my heart, it was a gut instinct, and my experience led me down that road." That might be a valid response, but that can be your ticket out the door. You need to throw some numbers up on a pie chart or under someone's nose to help justify your decision.

That is the root of the cause of the failure of products. Marketers lean on the data, to justify their existence, instead of relying on their intuition and instinct. If you are a successful marketer you need to possess superlative instincts and have the intestinal fortitude to make a decision that is not purely based on numbers but based on what is in your soul!

There are two types of data that can be collected, Primary Data and Secondary Data. Primary Data is new data. Primary Data is fresh data. Primary Data is collected to help solve the current Marketing Research problem. Primary Data is an effective tool because a marketer can target a very specific audience to build their case for why a decision was made.

Secondary Data plays a different role. At one time Secondary Data was Primary Data, someone collected the data and it has been sitting on a shelf somewhere since. Secondary Data can be defined as previously collected data, and data that was collected for some other Marketing Research purpose. Secondary Data can be a practical tool. Secondary Data supports the Primary Data discoveries. Secondary Data backs up the Primary Data. Secondary Data is cheap and readily available, literally at the marketer's fingertips, it's called the World Wide Web.

I was asked by the admissions office at a college where I was teaching Marketing to help them with their decision of how to spend a limited amount of resources on a marketing campaign. They had it in their heads that they wanted to advertise the college on radio stations in New York City. My first question to the committee was, "What is the budget for this?" Marketing costs money. You need to know how much money is at your disposal. My next question was, "What are you thinking about regarding Reach and Frequency?" They looked at me like I had two heads, "Reach and Frequency? What's that?" Consider the audience, career academics who never sold anything in their life!

I put together a survey (data) for all of my students as well as the students throughout the campus. The survey included demographic variables such as age, part-time or full time student, academic major, grade level, anticipated graduation date and the genre and radio station that you prefer to listen to.

Just itemizing the aforementioned demographic variables justifies the existence of the Primary Data and is an excellent example of how Primary Data can be customized to solve a Marketing Research problem. The goal of obtaining the Secondary Data was to support my Primary Data direction. I wanted to dig up previously collected data on what genre of music is popular for ALL college age students. I made a recommendation and it was a successful promotional campaign.

Five years later the same committee approached me about the same issue. They had marketing resources and wanted to consult with me on how to spend the resources. Again, they had the notion of radio advertising in their head. I agreed. I administered the EXACT same Marketing Research survey five years later (Primary Data). I dug up the previously collected data (Secondary Data) and specifically compared the results of the genre of music and radio station. The Secondary Data, the previously collected data from five years earlier, mirrored the results of the new, freshly collected Primary Data.

Quantitative Marketing Research Versus Qualitative Marketing Research

There are two philosophies or directions that you can steer your marketing research towards, Quantitative Data versus Qualitative

Data. What is the difference? The most elementary difference between the two approaches is that Quantitative Marketing Research is based on numbers, while Qualitative Marketing Research is based on something other than numbers such as words, observation or experiences. Quantitative Marketing Research is a superficial wound and shallow, while Qualitative Marketing Research is a deeper cut and a deeper dive.

Quantitative Marketing Research is the accepted, traditional method while Qualitative Marketing Research is more contemporary and potentially radical. What is meant by radical is not that it is fanatical, it is just different from the traditional accepted method. Qualitative Marketing Research borders on being a slanted premonition. Quantitative Marketing Research delivers an OBJECTIVE recommendation while Qualitative Marketing Research recommendations are more SUBJECTIVE.

Quantitative Marketing Research is rooted in Survey Research where numbers and data rule the day. Survey research is accepted for a few reasons. Survey research is quick to acquire, quick to collect, quick to analyze and quick to make a recommendation. It is neat and it is clean. I did not say that Quantitative Marketing Research is correct, I said that it is quick, neat and clean. With the advent of technology survey research continues to remain a popular form of Marketing Research, not because of its effectiveness, but because of how "user friendly" it is compared to qualitative methods of collecting data. Survey research collected via the Internet is an acceptable form of marketing research.

A flaw attributed to Quantitative Marketing Research is the legitimacy associated with the responses to survey questions. What is a normal way to respond to a survey question? As quickly as possible. Do you complete the survey to get it over with or do you complete the survey hoping that your responses can change the world?

Data can be manipulated. Data can be skewed. Data can be tailored to meet the desired result of the marketer. How do you trust the data? You cannot! A hospital boasted their success rate of a specific surgical procedure. The success rate of the data collected ranked them as one of the best hospitals in the country for this type of surgical procedure. What they did not tell you was that high risk patients were not a part of the study, to qualify for the clinical trial you could not be a high risk patient. A more accurate interpretation of the data would have to have include ALL patients and not exclude anyone. It reminds me of a sales tactic where you would actually ask the doctor to send me your worst problematic patient, and if my product could solve their problem, all of your patients could benefit from my product. This is the polar opposite, this research only included the patients who are not a high risk, and excluded the problematic patient who can skew the data away the desired objective.

Of course you have blind studies or double blind studies, infusion of placebo components into the research, all mechanisms put in place to add legitimacy into the research. You just do not know! Why this strong, not so positive endorsement for Quantitative Marketing Research? If the research method was so spot on accurate, why is the failure rate for new products so high?

Do not ever believe that you are answering an anonymous web based survey, your responses can be tracked back to your web address. About a decade ago all of the salespeople at a medical device manufacturer received a mandatory survey. The company was sluggishly moving forward, but had seen better days. A few of their Star products had become Cash Cows and were headed towards becoming a Dog. Management could have righted the ship with new Question Marks that could have paved the way for future success but they did not. Management believed that the lives of the Cash Cows would go on forever.

With this atmosphere of doubt hanging over the company, the management issued a survey. You were asked to rank your responses on a scale from one to five, with one being poor and five being outstanding. Here were a few questions that I remember that were very interesting. How would you rank the training that you have received from the company over the past few years? Over the same time frame how would you rank the way that your direct supervisor has treated you and managed your performance? What is your opinion of the direction that management is taking the company in? Are you kidding? You sit there, you answer those questions knowing that your industry and company are in flux, the chances of replacing the job that you have are grim at best, and you are supposed to answer those questions honestly? Come on, you need this job. Of course you are going to respond to the Likert scale in a positive way. Management crunches the survey responses and thinks that they are doing a bang up job, when that could not be the furthest thing from the truth.

Surveys that are too long can also be ineffective. I took a survey once and went to the end of the survey to see how many questions were on the survey. One Hundred and Fifty-Six! There is no way that the results from that survey were accurate. By question sixty-eight I was lost, finished and could not wait to complete it. By the end I was randomly answering questions just to get it over with. The problem with this is that someone on the other end is tabulating your responses and using your responses to help them make a decision.

The core of Qualitative Marketing Research is that there is a story behind the numbers. Words replace numbers in Qualitative Marketing Research. Qualitative Marketing Research is sluggish to acquire, sluggish to analyze and sluggish to make a recommendation. It is cumbersome and soiled. I did not say that Qualitative Marketing Research is correct, I said that it is sluggish, cumbersome and soiled.

Interviews fall under the umbrella of Qualitative Marketing Research. This can be extremely effective. However, a negative of the interview is that it will NEVER have the statistical significance that survey research can provide. There are a couple of components that are necessary for a successful interview. The questions posed have to be crafted in a way to engage the responder to open up and elaborate on their opinion. The responder has to play their part as well and offer insight that can be productive.

Time of the interview is also a factor. There is a difference between a five minute, half hour or two hour interview. Who has time for this? You then have to repeat the interview enough that a conclusion can be drawn. This is a resource and time line issue. The longer the interview, the more interviews that need to be conducted, the more resources that are needed. Are their deadlines in the timeline that must be met? All of these concerns push researchers towards quantitative methods because again, quantitative research is quick, neat and clean.

As everything in society is becoming less physical and more virtual, this notion has crept into the interview process related to Qualitative Marketing Research. I cannot emphasize this enough! There is nothing more productive than a face to face interview. You have to be in the room! A qualitative research interview has so many parallels with a sales presentation. A salesperson asks a customer a battery of questions. They ask the same questions to every customer during every sales call. It is the same with a qualitative research interview. The interviewer must be able to sense the body language of the interviewee along with the surrounding environment. This cannot be achieved over the phone. Even utilizing the technology today of the virtual meeting where you can see the interviewee through a device. It is just not the same! Resources come into play again. The physical location of both parties must be considered.

Focus groups are an excellent form of Qualitative Marketing Research. A group of customers are locked in a room and are asked a series of questions. Inquiries posed would include questions similar to this, "If our new product did this or did that would you purchase our new innovation?" While you can and should ask customers why they purchase your product, you should also ask customers why do they purchase your competitor's product?

A mistake made by marketers who access and utilize focus groups for the purpose of conducting Marketing Research is that you are asking questions to the wrong customers. Loyalty is a wonderful thing, and loyalty to a brand is essential in business. Too many focus groups are a reward, or a thank you, if you will, to loyal customers, who are invited to a junket or national sales meeting, conveniently located at a tropical location, to interact with the company's sales force. Focus groups are conducted during breakout sessions of the sales meeting enabling the interaction. What kind of a response do you expect? The company pays your expenses to and from the sales meeting, all meals and entertainment are picked up by the company, the customer has zero out of pocket expenses for their, "Focus Group" participation. What kind of responses do you think you are going to receive? Of course, it is a positive response to your new innovation. The customer wants to be invited back to the next free vacation. A more productive utilization of this resource is not to invite your best and loyal customers, but invite your worst and disloyal customers who pledge their allegiance to your fiercest competitor. You need to find out what is your competition doing to make these customers happy, so happy that they choose not to purchase your product.

Observation research is part of Qualitative Marketing Research. You can learn a lot by keeping your mouth shut and opening your eyes. Observation research casts a net that includes everything from the body language of the customer, the atmosphere of their office, the neatness of their desk, to the way that you are received when you arrive. The component of observation research that interests me is the way that salespeople approach a customer and the way that a customer reacts when they see a product that catches their eye.

You cannot be half pregnant. Yet, a solution to the debate of whether Marketing Research should be done quantitatively or qualitatively is a hybrid research design which incorporates the benefits of both the quantitative and qualitative approaches. Why not use the data that has been collected to mirror the conclusions determined by the qualitative findings? What if you feel good about the accuracy of the survey data that was collected, but you want a second opinion, something that confirms these results, the qualitative discoveries can support the quantitative data and vice versa.

Marketing Research must start with a problem statement. A problem statement means what is the issue that must be resolved. My research interests are rooted in the development of the relationship that can be developed between a salesperson and a customer. In simpler terms, can the relationship that a salesperson has with a customer influence the customer's decision to purchase a product? Of course it does! I have to prove that. I can use quantitative methods or qualitative methods. Here is the issue. The problem statement DICTATES the research method. Too many marketing researchers fall on one side or the other. Marketing researchers get married to one method versus the other. The beliefs of the marketing researcher should not be the determining factor of one method over the other, the problem statement should DICTATE the method. My research interests conform to qualitative beliefs because they have to. Solving the problem of determining if the relationship between a salesperson and customer can influence the customer's decision has to be answered qualitatively. A quantitative approach just does not solve the problem.

Table Of Quantitative Research Methods Vs. Qualitative Research Methods

	QUANTITATIVE RESEARCH	QUALITATIVE RESEARCH
CHARACTERISTIC	QUICK	SLUGGISH
	NEAT	CUMBERSOME
	CLEAN	SOILED
METHOD	SURVEY	INTERVIEW
	QUESTIONAIRE	FOCUS GROUP
		OBSERVATION
FOCUS	NUMBERS	WORDS
RECOMMENDATION	OBJECTIVE	SUBJECTIVE

Chapter 5

The Party Is Over

Ethical Behavior And Social Responsibility

There was a time when the direction of a company was a one way street and that one way direction was leading towards one goal, profit. It was a take no prisoners mentality, a steam roller mentality where if you got in the way of profit you were trampled. There was no such thing as collateral damage, and if there was collateral damage, so be it. Try employing that type of strategy today, you will be out of business before you blink.

A generation ago if the manufacturing process forced you to emit harmful gases or smoke through a smokestack into the atmosphere, so what? It was all in the name of profit, profit, profit. If your product harmed the environment, if your product was not biodegradable, if your product left a huge carbon footprint or presented a threat to society, so what? Again, nothing got in the way of profit.

Today green has a new meaning! Green used to mean money, profit. Today green means you have to be socially responsible. Today the one way street of profit has an expanded lane, social responsibility. Today you cannot just be profitable, today you have to be nice to society.

Strategic Giving

If you throw your hands up and concede to the notion of social responsibility, why not turn it into a marketing opportunity? The most sincere form of a charitable donation, is an anonymous donation with no fanfare, or photo opportunity. Save the anonymity for the wealthy donors who need the tax deduction. There is a cost associated with everything. If you are going to exhaust resources to be more socially responsible make sure there is something that can benefit the company in the long run.

The concept of strategic giving is increasing in popularity. Strategic giving means you know you have to make a donation, so why not help a cause that can provide some reciprocity on the back end? Consumers are creatures of habit. If a consumer becomes comfortable with a product they can become a customer for life. If you grow up with a certain brand and are brand loyal, why not donate your product to that specific demographic niche and create a win, win situation. The customer wins, they get the product, the marketer wins, and they act socially responsible.

Demographics paint the picture of who is your average everyday customer. If you have a segment of the market that is clearly definable, and let's use gender as a strong demographic variable, then strategically give to support that demographic segment. Support a cause that supports you. An overlooked element of strategic giving that gets overlooked is the currency of the donation. Your donation does not have to be cash, it can be your product. Mobile Devices are an excellent example, in this case a "Tablet." You are a mobile device manufacturer. Last year you sold so many devices that you generated an obscene amount of profit creating the need for a tax deduction via a charitable donation. Have your Public Relations people contact local school districts and ask them if they would like to participate in a program where the school district receives free devices to be distributed to students to utilize in the classroom to enhance their learning experience. You can even empty your warehouse of last year's model that was headed towards obsolescence anyway.

Here is the win-win. The students are introduced to the technology at an earlier age. The student goes home and questions their parents on why don't we have one of these devices in the house. The student is distraught by the fact that they are the only student in their class who does not have one of these devices at home and will not stop reminding the parent of this until the parent gives in and purchases the device for their student. The manufacturer wins by getting the tax deduction, by moving the unwanted inventory, by germinating a new crop of customers and creates an illusion of social responsibility that can be splattered on every format of marketing material possible that they support the movement of bringing technology into the classroom to enhance the education experience. Sounds pretty "Strategic" to me.

Entertaining Customers

There are so many unethical marketing practices from misleading advertising, to the manipulation of data, to deceptive packaging all designed to unfairly manipulate a customer. The one that I can speak to the most about is the entertainment of customers.

Is it an unethical practice to entertain a customer? The trend today is to make the transition from transaction selling and transaction marketing, where closing the sale and raising awareness needed to be established and completed on the spot. The establishment of a long term relationship with a customer is the rule of the day. Can entertaining a customer enhance the relationship between the marketer and customer? Is this unethical? When does entertainment cross over the line of unethical behavior? Moderation is the answer to so many things in life. Excessive behavior is destructible! Excessive entertainment crosses the line! At what point does entertainment cross over the line to buying the business? Thanking the customer for their business is one thing, and can be very gracious. But when the customer expects or anticipates the entertainment, this can cross the line.

I am the first one to admit that the medical device and pharmaceutical industry are the enabler of this unethical behavior. The blame, and what brought down, and was the death knell to the entertainment in the medical device and pharmaceutical industry lies at the feet of the doctor and the surgeon. Doctors and surgeons are the cheapest people on the planet. They are notoriously cheap because of fools like myself. Salespeople with unlimited expense accounts who provide the gamut of meals and entertainment from afternoon coffee to front row seats at a Broadway show. My how things have changed today.

I understood the practice of entertaining clients but never abused the privilege. Many marketers lead with entertainment as part of their pitch, "Can I bring lunch into your office for you and your staff?" Whatever the type of the entertainment I always kept it in my back pocket as a card that I would play only if necessary. My style and approach focuses on solving a problem for a customer as opposed to buttering them up with food and entertainment. I want my customers to think of me as a problem solver and not a party planner!

I am also saying that I was not exempt from this practice, as a matter of fact you were given an expense budget for the sole purpose of entertaining clients. If you did not exhaust that budget it was a negative on your annual review! Access to the customer is the key. Can entertaining customers open the door and provide you with the necessary access that is needed to make a presentation? Absolutely!

I have to commence with my first exposure to this practice. My first medical device job was in the homecare space. Our company could provide whatever type of medical equipment or service that the patient needed at their home when they were released from the hospital. It was a local New York City based company. I was assigned my first sales trainer, he was an old time "Salesman" who showed me the ropes. The end of the year was approaching. In early December he says, "We have to go to the office and talk to the boss." I asked, "Why?" He said, "It's the holidays and we have to go and see a bunch of customers in the next few days and give them a gift?" I said, "A gift, for what?" His response was, "Do you like this job?" I said, "Yes!" He said, "Be quiet and learn from me!"

We go to see the boss. He arrives with a list of customers and what type of gift they prefer. It was like a Santa Claus list for a group of kids, Johnny wants a bike, Mary wants a doll, and Jimmy wants a baseball. This was classic. He gives the itemized list by customer name and account with their gift preference to the boss. He knew exactly how to bribe them. Joe at hospital "A" wants Scotch, Jane at hospital "B" wants perfume, Ann at hospital "C" wants Broadway tickets, and Chris at hospital "D" just wants CASH! The boss agreed and approved the expense report/gifts and for the next two weeks we went to see customers and were able to play Santa Claus delivering Scotch, perfume, tickets, and cash to his best customers. Classic! Those were the days!

As you read through these examples of the abuse of entertainment you can understand why I always kept that card in my back pocket.

The government needed to step in. A watchdog needed to be put in place. Enough was enough. The Physician Payments Sunshine Act, commonly called the Sunshine Act,[6] was enacted by Congress in March 2010 as part of the Patient Protection and Affordable Care Act, or the healthcare reform law. The law is intended to make the relationships between the healthcare industry and healthcare

---

[6] Reference of Sunshine Act
https://www.google.com/url?sa=t&rct=j&q=&esrc=s&source=web&cd
=15&cad=rja&uact=8&ved=2ahUKEwjG16GJ1KneAhUxn-AKHcR7B4
oQFjAOegQIABAC&url=https%3A%2F%2Fwww.pharma.us.novartis.
com%2Fsites%2Fwww.pharma.us.novartis.com%2Ffiles%2Fsunshine-faq.
pdf&usg=AOvVaw1aigXIth3pdbBtsVENWfmq

professionals more transparent. The Sunshine Act requires applicable manufacturers of drugs, devices, biologicals, and medical supplies to report certain payments or other "transfers of value" provided to physicians, teaching hospitals and other research entities.

Dollar amounts and limits were put on the cost of each individual meal, and simple office gifts, while other marketing material such as pens and pads were eliminated. Food was deemed compensation. How can a bagel be compensation? Let's say the food costs two hundred dollars and the doctor has ten meals over the course of the year. That's two thousand dollars of compensation that the doctor has received tax free! Everything is being scrutinized today. The number of prescriptions that a doctor writes is monitored and tied into the amount of entertainment that was documented. Ouch! If the number of prescriptions or the amount of the entertainment does not match up, it can cause a red flag that goes up, and that can trigger an investigation. Ouch!

Today customer entertainment needs to be legitimized. How do you mask the entertainment or donation into something that just sounds better? Education! The medical device and pharmaceutical industry has figured out that the loophole around the stigma associated with entertaining customers can be cloaked under the guise of education. Today every meal, whether a breakfast cup of coffee and a donut, or a bottle of water and a sandwich for lunch, a late afternoon coffee break with cookies, or a dinner at a fine dining establishment with premium wine being served, somehow education has to be part of the conversation. It has to be documented what was spoken about over the meal, who attended, and can even require a signature page of all attendees. Doctors are not happy about this. There was a time when you could entertain and feed anyone, including the spouse of the doctor. Forget that today, spouses have to pay their own way. How do you think that conversation goes with the doctor? They are used to getting everything for free.

It was common for medical device and pharmaceutical manufacturers to have tremendous budgets for trade shows, conferences and symposiums. A manufacturer could easily spend a million dollars at a major event. A big chunk of the budget went for entertainment during the event. Throwing a party for ten thousand guests can get expensive when you consider food, adult beverages and have to hire some "Has Been" musician from a generation ago to perform at the event. Those days are over as well. They still attend the event and can still spend the same amount of money, but instead of the funds being spent on entertainment the money is donated to the association for education purposes.

I attended a symposium at one of the most prestigious hospitals not only in this country, but on the planet, with a Madison Avenue address in New York City. The symposium attracted physicians focusing on cutting edge technology where the hospital is noted as a "Center of Excellence." Attending the symposium cost the company a few thousand dollars. The physician running the symposium was a KOL (Key Opinion Leader) and a "Champion" for the product. A Champion is a customer who will stand up for your product and spout the reason why they use the product and why you should as well. From a marketing perspective I don't care what it costs to support a KOL, you need the Champion in your corner.

The KOL solicits support for the symposium for every vendor that they support. Multiply that figure by the number of companies that want representation at the symposium. Some customers want extra special exposure at the symposium and pony up more cash to be listed as a tiered sponsor from bronze to platinum. If you do not support the KOL, the relationship between the KOL and the marketer can begin to sour, putting pressure on the marketer to support the event. I lost count of how many of these events I have attended for the past three decades but the modus operandi is always the same. Squeeze or extract whatever you can from the marketer to generate revenue shrouded under the veil of education.

Does it ever get blunter than this? A doctor asking a marketer, "What's in it for me?" The doctor does not want to hear that your device or medication can help their patient and deliver overall better patient outcomes. What's in it for me means how much do I get out of it. In the old days that could have meant tickets for events, samples, lunches, dinners, the ability to bill insurance companies for the patient visit, support for their conferences or even cold hard cash. I had a colleague who was asked by a doctor to provide a laptop for their kid who was heading off to college. How does that look on an expense report? Deals are made all the time with entertainment providers, especially caterers who provide the food for the doctors' offices. It can be very lucrative for the caterer. The caterer bills the marketer's company credit card for the food, the caterer hands the marketer cash instead of the food. The marketer shows up at the doctor's office with a laptop instead of the food. That's creative accounting! That practice has been curtailed.

There was a vascular surgeon whom I had called on a decade earlier with a different product. I remember that he was one of the top doctors in town and I put him on my radar as a prospect for the new product that I was marketing. I tried every way to get in front of him to make a presentation. I was stalled by the gate keeper every time. I wanted to meet with the surgeon so I pulled out the entertainment card. As soon as I offered to bring lunch to the office I was given an appointment. It was a very specific date, with a very specific time, which was a little strange, but I booked it anyway.

I get to the office with bags of food in my hand and my briefcase filled with samples and marketing material for my presentation. The nurse at the front desk smiled when I walked in the door and said to me, "Great you are here!" She seemed enthusiastic about my arrival. She whispered to another nurse, "He's here." That nursed whispered the same thing to another nurse and then the nurse manager walked out and said, "Great you are here, come with me." I proceeded to the break room where they have the salespeople set up the food and the information for the presentation. Let me remind you that this is a high end surgeon's office, with actual patients in the lobby waiting to see the surgeon. This is how the drill usually works. You show up with the food, set it up, feed the staff and when the surgeon gets a few minutes they grab some food, call you in to their office and you get your five minutes to make your presentation. I have completed this drill so many times and it is effective. All you need sometimes is a few minutes with a decision maker to move you along the sales process.

This lunch was different. I notice that the break room was decorated with Happy Birthday decorations all over, specifically Happy Fiftieth Birthday signs. I figured it out, why the specific date and time? The office manager knew they were throwing a birthday party for one of the nurses on that day. Why not have someone else pay for the food? I get it. It is part of the drill. The nurses also planned some other entertainment beside the food that I was providing. They ordered a male stripper to the surgeon's office at twelve noon on a Wednesday afternoon. I got there before the male stripper, they thought that I was the male stripper! It gets worse. While setting up the food, who comes strolling in, a male stripper dressed as a doctor. An old male stripper. I was probably pushing forty at the time, the average age of the nurses was around fifty and the stripper was the oldest person in the room. The room was crowded and I was stuck in the back of the room and could not leave. I had to watch the male stripper go through the show. Nurses, in their uniforms, were tipping him with dollar bills, all of this going on with patients in the waiting room. I have never felt so violated in my life as a salesperson. I did get my five minutes with the surgeon and I had to ask him about the festivities. He said, "We get a little wild around here!" No kidding!

I reference a million dollar capital equipment deal several times throughout this book because there were multiple marketing applications throughout the sales process. This was a chain of more than ten hospitals with two flagship campuses making the decision on which product all of the members would use. I needed to get the blessing of the flagship sites in order to move forward. In one hospital, while it took close to one year to get there, gave me their blessing. In the second hospital it was a different story. Stonewalled to death. No progress. I needed to see the Chief of Anesthesia. I decided to take the entertainment route. I approach the nurse manager about setting up a lunch for the department where I could get a few minutes with the Chief. I needed face time with one physician. The nurse manager informed me that to see the Chief of Anesthesia I had to feed the entire department. Fifty-three physicians and nurses! I agreed to it because I had no choice.

Most times when you bring free food, the customers are thankful and respectful. I pick the food and bring the food because I need to insure that everything goes smoothly. Not this time. The nurse manager pulls out a binder filled with menus from the finest restaurants within the vicinity of the hospital. I said, "I order the food and I bring the food." The manager said, "That is not how we do it here. I pick the food, I order the food and you give me your company credit card so I can place the order." I said really? She then proceeded to thumb through the menus stating, "We ordered from here last week, next week we are ordering from there, here you go this is the restaurant I am ordering from." I said really? What Nerve! Close to one thousand dollars to feed fifty-three physicians and nurses.

The lunch comes. I feed fifty-two people with no sign of the chief of anesthesia. The one person I bought the food for does not show up! At the end of the lunch who comes walking into the breakroom, the Chief of Anesthesia. He was late because he is the Chief, and was stuck in the adjacent operating room with a problem patient. He had some food gave me some time and in five minutes I was able to convey the features and the benefits of the device. He had a previous positive experience with an earlier version of the device, looked at the next generation of the device that I was presenting, nodded his head and gave me his blessing. This meeting did move the project forward eventually leading to the closing of the million dollar deal.

I called on a small practice of physicians who were not current customers but were doctors that I wanted to meet with. The office manager informed me that the only way to meet with the doctors is to schedule a lunch. I was put on their calendar. When I gave them my business card I noticed that they had a ridiculous amount of lunches scheduled by sales representatives filling the calendar. Many doctor's offices tell their staff that a perk with working here is that you get free lunch. I did not think much about this, it was quite common. The lunch was on a Wednesday. Early that Monday morning I call the office to inform them that I was not canceling the lunch, I wanted to reschedule the lunch. Something came up. This is two days before the lunch! Here was the response from the office manager, "What do you mean that you are canceling the lunch. I said I am not canceling the lunch I want to reschedule. She said, what do you expect us to do for lunch if you are canceling? If you don't show up with lunch we are going to charge you one hundred dollars. If you do not pay the one hundred dollars you will never, ever see the doctors in this office!" What nerve! I never went there again!

A medical device manufacturer who had over ninety-two percent market share for their product had an interesting expense policy. When you market a product that has ninety-two percent market there is little need for selling skills. It is more Public Relations than Personal Selling. I had become friendly with the local sales representative in my territory. We had non competing products but we called on the same type of physician. I would frequently bump into him in a hospital or a doctor's office and he always seemed to be planning some kind of entertainment. I talked to him one day about it and he said that he does very little selling and mostly entertaining customers to make sure that they are happy with his medical device. He had an unlimited budget for entertainment. Unlimited meant unlimited. I asked him one day what is the most money he ever spent on a few doctors in New York City? Twenty thousand dollars! Are you kidding? Can a few people spend twenty thousand dollars in one night in New York City? Here is how you do it. You start with a dinner at the most expense steakhouse, ordering expensive wine and food. After dinner entertainment needs to be provided, so when a customer said I want to go to a Broadway show, or a sporting event they don't mean that they want to sit in the cheap seats, they want to sit in the front row. That costs money. Start adding it up and that's how you spend twenty grand on one night! A little excessive if you ask me.

When I started my medical device career almost thirty years ago there was a common marketing practice that many medical device and pharmaceutical companies employed. Research has proven that if a doctor becomes comfortable prescribing a medical device or medication they can become extremely brand loyal for many years. The strategy was to get to the doctor when they are very young and impressionable. How do you get to the doctor? How do you get access to the doctor? How do you get their attention? The answer if FOOD, FOOD, FOOD, all day every day. Young doctors are called residents. Yes, they have graduated from medical school, but they are still learning how to be a doctor. Where do they learn? Where do they get to "practice" on patients? Yes, a hospital is a hospital, but not all hospitals are teaching hospitals. Teaching hospitals are the hospitals where residents get to "practice" on patients. Teaching hospitals are affiliated with a medical school, who rotates the residents through their residency program at the teaching hospital. Residents are overworked, underpaid, impressionable and always hungry.

The strategy was to contact the department in the hospital where the residents reported to. It could have been the department of surgery, or a specific specialty department such as the department of orthopedics, cardiology, neurology etc.

All you need to do was find the name of the Chief resident, the most senior resident, who could coordinate a Resident Conference Lunch, and contact them. It was an easy conversation, "Dr. X, are you the Chief resident? Can I schedule a Resident Conference Lunch with the residents?" The response from Dr. X was always something like this, "You want to bring free food for the residents? You can come Tuesday, there are twenty-two residents." They usually did not ask ANY questions about your product. They were starving, and hungry and did the free food get you the access that was needed to make a presentation? All day!

The silver lining was not only the access to the young impressionable resident, it could open a much more difficult door to open, the door of the attending physician. The attending physician is the established doctor who is much more difficult to gain access to. If you take care of the residents and you have a pretty good product, the residents could and did pave the way to gain access to the much more important potential customer, the attending physician.

That sounds like a piece of cake, you bring the food, and you get the access. It was not that easy. The first few times I scheduled a Resident Conference Lunch I had the food delivered, what a mistake! Teaching hospitals are massive structures, with buildings that can spread across a campus. Having food delivered to your Resident Conference Lunch can be a challenge. Today's lunch is in the Jones building, in the Northeast wing, on the fourteenth floor, in the Smith conference room. What? Do you know how hard it is for that food to reach where it is supposed to go? Do you know how many times I would be standing in front of twenty-five residents, who really only wanted and agreed to meet with me for the free food, only to have to stall because the caterer could not find the Smith conference room, on the fourteenth floor of the Northeast wing of the Jones building.

What is the solution? I became the caterer's delivery boy. I delivered chicken in high school and delivered pizza in college so I knew the drill. Did I ever walk into a hospital carrying ten pizzas, or four dozen bagels, or five buckets of chicken, plus associated side dishes, drinks, plates, forks, knives and napkins? Yes to all! How do you keep food hot or cold in your car? Figure it out! I also had to carry in all of my marketing material for my presentation. Of course I did it myself, who was going to help? It was an effective marketing and sales strategy and in the end the resources that were spent on the entertainment did have a positive impact to support the development of the relationship between marketer and customer. Today that practice is frowned upon in teaching hospitals! This is an example of how entertainment has changed from thirty years ago to where we are today.

After a few years as a salesperson I expressed an interest in thinking about sales training as a future endeavor. This is what eventually led me into university teaching. I became a field sales trainer for two medical device manufacturers. This meant I remained in the field as a salesperson but took on the additional responsibility of training salespeople in the field. I loved it. For the most part the field training assignments revolved around showing the newly hired salesperson what the job was like in the field on a daily basis. They often rode shotgun and just tagged along with me to see what a typical day in the field was like. The most effective use of this activity was a salesperson spending two full weeks in the field with me as their field sales trainer, eight to five, every day for two weeks. By the end of the second week the trainee would have witnessed almost every type of sales situation that they would experience when they were in the field as a salesperson.

What I loved about it was that I was given the opportunity to work with salespeople from several different markets all over the country, and literally all over the world who had the same job that I had in their individual market. I was based in New York City. The corporate training philosophy was to send the new salesperson to the worst market in the country, with the most demanding customers on the planet. If the trainee did not run away from the opportunity after spending two weeks in the cesspool market of New York City maybe they were a keeper! I literally trained salespeople from all over the country including salespeople who sold the same products that I did in Asia and South America.

I have to write about my South American sales trainee, Fabio, who had the exact same job that I had for the global leader in the medical device industry. The only difference was that my geographical territory was New York City and his geographical territory was the continent of South America!

We spent the aforementioned two weeks in the field together. One common theme about our discussions about the difference between the domestic market and South American market was that here in the United States the practice of buying the business, or bribing the customer, was frowned upon, discouraged and often went against company policy. Fabio consistently responded that the first step in the sales process in South America was to initiate the sales cycle with a bribe to the customer. It was expected. It was acceptable. It was part of the sales process. It was part of doing business in that market. We went back and forth for our two week field visit with, that might be a normal business practice in South America, but here in the United States we are above board with our relationships with our customers.

I was having an issue with one of my largest accounts. This was a flagship account, the number one cancer hospital on the planet, where patients from every corner of the globe traveled to New York City to receive the best care for their illness. This customer spent several hundred thousand dollars a year on my products. My company was piloting a software product that could help the hospital manage their ten million dollar inventory of surgical instruments. The software Beta project, where we asked the customer to test our new software, was a nightmare. The software Beta project almost crashed the entire IT network of the hospital, straining my relationship with the customer.

My manager's decision to smooth over the situation was to take care of the manager of the Central Supply Department, the point person in the Beta software project, and the best advocate for our products throughout the hospital.

My manager instructed me to pull over the company car, with Fabio my South American trainee in the car, in Times Square New York, and go into a bank and take my company credit card out and charge three hundred dollars in cash and put it in an envelope and deliver it to my estranged customer. I doubled parked the car in New York City, I said, "Fabio watch the car." I went into the bank, back in the day when there were bank tellers at the window. I looked into the car and I could see Fabio watching the teller count out the cash.

We go to see the customer, he was not happy about the potential crash of their network due to the inefficiency of my company's botched Beta site attempt to manage the inventory of their surgical instruments. I placed the three hundred dollars in an envelope on the customer's desk, without personally handing it to him. When you just drop something on a desk you cannot be accused of handing something to a customer, our hands never met. We walk out of the office, Fabio states, "You just bribed the customer!" I said, "I have no idea what you are talking about, I just left a thank you card for a great customer. We are not in South America, we don't bribe the customer here, and we are above that." Within the hour the customer called and said, "I cannot accept this gift." I said, "What gift, I do not know what you are talking about?" The customer replied with, "If I accept this gift I can lose my job." I said, "What gift? If you cannot accept it can you use the funds for a holiday party for your staff?" He thought that was a great idea and it all worked out in the end.

What is the result? What is today's landscape when it comes to the entertainment of customers? Here is an apropos example. A high level meeting was scheduled with an existing customer. There were three salespeople/sales managers representing the company and one Vice-President representing the hospital. A dinner meeting was scheduled. The Vice-President agreed to attend the meeting under one condition, they would pay their own way. The salespeople looked at each other, and gave each other a wink, Ok! You can pay your own way, but at the end they would be picking up the check. The bill came, the Vice-President demanded that the restaurant put his meal on a separate check and that he paid with his own credit card. The Vice-President said, "I have to be able to show that I paid for my own meal, and I have to have a hard copy credit card receipt itemizing the charges." Again, my how things have changed!

SECTION 2

Why Your Product Drives The Bus

This section defines why your product
is the key to marketing success

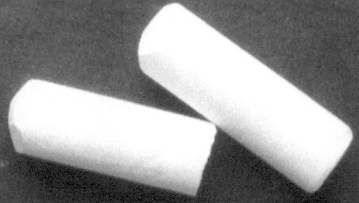

Chapter 6

....

No Product No Sale

Product Life Cycle

Products are like people, we both go through an incubation period before birth, are then born into this world, and eventually die. Some people are fortunate enough to live a long, full life and some people unfortunately meet their demise at a tender age. The same goes for products. Some products just seem to go on and on forever, and some products cannot seem to get their life off the ground and are discontinued by their manufacturer, hence ending their life.

The Product Life Cycle (PLC) is a tool used by companies to monitor where their products are in their life. Are they at the early stage, middle stage or latter stage of their life? The PLC has four stages, Introduction, Growth, Maturity and Decline.

Product Life Cycle Theory has been a key organizing principle in studies of innovation over the last twenty years and is promoted by leading management theorists as a tool for strategic decision making (Windrum & Birchenhall, 1998).[7]

----

[7] Windrum, P., & Birchenhall, C., (1998). Is Product Life Cycle Theory a special case? Dominant designs and the emergence of market niches. Structural Change and Economic Dynamics, 9(1) p.109-134.

PRODUCT LIFE CYCLE

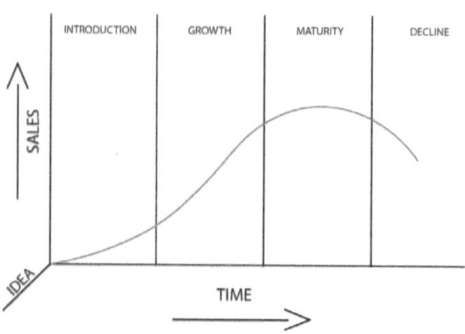

Idea Stage

This is the traditional model of the PLC, with the four stages. I believe in adding a stage, almost as a prequel to the traditional four stages. I call it the Idea stage, the stage of life of a product from conception to birth. This stage falls below the traditional graph. Why? It falls below the traditional graph because it has to. One axis of the graph measures sales, the other axis measures time. Every product starts out as an idea, it can be an astonishing idea, but it does not crack the axis where sales meets time (birth) until the idea is converted into a product and can generate revenue. The reason why the idea stage is below the graph is that if your idea is not generating any sales then it is actually costing you money.

Resources are needed for new product development, investment in the new idea (product) is necessary, salaries must be paid, all contributing to the negative line below the graph. It is an underestimating phenomenon that gets swept under the rug. The amount of time that it takes to transform the idea into something that makes money, must be considered. All kinds of forces are fighting against you. "Bring to Market" is the time it takes to transfigure your idea into a product.

Most new products fail. Pressure can be exerted from senior management to rollout a winner and digress away from the new product failure rate. Especially if your most recent batch of ideas did not experience the full product life cycle. Government regulation can be another consideration. In the medical device and pharmaceutical industry, you have to deal with the Food & Drug Administration (FDA). This is a lengthy and drawn out process. If you have a positive relationship with the FDA your application can be expedited. What if you do not? Your application for this new idea can be buried in bureaucracy and moved to the bottom of the pile. All of this can delay the birth of your product.

What this can lead to is tension from senior management to "Rush to Market" the idea. Resources are being allocated but revenue is not being recognized. Rush to Market means that the idea stage is accelerated due to the pressure to generate sales. New product development is hurried, prototype development is truncated, test marketing is curtailed, and the product may be born prematurely. Again, similar to people, premature babies are born every day but are not ready to enter the world in which they inhabit.

Eventually the product's birthday arrives and the product is hatched or launched. The new idea (product) cracks the perpendicular axis where sales meets time and you have something to sell. Revenue can be generated over time and you enter the next stage in the Product Life Cycle, Introduction.

Introduction

I would not say that introduction is the most important stage of the PLC, but it might be the most critical stage in the life of a product. To make another parallel about life it is similar to the impact that a parent can have on the nurturing of an infant and adolescent. A solid foundation in the early years can put a child on the road to success in life and the same goes for a product in the Introduction stage of the PLC.

What separates introduction from growth, maturity, and decline is that while you may want the latter three stages to last forever, you want the introduction stage to be as short as possible. Therein lies the problem. An immense amount of time, effort and resources can go into the idea stage, then when the product is launched, boom, a natural reaction is to exhale and let the product sell. Then the product gets stuck in Introduction. Moving a product from Introduction into the Growth stage can be a challenge. Unfortunately, people die at a very early age, from illness or tragedy and the same can happen to your product in the Introduction stage. Companies realize that maybe this idea, that was a great idea at conception, is really not worth the continued investment and they pull the plug and kill the product. Reasons for the lack of immobility in the Introduction stage can include being priced out of the market, the product can be over engineered, under engineered, or competitive offerings may be more attractive alternatives to your customers. This goes back to the Idea stage. At conception the innovation can seem like an impressive idea, but your competitor might beat you to the market. The dilemma is do you add all of the bells and whistles as possible (over engineer) or do you produce a product that is user friendly (under engineer)? Over engineering costs money which forces you to price your product at a premium. It is possible to miss the market, the window of opportunity might be short, and closing as we speak. Timing is a humongous variable and hitting the Introduction stage at the correct time is vital to moving onto the next stage, Growth.

Growth

Something needs to be triggered in the life of a product that moves the product from Introduction into Growth. Remember Introduction can be characterized with stagnation, uncertainty and doubt. Is this product truly an innovation? Is there a market for this innovation? What can be done to jumpstart the life of the product to move it out of Introduction and into the Growth stage are all legitimate concerns.

The spark or spurt can come from many directions. A reduction in price, or perhaps an increase in awareness, where your promotion begins to pay off can provide the fuel that launches the rapid growth that needs to take place to move from Introduction to Growth.

Once rapid growth initiates and the product clearly moves into the Growth stage a collective breath can be taken. High fives can be given but the best way to describe it is to say that you need to proceed with caution. The Problem Child has matured and is ready for adulthood, or perhaps ready to move out of the house and live their own life on their own. The proceed with caution tag remains because even though the product may be experiencing rapid growth, the product is still not out of the woods. It still may be part of the high failure rate of new products, or has it crossed the threshold into the low success rate space? It has not yet because the plug can still be pulled. The product, while growing, has to pay off the significant investment that was made during the Idea and Introduction stages. The product is still operating at a loss during this stage, while on the correct path, you still need to proceed with caution.

Midway through the Growth stage a noteworthy life altering circumstance occurs. Sales momentum is beginning to build. There is competition in everything in life, and the life of a product is not exempt from this phenomenon. Monopolies are not allowed in this economy, even if you market something that is truly unique it will face competition. Your competition has two choices, do they "knock off" your innovation and make their version of your product or do they dismiss the innovation? Do they copy or ignore your innovation? I can make a case for each competitive decision. If they ignore your innovation you can capture the entire market for yourself and not split the market share pie. Your competitor can copy your innovation, work around the patents that you have established, and possibly improve your idea and counter your product with a viable competitive alternative. You WANT your competitor to copy your innovation. It is natural to think that this is a gloomy day in the life of your product. This is a fabulous day in the life of your product.

Imitation is the greatest and most sincere form of flattery. If your competitor ignores your innovation, what they are stating is that this was not that great of an idea in the first place. If it was such a stupendous idea your competitor would market their version of your innovation. The first people that should be notified of the competitive threat are the executives above the new product development committee who have been pointing a gun at your head. They have been putting the pressure on the committee to crank out a winning product and stating that, "This is such an impressive product. Our competitors have decided not to ignore this innovation, but copy it!"

For a product to proceed in the PLC and have the full life it is going to have to face competitive threats at some time in its life. Why not face the competitive threat midway through the growth stage where the ball is starting to roll, and steam is building up. Why not go head to head with the competitive threat at this stage, where only the strong will survive.

As stated earlier you want the Introduction stage to be brief, but you want Growth to last as long as possible. During the latter stage of Growth the rapid growth begins to slow down and leads the product into the next stage, Maturity.

Maturity

Maturity can be depicted as the stage in the life of a product where growth still occurs but the rate or speed of the acceleration begins to slow down. The deceleration can be caused by competitive alternatives or the fact that the product has been purchased by customers who have recognized the benefit of the product. The solution to their problem has been satisfied.

Maturity is a celebrated day in the life of a product. At one time twenty-one was the age that signified the move from adolescence into adulthood. This might be extended today with the emergence of millennials occupying their parent's basement well beyond the aforementioned age.

This date needs to be celebrated because it represents the metamorphosis from potential product failure (High failure rate of new products) to entry into the club of product success (Low success rate of new products). If a product dies during the Idea, Introduction, or Growth stage it is considered a failure because profit can barely be recognized. There becomes a point late in Growth and early in Maturity where a break-even threshold is crossed, steering the product into profitability, hence a successful product.

If a product is discontinued at this point, look at where the product is in its life on the graph.

PRODUCT LIFE CYCLE

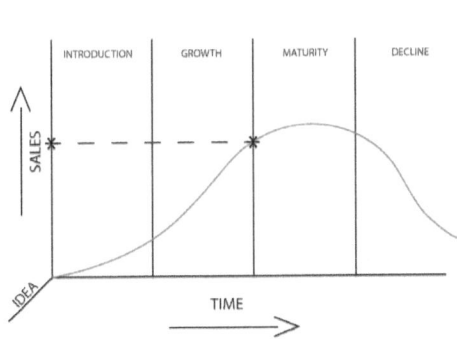

Over time sales have been accruing. There are enough sales to pay off the initial investment incurred during the three earlier stages of the Product Life Cycle.

Maturity should be fun, the best time in the life of the product. The challenge is how do you extend this happy time? The goal is to stretch Maturity as long as you can. Brand Awareness has been established, now is the time to extend the brand, and move through the continuum of Brand Intensity, from Brand Awareness, to Brand Preference, to Brand Insistence. Successful television shows are examples of products who are in Maturity. Shows where you guess the price of a product, search for your fortune at the spin of a wheel, give the answer to the question in the form of a question, or a network news magazine that plays off the number of minutes in an hour are all products that are in Maturity and seem to go on forever and ever, for decades! Finding new uses, new markets or new customers all contribute to extending the Maturity stage of the PLC.

Stretching Maturity does not have to be as complicated as it seems. The market is constantly changing and what was popular yesterday might not meet the needs of the market moving forward. A simple tweak, or modification to the original design or product offering can lengthen Maturity. Taking a chocolate candy, that is supposed to melt in your mouth and not in your hands and adding a peanut to its core can accomplish this. Adding pretzel flavors to it, making the product in green and red colors for the holidays, orange and black for Halloween, red and pink for Valentine's Day, or offering pastel colors for the spring all extended the Maturity of this product. This is the model or mentality that must be followed to prolong Maturity. Everything in life will eventually die, the same applies to the PLC. Eventually sales will begin to slow down and the product moves into the final stage of life, Decline.

Decline

Death is inevitable for people and for products. Some deaths are tragic and sudden and some are not. Decline does not necessarily mean that life has ended but merely changed. People can get sick and succumb to an illness in a short period of time, or drop dead of a heart attack and experience an immediate death. Other people can get sick and take medication that can prolong their life, sometimes for years. The same goes for products. A company can pull the plug, discontinue the product and it is gone immediately. Other products can have an elongated, prolonged and protracted decline that can take years for the product to meet its maker. Decline can still be profitable so why the rush?

What usually pushes a product into Decline is technology. New, more efficient technology that makes the current product obsolete. The problem is how do you know that your new technology will replace the current widget? Sometimes it is a seamless transition, sometimes it is not. Remember when you introduce the new technology you are actually starting a new PLC, and all of the aforementioned issues regarding the early stages of the PLC are applied again. There is no guarantee that the new innovation will be accepted. With that in mind there is no rush to kick dirt on the product that has been profitable and is in the latter stage of the PLC.

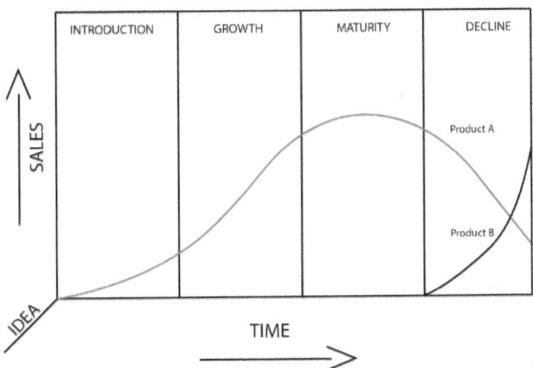

The key to success is to make the decision when to introduce the new widget and overlap the life cycle of both products. A strategy of planned obsolescence must be put in place. What is the timeline for the Decline stage? Just as the initial innovation is hitting the Decline stage the new innovation should be going through the Idea and Introduction stages. As the product moves towards the Growth stage and looks like it will be a winning innovation is the time to think about how long you want to prolong the Decline stage.

An example would be how we watch movies. There was a time when you had to go to a movie theater to see your favorite movie stars. Then movies were broadcast on television. An innovation called the VHS or VCR then took the market by storm. Questions were raised. Why would you leave your home to go to the movies when you could watch a movie at your convenience in the comfort of your own home? A competitive alternative to the VCR was introduced, the Laser Disc. It never got out of Introduction and it failed. The DVD player was introduced and it put the VCR into Decline. Blu-Ray was supposed to supplant the DVD, it has not. Digital on-demand formats have leapfrogged all of these modalities. The point is that do not be too quick to bury a product because you never know if the new technology is going to capture the market that you are looking for.

Market Share Versus Market Growth Matrix

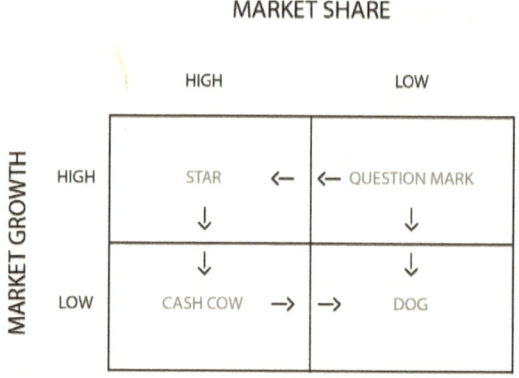

The Product Life Cycle is one way of taking a snapshot at where your products are in their life. Understand that most companies have more than one product offering or product line. A Product Line is what products are offered to the market by a company. Some companies can have several products, some can have hundreds and some can have thousands of product offerings, so the Product Life Cycle applies to every product offering that a company offers to the market. Managing where all of these product offerings are in their life can be a challenge. Another theory of product management is to utilize the Boston Consulting Group's (BCG) Market Share versus Market Growth Matrix. The product portfolio approach to marketing strategy formulation has gained wide acceptance among managers of diversified companies (Day, 1977).[8]

The four quadrant matrix measures Market Growth on the vertical axis and Market Share on the horizontal axis. Market Share is split between Low Market Share and High Market Share. Market Growth is segmented by High Market Growth and Low Market Growth. The four quadrants are Question Marks (Problem Child), Star, Cash Cow and Dog. Question Marks represent Low Market Share and High Growth. Star products signify High Market Share and High Growth. Cash Cows characterize products that are High Market Share and Low Growth, while Dogs embody the quadrant of Low Market Share and Low Growth.

There are a lot of similarities and parallels between the PLC and BCG matrix. There is a lot of overlap between the two theories. One has four stages that a product goes through (PLC), the other has four quadrants in a box (matrix) that products pass through. The correlation to the PLC is as follows: Question Marks are in Introduction, Stars are in Growth, Cash Cows are in Maturity, and Dogs are in Decline.

---

[8] Day, G., (1977). The product portfolio approach to marketing strategy formulation has gained wide acceptance among managers of diversified companies. Journal of Marketing. 41(2) p,29-38.

PRODUCT LIFE CYCLE

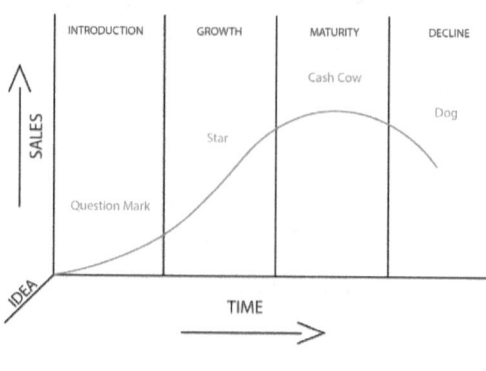

MARKET SHARE

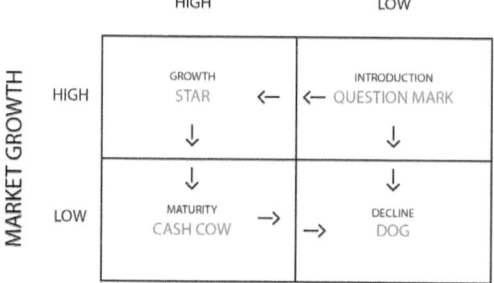

The overlapping and consistency of the two theories are an excellent way to judge where a product is, and where a product is moving in the future. The overlapping confirms and validates each theory and they play off of each other, meaning that it is prudent to look at both theories to make a judgment as to what is the overall health of your product line.

Question Marks (Problem Child)

Every product starts out as a Question Mark. Question Marks reside in the upper right quadrant where high growth converges with low market share. Question marks have low market share but high growth potential. Why the high growth potential? The company has identified a segment of the marketplace in which they compete in as a space where there is potential for innovation. The Question Mark is their answer to fill the space with their new innovation. Question Marks have low market share because they are new to this space, maybe new to the game and need to raise the awareness of their new product. Problem Child is another nickname for this quadrant in the matrix. Why Problem Child? It is a perfect analogy. A Problem Child can be defined as an adolescent who is at the crossroads in their development. Life is all about decisions and choices. At this stage in your life you are presented with many forks in the road that can either make or break your development as an adult and can impact your life for years. A Problem Child's life is filled with uncertainty, do you make the correct choices that can either set the Problem Child up on the right road, or does the Problem Child make the wrong decisions that can impact their development? It is the same for products. Does the product head west in the matrix towards becoming a Star product or does the product head south in the matrix towards becoming a Dog?

Too much ambiguity during this stage. Very similar to the Introduction stage of the PLC. You want the time that a product spends in this quadrant to be as brief and truncated as possible. Comparisons abound with the life of a young adult. Some get it very early in their life, and move on to becoming a Star, some are stuck in the stage and are searching for their identity and purpose in life, and unfortunately some Problem Children fall by the wayside.

It goes back to the definition of what a Question Mark really is. You just do not know the answer, this is why it is a Question Mark. Clearly, the same as the Introduction stage of the PLC, you just do not know if the Question Mark will ever reach its potential and move out of this quadrant. It can take a lot of time to get out of the Question Mark quadrant, and there is no doubt, that due to the uncertainty that is associated with being a Question Mark, it is the most problematic quadrant of the matrix to navigate out of.

Star

Star products are the best products to market and sell. Just look at their position in the matrix. The upper left quadrant where high growth meets high market share. Star products experience high growth and high market share. High growth means that something is going well, high market share means that the product is capturing the lion's share of the market. Star products do not just help you get out of bed in the morning, they force you to jump out of bed and get ready for your day. Marketing Star products is a great day, a fun day, a day to look forward to, a day that flies by and a day that you wish would not end.

All of this glee and enthusiasm is caused by the position of a Star in the matrix. High growth means that the snow ball is rolling downhill and awareness has caught on. Star products have assumed the position of market leader with fast-tracking growth rates. Star products do start to generate profits but these profits must be reinvested in other elements of the Marketing Mix such as distribution to capitalize on the momentum that has been generated to insure that distribution outlets are reached to maximize awareness and availability. A "Strike while the iron is hot" mentality must permeate throughout the organization while a product is a Star because this enthusiasm will not last forever.

Cash Cow

If Star products give you a reason to get out of bed in the morning, Cash Cow products give you a reason to go back to bed, sleep in, and eventually get out of bed in the morning. You can hit the snooze button if you are marketing Cash Cows. Cash cow products are in the lower left quadrant where low growth intersects with high market share. Growth begins to slow down, but a dominant market share position exists.

Cash Cow is one of the most overused and misunderstood words in marketing. Cash Cows sell themselves. Something has to pay the bills or as they say, "Keep the lights on" and Cash Cows provide the funding that keeps the organization above water. Milk the cow!

Dogs

If Stars give you reason to get out of bed in the morning, and Cash Cows give you a reason to sleep in, Dogs give you no reason to get out of bed in the morning. Dogs occupy the lower right quadrant where low growth coincides with low market share. Instead of hitting the snooze button, if you are marketing Dogs, you want to smash the alarm clock and bury your head in your pillow and go back to bed. I know that there are a lot of dog lovers out there, but the term Dog in marketing is not a good one. I do not know why it was not penned a fish, bird, or a turtle, but Dog has stuck and it is a stigma in marketing that is not going to go away. Some say having Dogs to market is a challenge but it beats you up, wears you down, and sucks the life and energy out of you.

The BCG matrix provides an excellent view of where your product line is heading. It is recommended to plot each product and plug it into where it fits in the matrix. There is much significance with each quadrant, and much meaning in the lines that separate each quadrant and form the matrix. Are you top heavy on one side of the matrix versus the other side? Are you deficient on another side of the matrix?

If you look at the matrix the vertical line that separates Stars and Cash Cows from Question Marks and Dogs is noteworthy. If your product line is weighted with more products plotted on the left side, meaning if you have more Stars and Cash Cows than Question Marks and Dogs, your product line is healthy. Hence, if your product line is slanted to the right side of this line, your product line is not as healthy. Think of what the consequences are of being on the right side of the line. That would mean that your product line is dominated by Question Marks and Dogs. Which means a lot of uncertainty (Question Marks/Introduction) and worry (Dogs/Decline) about the future of your product line. The horizontal line presents a different perspective. If you are below the horizontal line (Cash Cows/Maturity, Dogs/Decline) your product line has seen better days and the future of your product line is in doubt. After looking at the BCG matrix through this lens you can conclude that you want your product line skewed towards the left side of the matrix. Strategies that can be implemented include discontinuing the Dogs, yes, putting the Dog down and moving forward with the Stars and Cash Cows, while still attempting to develop the Question Marks because they are the future of the product line.

Another outcome of the BCG matrix analysis are expectations. If it is concluded that your product line is in good health senior management's expectations for success can be elevated. Again, there is nothing better than getting out of bed with Stars and Cash Cows on your side, but be careful what you wish for. There are no excuses. What happens when external market conditions such as the status of the economy and government regulations come into play? An example is what has happened in the medical device industry. The combination of the economic downturn coupled with the changes that the government has implemented in healthcare have brought the medical device industry to its knees. It does not matter that you are marketing Stars and Cash Cows, the industry upheaval has had a dramatic effect on the marketing of medical devices. Senior management does not see it this way, from senior management's perspective all they see is that their product line is filled with Stars and Cash Cows and the expectations are not being met. No excuses! Marketing Question Marks and Dogs can reduce these expectations and can provide a built in excuse for why the sales for these products are so sluggish.

The Importance Of New Products: The New Product Development Process

All products have a life. What happens when a product is at the end of its life? Do you pick up your marbles and go home? Of course not. You need new blood, you always need an infusion of new products to prolong the life of an organization.

New product development is an essential cog in the wheel of not only marketing success, but it can impact the vitality and future of the entire organization. The new product arena is as dynamic as any other element in business. You need new products! With that being said, new products fail at an alarming rate.

Despite the high cost of developing and testing new products, eighty percent of all new product introductions fail (Boone & Kurtz, 1995)[9]. Reasons for new product failure abound. Why such a high failure rate? The prime cause of failure is the lack of need of the new innovation coupled with the fact that most new innovations do not differentiate themselves from current competitive offerings. Why venture into this sea of failure? Why not focus on your existing successful product line? Every good thing in life must come to an end. If a new product development strategy is ignored, or placed on the back burner it can place the future of the organization at risk.

New product development needs to be embraced not frowned upon. When top companies, blue-chip companies, who have been around for a century take a step back and review their product portfolio it is popular to simply dissect their products into two categories, their new products and their old products. Does it get any more basic than this? New products are classified as any innovation that has been introduced to the market in the last five years. Any product that has a life of over five years is classified as an old product. When you add up the new and the old if the percentage of sales for the new products

---

[9] Boone, L., & Kurtz, D., (1995). Contemporary Marketing. 8 p.403.

compared to the previous year's sales increases, then it is deemed a successful year. The message is clear, while a company's old products may have put the company on the map, it will be the new products that drive the company into the future. That type of mentality is how you stay around for a century as a company!

NEW PRODUCT DEVELOPMENT PROCESS

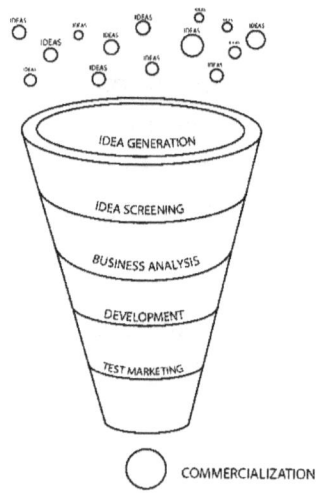

Idea Generation

I was given the opportunity to sit on a new product development committee for a medical device company. It was an eclectic committee which included members from all of the stakeholders involved with the marketing, manufacturing and selling of the device. There were members of the field sales department, who actually sold the product to the customer. Members of the marketing department who were tasked with marketing the innovation were there, along with representation from manufacturing, who assembled the innovation. Research and Development was in the room to mold the idea into a prototype and eventual product. Finance had a seat at the table to run the numbers to see how this innovation could generate revenue for the company.

Everyone who sat in that room played a different role in the new product development process. As you can track the progression of the idea through the funnel, each department's role became more apparent. Each stage of the process gave each department the chance to step up to the plate and make their contribution.

The Chairperson of the committee was a regional sales manager who walked in the room at eight AM on Monday morning and said, "You are locked in this room until five PM on Friday. You are being charged with coming up with new ideas for products that we need to focus on in the near future. Think of a blue sky!"

Blue sky? What does that mean? I raised my hand and said, "What's a blue sky?" His response was, "A blue sky means a perfect day in a perfect world. In a perfect world what products would we be offering to our customers?"

During the idea generation of the new product development process the funnel is as wide as possible, juggling as many balls in the air, hoping that someday one of these ideas will actually be spit of the funnel.

Idea Screening

If the blue sky is the perfect day, then what happens when clouds arrive? What about more challenging weather? A blue sky answer in that committee meeting can be, what about a product that cures cancer or cures heart disease? How about this blue sky idea, a cure for the common cold? How long have pharmaceutical companies been working on that innovation? The filtration process from the pie in the sky idea compared to concrete product innovation commences.

Business Analysis

What holds back the magnificent idea from commercial success? Ideas are great and profound but if the innovation cannot be monetized and converted into a profitable endeavor then it will just remain a pie in the sky illusion. Early in the new product development process a business analysis must be conducted. Every potential cost associated with the new product must be factored in. Including manufacturing costs, advertising, promotion, distribution and any other marketing related or business development cost must be estimated. Once this baseline cost is established a pricing structure must be put in place. Profit is simple to calculate. What am I charging the customer minus what does it cost? What is a gross profit margin that the company can live with? Getting over this hurdle is significant. Once the business analysis is completed, it might be determined that while a great idea, the company cannot monetize the idea and the idea can be stalled in the funnel. Let the number crunching begin!

Development

Once the financial and business analysis hurdle is cleared the project progresses into the development stage. The ball is now handed off to the research and development engineers. Here is where the blunder can occur. Research and development might have their vision for the product while sales and marketing can see the innovation through a different lens. The research and development vision is more laboratory driven while the sales and marketing lens presents a view that reflects what is going on in the real world. If research and development does not listen to the feedback given from the field, it can be fatal. What type of feedback from the field? Salespeople are the boots on the ground, they are in front of the customer all day every day. Customers can provide valuable information with regards to new product development, "I like your product, but if it could only do this I would love your product." This type of intelligence must be channeled through research and development in the initial design of the innovation.

Now the fun begins. Do you make the innovation bigger, smaller, over engineered or more user friendly? There are always tradeoffs. An advantage of one strategy is typically a disadvantage of the other. If you think of the success that the smart phone has had it combined the notion of a small device that is both high tech and user friendly.

All breeds of setbacks and delays can impair the progress of the projects. There can be regulatory setbacks. In the medical device and pharmaceutical industry the FDA acts as the watch dog over the industry with regards to new product development. Do we need this regulation? Absolutely, without this regulation companies would rush to market products that might not be safe for consumers. Remember it is a rush to move the idea through the funnel and avoiding any setbacks or delays is crucial.

What is the company's relationship with the FDA? A positive relationship with the FDA can accelerate the process. A negative relationship with the FDA can tie up your application process in meaningless federal government red tape. How do you develop a positive relationship with the FDA compared to the ill-fated negative relationship? The FDA works just like another popular government agency, the IRS. Just like the IRS, the FDA can show up on your doorstep unannounced and conduct an inspection (audit) of your corporate headquarters including your manufacturing facilities. It is a white glove test. If the FDA cites anything that potentially can be out of order they might give you a warning and leave. The next time that the FDA knocks on your door, if you have corrected the infraction, now you are on your way to a positive relationship which can lead to FDA clearance. Something for the record. The FDA does not approve products, you hear that all of the time, "Our product was approved by the FDA." The FDA clears products. The correct statement is to say that. "Our product was cleared by the FDA." If you ignore the FDA warning, and the next time they show up they cite the violation again, your application for FDA clearance can be stuck in the middle towards the bottom of the pile and who knows when clearance will come. Most medical device and pharmaceutical innovations are marketed and sold overseas first before they are introduced domestically because the global regulation does not exist to the extent that the domestic watch dog does.

Other setbacks and delays can occur during the development process including issues with prototypes and the actual sourcing of components that are to be utilized during the manufacturing process. Back to the rush to get through the funnel. While you are navigating through this process, your competitor can be doing the same thing and if they are more successful than you are can create a leapfrog effect. You might have conceived the idea first, but your competitor can bring the product to market quicker.

Test Marketing

Rush to market, or pushing the ball through the funnel, is always on an accelerated schedule. There is tremendous pressure not only from the higher ups in the organization, but from competitive forces that are also trying to push their ball through the funnel as well, to beat you to the punch and launch their innovation while your product is stuck in the funnel. How can you truncate the new product development process? How can you shave dollars off of the new product budget? By minimizing the impact that test marketing can have. There are several reasons why new products fail, one of the major culprits is diminishing the value of test marketing. Test marketing is an absolute component of the new product development process that needs more attention and more resources. Test marketing involves engaging a sample of the market where you can monitor the customer's interest in the new innovation. Test marketing gets truncated by limiting the amount of time for the product testing. Test marketing takes time and cost money. To test a product in three markets takes "X" amount of time, but testing a product in thirty markets increases the amount of time. To test a product in three markets costs "Y" amount of money, and testing a product in thirty markets blows the test marketing budget through the roof.

There is a sliding scale for the amount of markets tested versus the amount of time, divided by what is the budget for test marketing. What becomes statistically significant? Statistically significant refers to the amount of the sample size compared to the total population. Someone has to make a decision about how many customers are tested, in enough markets, for enough time to generate a consensus that there is a statistically significant amount of test marketing for the company to move forward with the new product development process. There is the pitfall, underestimating the statistically significant amount of customers tested which can contribute to the miscarriage with regards to the innovation.

Here is the argument for maximization of the test marketing process which includes testing in multiple markets over an extended period of time. It plays into getting away from the enormous cavity known as the amount of new product failures. When a product fails, resources are flushed down the toilet. The resource is wasted and gone forever. If a product fails because a limited budget for new product development was proposed, it does not matter what the dollar amount was, the resource is gone.

Where are the shortcuts? Test marketing in your backyard. Companies are famous for test marketing in the market near a corporate headquarters. This ties in with the increase in Corporate Social Responsibility. Most companies support the local causes and charities in their backyard. When a test marketing program is implemented in this market it is common to hear positive comments about the company's next innovation because of the brand recognition in this backyard market. "Sure I think this would be a great new product?" Here is where the judgment is jaded. The customer who you are asking could have a neighbor, friend, or relative who works for the company. The customer who you are quizzing might be a benefactor of one of the causes or charities that the company supports, they recognize the corporate brand name and say, "What a great idea!"

Another tactic is to penetrate markets where you have a stronghold over your competitor in that specific market. This can be a mistake. These are the wrong types of customers to test market. The same goes for focus groups who are assembled to ascertain feedback regarding a product, policy or corporate decision. Most focus groups are a collaboration of your elite loyal customers. Of course they are going to tell you what you want to hear.

An alternative test marketing strategy is to penetrate a market where your competition has a stranglehold on market share. Competition might be more open to be more forthcoming with their opinion on your shiny innovation. This is not as comfortable as test marketing in your backyard. How about a focus group of your competitor's best customers? Imagine what type of intelligence can be discovered from asking elementary questions to your competitor's customers such as, "Why you buy their product, what is it about our product offering that pushes you towards our competition?" What a novel concept!

The domestic market is a huge market with over three hundred plus million customers, three thousand miles from east to west and two thousand miles from north to south. Market Research can drill down a market by region, state, city, county and zip code. A limited, narrow approach to Test Marketing is to test in the three biggest markets in the country, New York, Los Angeles and Chicago. Why is this a popular strategy? In these three markets you can gather an opinion from the east coast, west coast and the mid-west. This is such a shortsighted strategy but may be hamstrung by the test marketing budget. A more accurate indication would be to sample not just the top three markets in the country, but the top thirty markets in the country to learn what is there opinion of this new innovation?

Thirty markets tested can blanket the country and give more of broad understanding of the value of the novel product offering.

I have had some interesting test marketing experiences with customers that support the aforementioned arguments. A medical device company located in the heart of the Southeast, clearly in a top fifteen market at the time of the test marketing, made the decision to parade around their new device to hospitals only in their backyard. Here is the problem. Yes, they may have tested a statistically significant amount of hospitals, but they were all backyard hospitals, who embraced the concept of this medical device manufacturer being part of the local medical community. They did not test outside of this market. Big mistake! Hence, this was the beginning in the dagger in the heart of the launch of this product. The test marketing only focused on the influencer of the product decision, in this case the surgeon who ordered the device for their patient in the hospital. Where they dropped the ball is with the end user of the product, the nurse. The end user applied the product to the patient. They never asked a nurse's opinion of the new innovation. They only asked the influencer. So what? The device weighed a whopping twenty-five pounds, was bulky to apply to the patient, and caused the patient to complain about the entire process. The company was blind to this feedback because they only cared about what do "local" surgeons have to say about this innovation. Another nail in the coffin of this dog of a product! This occurred during the test marketing phase of new product development and was ignored by management.

One of the most prestigious and top hospitals for cancer treatment on the planet is located in New York City. Patients travel from all over the globe to this institution. At the time this was one of my largest accounts, one of my greatest and favorite customers of all time. Why? All they ever did was call me up and say we want to place another order. At the time they would purchase close to three hundred thousand dollars of surgical instruments annually, with NO complaints.

My company was trying to make the transition into the Information Technology world, by marketing software that helped to manage the inventory of surgical instruments in hospitals electronically. This customer literally had a few million dollars' worth of surgical instruments in their physical inventory. They, along with other hospitals in the country, were looking for a solution as to how to manage this asset.

We decided to test market a software product that attempted to electronically track the inventory of surgical instruments as opposed to physically tracking the inventory, which was the current process. The customer was selected as a Beta site, a guinea pig, to gain necessary customer feedback. Here was the issue. The company was a medical device manufacturer, not a software development company. Bugs, glitches and errors were so prevalent that the software that was installed at this flagship account during the test marketing phase actually corrupted their entire IT network! So much for test marketing!

Commercialization

The innovation is at the end of the funnel and ready for the market. This is an exciting time in the life of the product. Marketers plan a launch of the innovation hoping and praying that the innovation becomes a success.

CHAPTER 7

···

A Brand Is a Tattoo

Levels Of Brand Intensity

This book commences with the one word definition of Marketing, "Awareness." Every product starts as an idea, how do you go from idea to awareness? Through the continuum of Brand Intensity, by reaching your ultimate goal of becoming a Master Brand. It begins with a belief in the development of a brand strategy. Do not ever underestimate the power of the brand. Do customers purchase products because of their brand name? Can consumers become so loyal to a brand that it shuts out your competitor? Of course they can. What is interesting about this continuum is that certain products for certain consumers carry different levels of intensity. While you may prefer a particular brand somebody else may be more finicky and insist on a specific brand.

What I find compelling about the Levels of Brand Intensity is that this practice does not only apply to consumer products but commercial and industrial products as well. The continuum is applicable to an occupation or a specific industry. I cannot tell you how many times a surgeon insisted on a specific brand name of a product. To the general public you have no idea what the brand name is associated with, what company manufactures the product or what the product actually does. Yet, it is important to that surgeon, so important that they will not accept a substitute and insist on the obscure brand name.

LEVELS OF BRAND INTENSITY

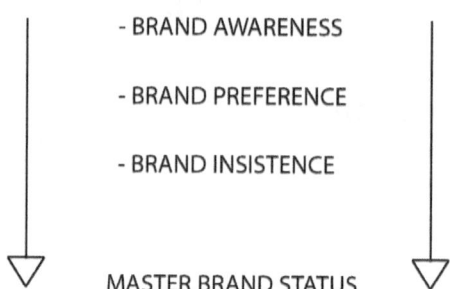

- BRAND AWARENESS

- BRAND PREFERENCE

- BRAND INSISTENCE

MASTER BRAND STATUS

Brand Awareness

Brand Awareness can be defined as a consciousness that a brand is available. There is no preference or insistence and substitutes abound with not much difference in product alternatives in the mind of the consumer. It is the commodity mentality, where there is not much difference between alternatives, Sugar is sugar. However, it is imperative to establish some form of Brand Awareness in the marketplace.

Brand Preference

A separation occurs between Brand Awareness and Brand Preference. The consumer begins to form opinions and influences in their product decisions. All of a sudden slight penchants for products pop up. During Brand Preference substitutes will be acknowledged and accepted. Most restaurants do not carry both lines of the global leaders in the cola business. It is one or the other. Some consumers prefer one brand over the other, and it is an individual decision, and some will accept the substitute even though they prefer the other brand.

Brand Insistence

Brand Insistence takes the level of Brand Intensity to new heights. Brand Insistence means that the consumer demands a required brand and NO substitutes will be accepted or even considered. Brand Insistence infers that the consumer will walk out and walk away from the transaction. Brand Insistence necessitates that the consumer will not even entertain the concept of accepting a substitute. Cigarettes are products that have high levels of Brand Insistence. When a consumer walks into a store they do not say, "Can I have a pack of cigarettes, they say can I have a pack of "Brand X." If the vendor is out of stock on Brand X, brand insistent consumers walk out empty handed.

Master Brand

Master Brand status is utopia. A Master Brand means that you have been beating your competitor for so long that the market thinks of your brand name when thinking about a product selection, thinking that the product is actually called by a name, but not realizing that the consumer is referring to the brand name of a product. Master Brand status is your goal in life as a marketer. Your goal starts with Awareness and ends with Master Brand status. This must be the mentality of every marketer. Consumers do not even realize they request Master brand products. Here are some examples. What is Jell-O? A gelatin dessert. Did you even know that was the product category, or do you walk in the store and ask, "Where is the gelatin dessert?" Or do you ask, "Where is the Jell-O?" That is Master Brand status at its best. Most consumers do not even realize that there are other brands of gelatin desserts, including store brands. The same goes for cellophane tape and adhesive strips. Do you walk into the store and ask, "Where the cellophane tape is and what aisle the adhesive strips are in?" Of course not. The store employee would look at you as if something is wrong. Instead you inquire with, "Where is the Scotch Tape and where are the Band-Aids?" Again, there are competitive alternatives, but the Master Brand name is what the customer requests.

In the corporate space do you say, "Xerox this, or do you say Canon this or Ricoh this?" All fine companies but not the Master Brand. A phenomenon for developing Master Brand status that has exploded today is the time that it takes to develop Master Brand status. All of the aforementioned brands have had long, successful lives as a product and it took years to become a Master Brand. That is not so today and it is a function of the information technology world that we live in. Microsoft is still a relatively young company compared to the companies that were listed above as having Master Brands. If you say, "I have to have Windows software" you are not talking about a pane of glass. How did a Polaroid get replaced by a selfie? Ask a millennial what a Polaroid is, they have no idea, they think it has something to do with a bear on steroids. If some say's to you, "Go Google it, or go Google yourself, they do not say go look it up on a search engine." Nobody ever says, "Go Bing yourself, or Yahoo yourself." All fantastic information technology innovations, but not the Master Brand.

Product Mix Width Versus Product Line Depth

Some companies market one product, some companies market fifty, while other companies market thousands of products. Some product strategies are very narrow and deep in their focus which is vertical in nature, while an alternative strategy is to be more broad, wide and horizontal with your product offering to the market.

A product line is a cluster of intently linked products. They are linked because they operate in a parallel fashion. A product line can be sold to similar consumers and can be sold through common distribution channels. The product mix are all of the products that a company sells. They can be related and linked but they can also can have a loose affiliation or no affiliation at all.

There are advantages and disadvantages of each approach. A common visual that can compare both approaches compares the Product Line Depth versus the Product Mix Width.

Here is the issue with initially having a product line depth strategy that over time moves towards a product mix width strategy. Your successful product line is what built your company, it is what pays the bills, it is what keeps the lights on, it is what helps you make payroll every week. Now you decide to venture into a market that while maybe related to your area of expertise and competitive advantage but is not really your strength? Mistakes are made by marketers because they think that they know how to be successful in the related product category, but they fail because they are not the expert in that product category. Which bodes the question of, "Stick to your knitting", stay with what you are successful with, as opposed to venturing out to an opportunity beyond your capacity of proficiency. There is a reason why you have been successful with your product depth strategy and focus on making that strength stronger. The counter argument is what if the market for your product dries up? Every product goes through the product life cycle and everything in life will come to an end. If you are too deep with your focus and ignore the concept of the diversification of your product line, even though it may be successful for decades, and kept the lights on for decades, it can be headed for the graveyard and you and your company are left standing on death's door!

Product Line Extension

Tying all of these marketing concepts together is like putting a puzzle together. Once a brand is established, and it crosses over the thresholds of success established by the Product Life Cycle and Market Share / Market Growth Matrix the dilemma of what to do with the "Brand" comes to the forefront. A Product Line Extension is an integral puzzle piece. How do you stretch Maturity in the Product Life Cycle, how do you keep milking the Cash Cow? A Product Line Extension! A Product Line Extension capitalizes on the success of a brand and takes the core of the product to new level. Something is altered in the Product Line Extension.

Instead of creating a new product with a new brand name and a new life, why not take advantage of the success of the original product and hitch the wagon of the new idea (Product Line Extension) to the successful established brand name. Remember the failure rate of new products. A new product needs all the help in the world to experience a successful product launch. If labeling the product as an extension of the successful brand helps launch the product, so be it!

Big Tobacco is the poster child to use as an example of a Product Line Extension. Especially the Big Tobacco Company with the "Red" box. They have incredible Brand Insistence, meaning if you do not have it in stock, the customer walks out! They have stretched the maturity so far and have squeezed so much milk out of the cow with Product Line Extensions that are lighter than the original brand, longer than the original brand, taste different than the original brand and literally come in sizes such as medium! Enough!

Other examples of industries who play the Product Line Extension game are television networks with their crime shows, soda companies with their endless extensions of the initial brand, beer companies who dilute the taste of their product and sports television networks that splinter their programming so much that you need a tweezer.

There comes a point when the stretching and the milking is extreme. I am all for evolution, and agree that change is necessary to stay competitive, but when the performance of a product has been diluted so much that it has run its course, there comes a time to end the belligerence associated with extending the brand. The marketer should start to map out a planned obsolescence time line for the decline of the brand.

Why would a company take the risk of extending the brand? It is elementary, if the established brand does not extend the product line the competition will. Rarely does the Product Line Extension ever overtake the overall success of the original. Let's face it, it is called an original for a reason, the original broke ground, the original planted the flag, the original put the footprints in the sand or the snow and blazed a trail and the original should be hailed and exalted for its strengths and not be remembered by its diluted geriatric image that can be the result of an excessive Product Line Extension!

Cannibalization

Marketing theory is filled with examples of terms that in the real world have one definition, but in the world of Marketing mean something else. Cows and dogs are on that list and you might as well add cannibals to the list. What comes to your mind when you think of a cannibal? The natural default is to a movie made a generation ago where a psycho wanted to keep the sheep quiet. The pure definition of a cannibal is one that consumes their own species. In Marketing, Cannibalization is defined as when sales of a new product cut into the sales of an existing product. Why would you do this? Why would you cut into the sales, and literally wound or stab at the sales of an existing product? Think about the resources that have been poured into the life of the existing product, now you are wielding the dagger of cannibalization in the face of the successful, existing product? A very interesting decision!

111

The reality is that if you do not cannibalize the sales of your existing product your competitor can cut into the sales of your existing product. At least you are keeping the business within the family. Cannibalization can also be part of a planned obsolescence strategy where the marketer knows that their product has seen better days and is moving towards the decline stage of the Product Life Cycle. While this can hurt the sales of the existing product it can jump start the life of the new product.

Cannibalization

Packaging & Labeling

Marketers and consumers underestimate the power of packaging. As a salesperson by trade, you need as much help as you can to convince a customer to make the decision to purchase your product. If your packaging nudges the customer in your direction, so be it.

There is an old marketing story about a global leader in the soda marketplace regarding their packaging and labeling. The can and the resources that were exhausted into what goes on the side of the can costs more than the soda that goes into the can. Think about how insane that sounds. Are you kidding me?

Can a product's packaging mislead the customer? Again, I love innovative, influential packaging. But I do have a few pet peeves.

The breakfast cereal market is humongous. Cereal is not cheap. How come when I buy a box of expensive cereal and open the box it is half empty? Why? Fill the box or make the box smaller! When I buy a bag of chips why is the bag half empty? I open the bag and I say, "Where are my chips?" They even make small bags of chips and they fill them half way. Why?

Packaging has many functions. Packaging helps to promote a product, protect a product and facilitate the recycling and storage of a product. The importance of this is often overlooked. Have you ever reached for a product only to notice that something is damaged with the packaging? There might be nothing wrong with the contents of the packaging, but the optic associated with this can create a negative connotation of the quality of the ingredients inside the package. Packaging is advertising. I remember as a young salesperson walking the floors of the hospital noticing the brands names of the boxes stacked up in the supply room or even on the floors of the hospital. My packaging was just a plain brown box with no mention of the brand name of the product. Not only was the packaging bland, but so was the quality of the corrugated box. I received a delivery of samples to my home office. The boxes were crushed and just dropped on my porch. I looked at the quality of the packaging and said to myself, "If I was the customer and I received this shipment I would not be happy". I took pictures of the packaging and sent them to the president of the company with a note about the quality of the packaging. That upset a few people in the marketing department!

It goes beyond just how your product is packaged. It is how your product is displayed. When you walk down the aisle of the supermarket which products are displayed at your eye level, below your eye level, or where the consumer has to reach either up or down to select a product? You can have the greatest box in the world but if the consumer cannot see it, it can diminish the importance of the emphasis on excellent packaging.

Does placing the image of a famous person or fictional character on the front of the box influence the purchasing decisions of the consumer? Of course it does. Have you ever walked down the aisle of a supermarket with a child in the wagon who notices someone famous on the packaging? Try to tell the kid that, "No we are not buying that today!" Good luck!

I was in the supermarket with my son who could not have been more than six years old. We walked down the snack aisle and there was a popular brand name of crackers on the shelf. On the front of the box was a promotion where if you found the cracker in the box that was shaped like a baseball with the seams of the baseball on the cracker, a famous baseball player would come to your house and have a catch with the winner. My naïve son said, "Dad we have to buy these crackers because I want him to come to our house to have a catch!" I said fine and he puts ten boxes of crackers in the wagon. A year's supply of crackers. We went home and I went up to my office leaving him alone in the kitchen. His mother was not home. I went down to the kitchen about twenty minutes later, only to find ten boxes of crackers spilled all over the kitchen. He was looking for the magic cracker, which of course was never found. Ten boxes of crackers down the drain. Great packaging!

Positioning

The word position has many interpretations and definitions. It can vary from where you play on a sports team to what is your stance on an issue. In marketing it has a different meaning. In marketing Positioning, or your position, is defined by where the customer perceives your product in their head compared to other competitive alternatives, substitutes and offerings.

The importance of branding has been documented. Creating a strong brand name is imperative. Attaining master brand status is your goal. Following this model leads you, or forces you, to create a position in the market. When the customer closes their eyes and thinks about your product where do they position you compared to your competitors? Does the customer think of you on the high end? The low end? In the middle? I can make a case for each and every possible position. The point is that once this position is established it is virtually impossible to change this perception in the mind of your customer. It is a brand, and I do not mean the name of a product, I mean a brand like the way cattle are branded. It is a tattoo an indelible imprint that can be permanent. Removal of this tattoo can be painful and time consuming. This is not necessarily a bad thing, if the proper position is established. The issue arises when the wrong position is created and a decision is made to re-position the product.

The automobile industry provides the classic example of how positioning can be used as a marketing tool. In this industry and in many industries there is a high end, low end and middle of the road position. In the 1980s three Japanese auto manufacturers who had solidified their middle of the road position, wanted to change their position in the marketplace. They developed a very strong brand position of value and reliability. A position in the middle, not the cheapest alternative and certainly not the high end position of luxury automobiles.

They wanted to compete at the high end, but recognized the problem of how they were perceived (position) in the marketplace. What did they do? They continued to manufacture cars, but created three new brands that kept their distance from the established brand and position. The brand names were shiny and sexy. The companies did not promote these new lines as an extension of the established brand but almost like three new automobile manufacturers. The reason for this was clear. If they would have promoted the luxury car as part of the middle market position, it would not have worked. It would not have worked because of the position created in the minds of the customers. Instead a strategy was employed where they went right after the high end luxury market with their new shiny and sexy brand names. They were so successful with this strategy that you did not even realize that they were the same companies, all they did was dress up their reliable and value based product with cosmetic upgrades from dashboards, to leather seats and fancy door handles. If you opened the hood of each alternative many of the same engine parts were used for the value brand as well as the luxury brand. They kept this under wraps. The high end position was established, it worked and the rest is history. Brilliant marketing!

POSITIONING

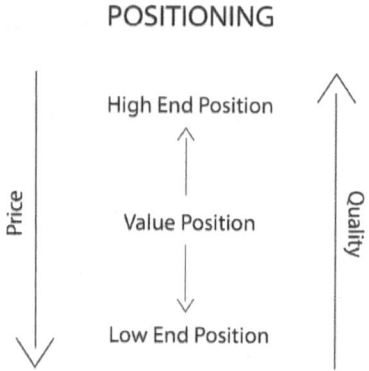

Market Share

Market Share is defined as what is your percentage of sales for all competitive offerings. In other words, what is your piece of the pie compared to all of your competitors? The sum of all market shares is equal to the Total Available Market for a given product category. Pie charts are a popular visual component for presentations and reports, and no other pie chart has been more overused, analyzed and abused than the market share pie chart.

Market Share Pie Chart

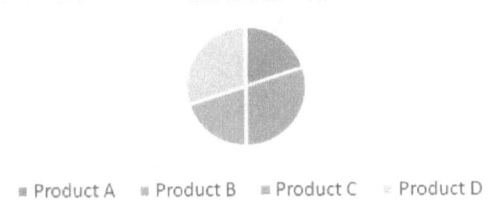

The slice of the pie becomes an obsession with marketers. Here is the problem with the "slice of the pie obsession". Marketers throw a party when their slice of the pie expands. Why are they obsessed? This obsession can cloud their ability to judge the greater long term marketing landscape. There is support for the touting of market share. For branding purposes, it is important to be able to publicize the strong market share performance. There are packaging advantages as well. Having the ability to advertise your market share status on your label is a positive. Salespeople need any kind of ammunition they can get to respond to the age old question, "Why should I buy from you?" Plugging your market share status during a sales presentation is always beneficial in reassuring the customer that your product is the solution to their problem. Being a market share leader builds morale throughout the organization and can enhance team work within the organization. As for marketing yourself, it does not hurt to be able to flaunt the success of the increase in market share when you have to answer the question, "Why should you get promoted, or why should I hire you?"

I have no issue with the pie chart analogy, pie is a beautiful product and comes in so many variations from apple to pizza. If you had to ask me I do prefer pizza pie to apple pie. To this day when I am in the field pizza is my favorite lunch. It is cheap, fast and good. When you walk into a pizzeria there are many pies that you can choose from. The same applies to the market share pie. There are pies with every available competitor including commodities, substitutes and alternatives. Everyone and every product. It is referred to as a garbage pie. When you order a garbage pie in a pizzeria they put everything in the kitchen on the pie including meats such as meatballs, pepperoni and sausage plus vegetables including onions, mushrooms, tomatoes and associated cheeses. I love garbage pies!

You can also analyze market share pies that are more specific, only you and your direct competitors. A specific pie, such as a clam pie, which is not as widely distributed. An example of the commodity pizza pie, where it is hard to see the difference between alternatives, is your plain cheese pie that you can find on any corner. In the end it is all good, I love pizza!

Market share pie charts need to be scrutinized differently. You cannot just look at a generic market share pie chart. Multiple pie charts need to be dissected to create a solid consensus of overall Market Share. Multiple pie charts can include who directly competes with us as a commodity, who competes with us as a substitute, and who competes with us as an alternative.

What is the difference between a commodity, a substitute or an alternative? Let's use the soft drink market as an example. The cola market is the commodity, with not much difference between the two market share leaders. The substitute can be another brand of soda. The alternative is another type of soft drink such as bottled water, iced tea, or sports drinks. Right there you have multiple pie charts that need to be studied.

A commodity can be defined as a product where there is no distinctive advantage over a competitor and is sold at the lowest price possible without going out of business. Can you make money selling a commodity? Of course you can but you have to generate a tremendous amount of sales volume to stay in business. In the soft drink cola market the two market leaders run at about forty-three percent market share versus forty-two percent market share, give and take a point here or there depending on who comes out with the latest trend. Why do they fight over the one percent market share? They fight over it because the global soft drink cola market is a huge number with a lot of zeros at the end and one market share point adds up.

We live in a commodity driven market. Everything that we purchase is being pushed towards a commodity driven environment. There is the polar opposite approach of driving the customer towards the brand, away from the commodity, substitute and alternative but that is becoming an uphill battle.

The pharmaceutical industry is famous for weighing market share more than it weighs sales volume. A mentality of placing more of an influence on market share versus sales volume is misguided. When salespeople are being compensated based on market share instead of the bulk of their incentive compensation being based on sales volume growth, the compensation plan needs to be reevaluated. Focusing on market share centers on increasing your piece of the pie. Stealing share from competitors is the order of the day.

A more robust and long term view of the market involves observing the market not as this limited pie where stealing share from competitors is the goal. What about the concept of making the pie bigger? Growing the total available market. Instead of a six slice pizza pie why not an eight slice pizza pie. Yes, you are expanding the pie, making more pizza for everyone. The mentality is, only the strong will survive. In this world of a market that is driven towards the commodity, if your brand is going to survive it is going to face competition, substitutes and alternatives, so roll the dice and live with the consequences. Pizza for everyone!

How do you make the pie bigger and more expansive? Yes, hunting and searching for new markets is a popular plausible strategy.

Remember when the total available market reaches saturation it has exhausted the notion of new markets that need to be penetrated.

Where is the gold? Where is the genius? What is the equivalent of hitting the marketing lottery? Finding new uses for your product is the solution. Here are some examples.

Baking soda has been around forever. I have never seen anyone actually bake with baking soda, but I have seen baking soda promoted in tooth paste and as a toilet bowl cleaner. How can something that you brush your teeth with be also used to clean your toilet? Onion soup mix in a box was intended to be an alternative to homemade soup or soup in a can. Someone figured out that if you combine onion soup mix with sour cream you can create a dip for chips. They probably sell more onion soup mix in a box that is used as a dip than when it was originally marketed as a soup.

A popular medication, did not start out that way. It started out as a medication for men suffering from heart disease. Once it was discovered that there was another use for the drug, a medication for a men's health disorder, sales exploded and it became one most successful products in the history of the company.

There is a market for orange juice. The primary market for orange juice is as a morning beverage to start your day with. Somewhere a bartender figured out that if you mix orange juice with alcohol it tasted unique, hence the birth of the screwdriver. How do you think that innovation impacted sales of orange juice and grew the total available market? The same was for cranberry juice, a commodity with a limited market. I would love to research the sales of cranberry juice since a bartender figured out it mixes well with alcohol. Energy drinks were introduced to the health conscious market who loves to spend their time at the gym working out and putting their health first. I have not heard of the energy drink companies crying that mixing their energy drink with alcohol is a misuse of what their product is intended for. The same goes for Jell-O, mixing gelatin dessert with alcohol became a popular adult shot. How about sales for the little paper cups used for the gelatin shots, the best cups were the cups used in fast-food hamburger franchises, initially intended as a place to put your ketchup in to dip your fries, now another use. Again, growing the total available market.

I played a lot of sports growing up and come from a sports family. For some reason I started playing ping pong around eight years old on a family vacation. We vacationed at the same location for several years and the ping pong table was in the clubhouse year after year. I coerced my parents into purchasing a ping pong table for our house. I continued to enjoy the game of ping pong. Why was the ping pong ball invented? Was it invented to be a prop in a sporting competition or was it invented to be bounced on a table into a red cup during a beer guzzling competition? Marketing is about distribution. When I think back about where did I purchase ping pong balls, FOR PING PONG? I would have to go to a sporting goods store to purchase the product. Where can you purchase a ping pong ball today? A sporting goods store, a gas station, a convenience store, a liquor store/ beer distributor, a chain of pharmacies, a supermarket etc. The same explosion of distribution applies to the red cup. This is hitting the marketing lottery! This is marketing genius! Brilliant marketing!

Yes, these are not complex products and finding new uses for these products was not rocket science. Here are some examples of expanding a more complex and sophisticated market. At one time I was selling a syringe pump to hospitals. A syringe pump is designed to deliver small, precise doses of medication and nutrition to premature babies located in the Neo-Natal Intensive Care Unit (NICU) of the hospital. Figuring out how to feed and deliver medication to an at-risk, pre-mature baby, living in an incubator is as close to life and death as it gets for a product. If the product performs you are a hero, if the product fails the consequences are unmentionable. This product became so popular that over ninety percent of the NICU's in children's hospitals purchased this product. That's over a ninety percent market share. Do you understand what it is like to sell a product with over ninety percent market share? A day at the beach!

Over time this market became so saturated with dominance that sales began to flatten out. When I say over time, we are talking about an over twenty year run of dominance. A competitive device used in the operating room of the hospital for a completely different use, to place a patient under anesthesia during surgery, went through some product challenges. This opened the door for the use of a syringe pump in the operating room to deliver general anesthesia, a completely new use and opened the door to expand the total available market for syringe pumps.

Another medical device was designed to reduce the incidence of Deep Vein Thrombosis (DVT), or a blood clot, which can lead to a pulmonary embolism and kill you during surgery. The highest incidence of DVT occurs during hip and knee surgery, with the target market being the orthopedic surgeon. After the product was released additional research indicated that not only are orthopedic surgeons, targets for DVT pumps that ALL surgeons put their patients at risk during surgery and are excellent targets for DVT pumps expanding the Total Available Market beyond just orthopedic surgeons.

SECTION 3

How Do You Get The Word Out?

This section describes the magnitude of
raising awareness through Promotion

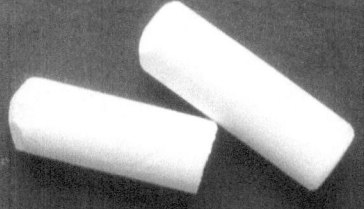

Chapter 8

....

Delivering The Message

Promotional Mix

P romotion, the third "P" of the Marketing Mix, can cause a bit of confusion. The promotional mix is not the same thing as the marketing mix. The promotional mix is part of the marketing mix. First of all, I want to define promotion from a marketing standpoint. Promotion in marketing does not mean that yesterday you were a salesperson and did such a great job that today you were promoted to sales manager. Another example is that at the end of the third grade you received your report card and it said that you have been promoted to the fourth grade. Promotion in marketing has a different definition. Promotion in marketing means how do you get the word out to the market, albeit raise awareness, about your company, your brand or your product.

The Promotional Mix means how you as a marketer use the tools available to you to raise the aforementioned awareness. It does have some parallels with the Marketing Mix where marketers are charged with making the decision to create the right mix to match your promotional options with the targeted market.

Think of the Promotional Mix, as illustrated by the bullhorn, as the engine or method that raises awareness of the product. The traditional Promotional Mix included, in no particular order, is the integration of:

Promotional Mix

Advertising

Personal Selling

Sales Promotion

Public Relations & Publicity

Social Media

Can the third "P" promotion be utilized as a competitive advantage? Meaning can your promotion be more of a strength than the other three "P"s? Here is an example. How does a movie studio promote a new motion picture? Producing and distributing a trailer. I remember this, it was a trailer for a comedy. All the studio did was splice together a few funny clips from the movie and released it as a trailer. If you watched the trailer you said, "Wow, that looks like a funny movie!" Persuading consumers to pluck down their cash and go see the movie. It was a successful trailer. It was an example of excellent promotion. The problem was that the only funny parts of the movie were the few clips that were interwoven together to make up the trailer. That was it, nothing else was funny, and the movie was a dud, a bomb. Great promotion, poor product!

Advertising:

Advertising

Medium	Characteristic
Television	Expensive but Effective
Radio	Genre Specific
Print (Newspaper,Magazine)	Seen Better Days
Outdoor	Underrated
Internet	Evolving

Marketing is awareness and one of the most misunderstood elements of marketing is advertising. The core definition of advertising is a message delivered to a customer. Advertising elevates awareness to new heights. Advertising is a mentality, a necessity, and something that cannot be ignored. When I hear business owners or companies state that they do not need to advertise, they have enough business, and that word of mouth is the way that they advertise their product. This is a foolish statement! Why all of this negative connotation associated with advertising? Is it warranted or just a myth? Yes, advertising is persuasive, misleading and can and does make false claims. Is it unethical or just smart business for a company to mislead their customers through deceptive advertising? Is it unethical for a pancake company to place cardboard between each flapjack to add height to the stack during a commercial? Or is it worse to pour motor oil over the stack instead of syrup because motor oil does not absorb into the pancakes? What about the cereal company that in their commercial creates a base of a gelatin dessert in a bowl, then covers the gelatin with white school glue creating an image of milk in a bowl. Then the cereal is placed on top of the white school glue, the glue prevents the cereal from sinking and getting soggy. Is this unethical or just Brilliant Marketing?

This is not the real culprit. The problem with obtaining more buy in on the importance of advertising a product has to do with the intangibility aspect of advertising. All marketing is expensive. Advertising always has to answer the question of, "Is this expense worth it?" It is very difficult to measure the effectiveness of advertising. You cannot put your finger on it. Did the message increase sales? Did the customer receive the message? Did the customer pay attention to the message? Did the customer take the garbage out during the commercial? Did the customer zip by the billboard because there was no traffic? Did the customer fall asleep during the television show and miss the commercial even though the television broadcasted the commercial? Did the customer delete the commercials and consume the programming on a device that deletes the commercials? How many customers are actually in the room to view the commercial?

There are metrics that can be put in place to measure the effectiveness of advertising, but the intangibility factor will always loom in the back of the mind of the advertiser.

Students ask me all of the time, "Why do famous, well known, companies, with established brand names advertise their products?" This is a great question. A legitimate question. Why spend money on a product that sells itself? Understand this about any and all types of advertising regardless of the format. If it did not work they would not do it anymore. Why do you consistently see companies invest millions of dollars on advertising during the broadcast of the professional football championship on the first Sunday of February? Let's just call it the big game. It works! If it did not work they would not do it anymore. If it did not work then the networks would not be able to command the price that they do for the thirty second message.

Here is why there is a continued commitment to advertising. The beer industry is the best example. Why do established, successful, cash cow beer brands spend millions of dollars on advertising? Every day someone turns twenty-one in this country. Every day, new potential customers are exposed to the brand. The same goes for other popular brands that rely on aggressive, expensive advertising campaigns. Every day there is a new generation of customers that must be made aware of the brand. How do you raise this awareness? Advertising. Fast food burger chains are another example. If they decided to stop spending millions of dollars a year on advertising eventually a generation of customers would grow up not being aware of their product. The same goes for the soda industry. If one of the major players decided not to advertise anymore that would open the door for a competitor to swoop in and make their product offering more aware to the next generation of potential customers.

There are a multitude of advertising formats. Which is the most effective? I had a marketing professor of mine pose that question to a class many years ago, "What is the most effective form of advertising?" Television? Radio? Internet? Newspapers? Magazines? Billboards? It was a trick question. The professor's answer was, "The most effective form of advertising is the one that works!" Brilliant! The term is referred to as, "Bang for your buck." What does that mean? Bang for your buck means what was the return on the advertising investment? If a company spends a million dollars on advertising and that million dollar investment generates an increase in sales that covers the cost of the advertising, then there was bang for the buck. If a company spends one thousand dollars on advertising and it does not increase sales, or cover the advertising cost, then it was a mistake to utilize those funds on advertising. No bang for your buck!

There are two elements at the heart of the significance of advertising. Reach and Frequency. Reach is defined as how many consumers are exposed to the message. The more expansive the reach the more expensive the advertising message. The most expensive advertising is a commercial during the big game. Why? The reach is off of the charts. Think about this. There are over three hundred million consumers in this country. On one Sunday evening in February more than one hundred million consumers are doing the same thing, at the same time, watching a football game. That is approximately one out of every three consumers in this country doing the same thing. That is an insane reach! That is why it costs millions for thirty seconds of air time. It is all driven by reach!

Managing reach is a key to advertising success. How can you manage the reach of your advertising? How can you control the reach of your message? Television advertising is an effective yet expensive form of advertising. Network advertising has a tremendous reach, with a significant cost because of the reach. This is a broad audience where you might reach targeted consumers but not everyone in the reach is a target. Here is an example of controlling the reach. Television advertising has evolved into the splintering of the audience into specific demographic channels. Everybody needs to eat and while a commercial for a food product can have a great, yet expensive reach on network television. Critics laughed at the concept of a twenty-four hour a day television network dedicated to food. Who watches a television network about food? Consumers who like to eat but also love to cook. If you have a new line of pots and pans, or other related cooking products it makes more sense to advertise your product on this demographic specific network at a much more reduced advertising cost. Bang for your buck!

Another example is the golf business. Golf is televised on network television. You can advertise golf products on network television and you can also advertise golf products on all sports networks, all with their associated reach. However, there is also a twenty-four seven channel dedicated to golf. Another cable channel scoffed at by critics at its inception. Who watches the golf channel? Who is tuning in to the golf channel at two in the morning on a Tuesday? A golf fanatic! What a fantastic opportunity to advertise your latest and greatest golf related products such as golf balls, golf clubs, golf shoes and golf courses. It is all about maximizing and controlling the reach. Bang for your buck!

Frequency can be defined as how often the advertisement is repeated, what is the frequency of the message. Advertising is subliminal, meaning it is designed to plant a seed in the back of your mind. The more frequent the message, the more touches to the subliminal portion of the back of your mind. It is amazing that when a consumer is faced with a purchasing decision, something is triggered in the back of your mind that creates the awareness of the product. This is the result of the frequency of the advertising message. A superb illustration of the effectiveness of frequency of advertising is the lottery. When is the frequency of lottery advertising increased? When nobody wins the jackpot. When the jackpot increases the frequency of advertising increases. Once a lottery winner is chosen, frequency of the advertising, or awareness of the jackpot is reduced.

Something that I find interesting about the mix between reach and frequency is with regards to commercials during the big game. The production cost associated with a big game commercial is astronomical. It better be! If a company is potentially flushing millions of dollars down the toilet for a big game commercial it better be a quality commercial. For the most part if you analyze the production quality of a big game commercial compared to your run of the mill everyday commercial you can see the quality. Big game commercials are better. Why do they disappear after the game? Why is the frequency diminished? Especially the good commercials, they are sent into the witness protection program, gone from our consciousness, wiped from our memory. As opposed to the frequency of commercials that we are bombarded with every day. The car insurance business is an excellent example. They are all in a battle to reach that subliminal piece of the back of your mind with frequent nauseating messages. If you ever find yourself singing the jingle of a commercial chalk that up to the success of the frequency of the message planted in the back of your mind.

Television

Advertising runs television. Without advertising there is no television. The impact that the innovation of television has had on our society is underestimated, yet it ranks with other profound innovations that truly have changed our lives such as the automobile and the light bulb. Ratings are the rubric, the metrics and the analytics that measure the amount of consumers who were exposed to the message.

Television ratings are down across the board. Why? There are several factors. The biggest factor is choice. One of the highest rated television shows of all time was from a situation comedy based on the Korean War in the 1950s which aired on television from the early 1970s until the early 1980s. The final episode was riveting television. The ratings soared through the roof. It was exceptional entertainment. While all of those factors contributed to the high rating the prevalent factor that drove the rating was that there were limited choices. You had no choice. Pay per view was in its infancy, there was no on-demand binge watching, recording devices that let you watch the programming at your leisure were expensive, you were a captive audience. Today the ratings are splintered. Not only can you consume the programming on a device other than a television, the content can be consumed when you want to consume it.

Do you want proof of the power of advertising? When a television or radio personality gets in trouble off the air, either in their personal life or in their professional life off camera, there is tremendous pressure put on the network to remove the personality immediately. Whether they are guilty or not guilty, with the latest trend of guilty before trial, whether legally or in the court of public opinion. The genre is irrelevant whether it is a star from a situation comedy, or a network news show, to a talk radio, nothing is off limits!

It is all driven by ratings. The higher the ratings the greater the advertising revenue generated by the content. If the ratings of your content are soft and an issue arises. Goodbye! No questions asked! You are ushered to the door, kicked to the curb, your email account deleted and your card swipe for office access is shut off before you know it!

What if the ratings are solid? What if the programming is a star or cash cow product that generates millions of dollars of profit for the network? Now you have an investigation. Not an immediate dismissal but a suspension until all of the facts and details are investigated. The network starts to do the math. Is the issue serious enough to pull the plug on the programming? What type of pressure is being put on by the advertisers? Are the advertisers catching heat from the public to pull their commercials? If the advertisers do not force the network to make a decision on the programming they are sending a message that they condone the behavior of the accused. It is so similar to other production based occupations. If a top producing salesperson has some issues, are they tolerated because of the revenue generated by the salesperson? If the professional athlete performs on the field, but is not a model citizen off of it, is the headache and baggage associated with the non-job related issues worth the production value on the field?

Television is an effective medium to deliver your message (advertisement). Television advertising, while expensive, delivers tremendous bang for your buck. Are commercials annoying? The rule of thumb for television is for every thirty minutes of air time there should be roughly seven minutes of commercial time. Is that too much? Is that too little? Where is the tipping point where the break in the action causes the consumer to leave the broadcast? Should you have fewer commercial breaks that last longer or more commercial breaks that are more concise? Should you have less commercial breaks and just charge more for the air time or have more commercial interruptions and reduce the cost associated with the message?

Are things changing in the television advertising business? Of course, like any industry, if it does not evolve, it will die. Television is about content. Content is king! Someone has to make a decision what to put on this channel at two o'clock in the afternoon on a Tuesday and what to put on this channel Thursday night in prime time. It is referred to as programming.

How does a network generate revenue and turn a profit? It is very simple. Profit is defined as Revenue minus Expense. What is left over is profit. The revenue comes from the commercials that are sold during the commercial breaks of the programming. The higher the ratings for the programming the higher the cost to advertise your product on that show. Expenses include production costs and rights fees. Here is how it works. A sports league puts out a bid for the broadcasting rights of their live competition. A network signs a contract for a specific broadcasting package.

Professional football has to be used as the textbook example. Why? Despite a recent softening of television ratings if you were to look at the highest rated television shows of all time, the highest rated television shows from the last year and in recent history, professional football dominates those rankings. Professional football dominates the top ten television shows very year, and also dominates the top one hundred television shows in a given television season. Content is king! Professional football is the model of all programming and content. The content associated with professional football and the impact that it has on television ratings justify the exorbitant rights fees that professional football commands.

Using football as an example. There is a rights fee associated for the following packages. Early Sunday afternoon, late Sunday afternoon, Sunday evening, Monday evening and Thursday nights. They now even offer a Sunday morning package. Plus playoff packages. If the networks had their way professional football would be broadcasted every night of the week during football season. Of course there are scheduling, logistical and safety issues associated with this, but a professional football game on a Tuesday, Wednesday, Friday or Saturday night will record a rating that is higher than your typical network rerun or reality show based on duck calls or matrimonial competitions. Broadcasting rights fees are in the billions. Remember the network needs programming, they need to be able to broadcast something on their channels otherwise they will go out of business. How do they turn a profit on this billion dollar investment? Selling the commercials. Hopefully the advertising revenue covers the rights fee and production costs. If this was not the case there would be no market for the astronomical rights fees. Back to, if it did not work they would not do it anymore.

Even in a market where professional football ratings have dipped, compared to the other content and programming that is available, it is still a domineering product. A mid-season matchup between the two worst teams in the league, from two of the smallest markets, in a meaningless game will generate a rating that crushes all competitive programming including playoff baseball games played in the middle of October.

Professional football generates a rating for their college football try outs in February. Potential professional football players assemble at a combine in the Mid-West and are tested on physical metrics such as speed, quickness, and their athletic ability. The players are dressed in shorts, and it is similar to how cattle are selected. There is no game, yet this activity generates a rating. The same goes for the professional football draft. It is an exercise where each team picks their new players in sequence from last year's worst team to last year's champion. It is not a game but yet this event has been turned in to a prime time television event that draws a rating that would blow your mind.

This is what I find fascinating about broadcast rights fees for sporting events. Let us use the big game as the example. When you sell the rights to broadcast your event you are selling your soul. You give up all control over the content. What do I mean? The kick off for the big game is approximately at six twenty-two, Eastern Standard Time. Who makes that decision? Think of the stakeholders. Does the league make that decision? No the league sold their soul to the network. Do the owners of the teams make that decision? Do the referee's make that decision? Do the coaches or the players make that decision? No, none of them have a say as to when the game (programming) starts. The network makes that decision. The network purchased the right to make that decision. Why six twenty two? That maximizes the ratings for the event.

There was a time, and I remember a generation ago when the big game was on during the day on a Sunday in January. Why the shift from a Sunday afternoon in January to a Sunday evening in February? Ratings! Everything is driven by ratings. The ratings are higher on a Sunday night in February compared to a Sunday afternoon in January. February is also an important month in television advertising. There are a couple of months during the year that set the market for advertising rates, including February and May. The big game has become an unofficial national holiday. The day after the big game is the most popular day for employees to call in sick at work for the entire year.

It is sacrilegious to even suggest this, because the big game is a Sunday thing. If the network wanted to broadcast the big game on a Saturday night instead of Sunday because the thought that the ratings would be higher on Saturday compared to Sunday, they could make that bold move. They can do it because they own the content. Look for this in the near future. Football traditionally starts at the beginning of September. Ratings in early September are weaker than ratings in February. The weather is still nice, people are just returning to their routines while summer winds down. Summer time used to be a wasteland for television ratings. Today with the importance of creating content that can build an audience it has become a trend to introduce new programming not necessarily at the beginning of the television season in September but to introduce new programming during the summer months to see if the new programming can generate a pulse, or a blip, on the ratings radar screen.

The start of football season will be pushed back for two weeks into the middle of September. Why the sliding of the "programming"? This pushes the second highest television ratings day of the year, the day it is determined who will play in the big game into the valuable February ratings month. It pushes the big game to the third Sunday in February, the night before a National Holiday, where many people are already off from work. If the network believes that this will generate a higher rating for the big game, they will push it back two weeks. They have the power to make this shift, they own the rights.

The big game has a built in audience and the rating for the event is as closed to bullet proof as any other content that is broadcasted on television, almost a guaranteed rating. This makes the investment in this property so appealing, as opposed to other sporting events where the ratings for their championship games can fluctuate more than the ratings for the big game.

Moving the needle in ratings refers to someone or something that causes a spike in the ratings. What can move the needle for the big game? A big market moves the needle. A team from New York, Chicago, Los Angeles or other major metropolitan area can move the needle more than a team from a smaller market like Jacksonville, or Indianapolis.

A star player can move the needle, specifically a star quarterback, regardless of what market they are from. A team with fans all over the country, a national team, with a nationwide legion of followers can move the needle. A team that hails from the steel city or a team named after a meat packing plant in Wisconsin have fans all over the country and can move the needle if they are in the big game.

Which brings us back to football. A concern of professional football and all live sporting events is how can the in-person experience compete with the in-home experience? The advent of television technology is so advanced that the quality of the broadcast puts you right in the middle of the action. Why go to the game? With flat screen and smart televisions many can argue that while there is no other greater experience than tailgating at a football game, the in-home experience of consuming the game on television rivals the in-person experience of attending the game in person. It is warm and comfortable in your living room, the rest room is clean and only a few steps away, you do not have to pay an exorbitant of money for a hot dog, beverage, parking, ticket prices and deal with unruly obnoxious fans and inclement weather! Other reasons supporting the in-home experience include the lack of travel and traffic associated with going to the game, all make the in-home television experience appealing.

Televised sporting events are as much of a television show as it is a competition. The job of the network and the desire of the professional league is to maximize the ratings. Why? Future negotiations for broadcast right are based on previous ratings. Certain teams move the ratings needle. I am not saying that there is a rooting interest for certain teams by the networks, the league offices and league commissioners, but there is! Teams with national followings drive ratings. It is good for business that in professional football for the team from Texas with the star on their helmet, or the professional baseball team from The Bronx with the pinstripe uniforms, to be competitive and make it to the championship game. It IS good for business. Those two examples, while they have legions of fans that will tune in and drive the rating up, there are an equal amount of fans who will view the broadcast because they loathe the performance of these two franchises and love to watch them lose. It is all about eyeballs to the television and it is good for business for certain teams to be successful.

Content is all about the first "P" Product. While live sporting events are competitions and a form of entertainment they are also television shows. Football is a perfect match for television. Football and television are a match made in heaven. Remember it is still a television show. Programming of the content rules the day. Most football games are completed within a three hour window. Of course once in a while there is overtime or a game stretches beyond the three hour window but you can set your watch by the time it takes for a football game. The multiple camera angles, with replays of action, with built in stoppages of the game, making commercial breaks look seamless along with the length of the game make it a natural fit as a television show. Programming and scheduling football games is more predictable than other sports. It is a neat and clean programming product. As opposed to baseball, with no time clock, who knows how long the game will take. This causes programming nightmares.

Other sports have issues translating to television. Baseball is too slow compared to football. Baseball has too many meaningless stoppages in the play all effecting its translation to television. Of course this is part of the charm of America's pastime. Hockey has the widest gap between experiencing the action live compared to watching a hockey game on television. It is just not the same experience. Hockey has two slightly less than twenty minute breaks in the action during periods. That is too much of a break in the action hampering its ability as a television show. Basketball has too many time outs at the end of a game which can be agonizing. What is attractive to the networks about the other three major sports, Baseball, Basketball and Hockey is that their lengthy regular seasons can help fill a Regional Sports Networks programming schedule. Golf is rough to watch on television. While a compelling major golf championship can be exciting, the regular weekly golf tournament can be painful to watch on television. Soccer, the world's sport, also has issues. There is not enough scoring in soccer and there is a running clock making it difficult to embed commercial breaks which pay for the rights fee for the event. It comes down to the programming of content. Something has to be put on the network. How many re-runs of recycled television shows can you utilized to fill your programming slots?

There have been several rule changes in professional football that have not only enhanced the game but have believe it or not, made it a better television show. The most recent rule changes have been legislated into the game to make the game safer for the players. Quarterbacks cannot be touched anymore. Why? Quarterbacks are the stars, fans want to see stars, not understudies. It is the Broadway analogy, nobody in the audience is happy that when at the start of a Broadway show they announce that the star will not be performing that night and their role is being played by their understudy. Other rule changes have been made to add offense to the game. Why? Offense increases ratings. While a hard fought low scoring game can be entertaining, ratings are higher for a game loaded with scoring and ends up a being a shoot-out with the team who has their hands on the ball last wins.

There was a time during the 1980s when the big game was not competitive. Teams were able to dominate professional football, dynasties were popular, at least a team if not a dynasty, could go on a run that lasted for several years. This led to a competitive imbalance. This was prior to when free agency and a salary cap were instituted. Once this happened massive movement of the talent shifted the competitive balance. The super team was done. What does this have to do with ratings? The league would prefer parity where "On Any Given Sunday" anyone could beat anyone. What this did was move all of the teams toward mediocrity keeping more teams in the hunt as the season went on. Hence, more awareness and interest in your team yielding stronger ratings. If you look at the past twenty years of the results of the big game, there have been more competitive games gluing the audience to the television driving up the ratings. Brilliant Marketing! These subtle manipulations of the product all are made to of course improve the game, also but to make it more of an attractive television property.

Impact Of Gambling On Ratings

The elephant in the room that nobody from the league or the network wants to address is the impact that gambling on sporting events has on television ratings. Another example of why football laps the field when it comes to the combination of gambling and ratings is the seamless interaction between football and gambling. It is pure and simple. It is easier to wager on football than the other sports. If you are betting on a random hockey game in February or a meaningless golf tournament in July maybe you need some counseling.

The other elephant in the room is not just how football and gambling are synergistic, is the impact that "Fantasy Football" has on television ratings? Fantasy sports, where you pick players from different teams to form your own team, where you win when the statistics from your ensemble of players accumulates more points than your fantasy competitors. This was laughed at when first concocted. Baseball was the first to try this notion. Again, football was a better fit.

Today there are television shows dedicated to fantasy football, websites, publications, and other social media outlets dedicated to the promotion of fantasy football. Football broadcasts inundate the viewer with updates of statistics. Traditional fans loathe this while the contemporary younger consumer eats it up. Here is all that matters from a network and league perspective. If "Fantasy Football" increases awareness for the brand and contributes to an uptick in ratings, so be it! They love fantasy!

The next wave of gambling that will impact ratings for live televised sporting events is in-game wagering. Traditional gambling practiced the notion that a wager had to be placed before the live event commenced. It had to be. The technology was not available to place a wager once the event started. That is out the window today! The combination of the legalization of gambling and the technology at our fingertips has spawned the notion of placing a wager from a device right before the kicker lines up for a field goal. Does the kicker make the kick or not? That opens the door for so many potential issues. Will this impact your decision to view the event? Of course it will, driving ratings up.

While the week to week aspect on wagering on football games is a cash cow, the amount of money wagered on the big game is in the stratosphere. Forget about the wagering that goes on the final score of the event. It is the "Office Pool/Restaurant Pool" plus the "Prop" or proposition wagering that goes on.

Proposition wagering involves taking the chance that something is going to happen, and it might have nothing to do with the outcome of the event. I love the prop bets. I love the prop bets that have nothing to do with the game. You can wager on the color of the sports drink that gets dumped on the winning coach, how many times someone famous was shown on television in their seat or luxury box, how long did it take the artist to sing The National Anthem, or which player has the best chance of getting arrested in the nights leading up to the big game!

The "Pool" wagering is much more serious. A grid is formed and consumers pick a box without knowing the numbers associated with their box. The numbers are random. So what? What does this have to do with ratings? The random numbers translate into winning the pool. If the game is not competitive the numbers still are. This holds the audience delivering a consistent, robust rating that is simply just not achieved through other programming options.

Loss Leader

A loss leader is a commodity product that generates pennies on the dollar of profit. Many products sold in a supermarket are loss leaders. Why would you sell a product that may not be worth the effort? The loss leader brings in the customer. The profit margins on milk, cigarettes and lottery tickets are infinitesimal so why carry them? Without the loss leader traffic can be diminished. The same goes for television programming.

Professional football can be looked at as a loss leader for a network. There is a compelling argument. Are the massive broadcasting rights fees worth it for a network? It is a resounding yes to this argument. Here is why. The loss leader of professional football allows for the exposure of your entire programming lineup. Cross promotion involves integrating multiple aspects of your product line to capitalize on the opportunity to raise the awareness of all of your products.

How many times during a football game are you reminded what is coming up on the network after the game, this Tuesday night, and reminding you not to forget about the debut of the network's new show this season. It is called a "Drop In". Whether it is a verbal message or a graphic that shows up on the bottom or the side of your screen it is free advertising for the network. I have no issue with the subliminal or mentioned message. The network owns the broadcasting rights, the network pays through the teeth for these rights, the network has the right to exhaust every opportunity to cross promote their programming.

Radio

Radio commercials also have the same pitfalls that television commercials have. Did the consumer actually consume the commercial? You are driving down the highway listening to the radio, your phone rings, you mute the volume on the radio, to answer the call, hopefully hands free. The radio is still playing, you are still tuned into the radio station, but you cannot hear the radio. You miss the commercial to take the call. How does the advertiser on the other end know this? They don't! More evidence of the intangibility of advertising.

Radio advertising also can be targeted to a specific market the same way that television advertising hones in on an identifiable customer. Certain products sell better when they are advertised on AM radio stations while other products generate a better bang for their buck when they are advertised on FM stations. FM radio stations that play a specific genre of music all day attract a different type of audience. A radio station that plays Classic Rock all day has a different audience than a radio station that plays Hip Hop and Rap, hence different advertisements for different genres of music. AM radio stations with a sports radio format attract a different audience that a radio station that hosts political opinion shows.

Certain products are a better fit for radio than for television. Here is a great example. Same product, a community college. One is a perfect fit for a radio advertisement while the other is a natural fit for a television commercial. The first community college is located in the concrete jungle of New York City with a location in an industrial area situated literally next to a prison. Very urban. Not the most cosmetically appealing location, nothing pretty or appealing about the scenery. This is a perfect fit for radio. Why? You cannot see the location and do not want to see the location on a television commercial. The other community college is also located in New York City but on the border of the city limits of New York and the suburbs. Before the location was a community college it was a golf course, tucked away in a secluded location that was hard to find. Golf courses are beautiful places, very scenic. This campus was the polar opposite of the urban campus next to the prison. This location had tremendous aesthetic appeal. This location was tailor made for a television commercial. A radio commercial would do the same injustice that the television commercial would have done for the urban campus. This is a prime example of how to utilize the Promotional Mix, certain products are just a better mix for one form of promotion while another product, albeit the same product, a community college, can deliver a better bang for your buck based on something as simple as the physical location and appearance of the product.

Satellite radio has crept into the marketplace. Satellite radio faced the same challenge a generation ago when cable television burst onto the marketplace. Before cable, television was free. You have to pay for cable television. This was not received well. Why would you buy the cow when you get the milk for free? The same applied to radio. Radio is free and now you want to charge customers to listen to the radio? This did not go over well. The sales pitch was that Satellite radio had no commercials. Satellite radio can have very specific genres of channels, much more pointed genres than terrestrial (traditional) radio stations. I love sports and the range of genres that satellite radio can provide is unmatched by traditional radio. I can listen to local sports shows that cover local sports issues, I can listen to national sports shows that focus on national sports stories and I can listen to radio stations that are dedicated to a specific sport.

I also love music. I am a big believer in that the music that was popular during your early pre-teen and teen years is the music that you grow up with. For me this was the mid-1970s through the mid-1980s. What genres of music were popular then? What is now considered classic rock with groups associated with the color pink, and heavier metal groups that have letters in their name separated by a lightning bolt became standards. This was also the era when they referred to a certain type of rock that punks listened to creating a fresh wave. Growing up I was also subjected to listen to the music that my father worshiped including the genius of the crooner they called the "Chairman of the Board" with his "Ol' Blue Eyes". Sinatra sang about doing things his way and singing about the city that has the same name of the state that is located in. Each of these genres have their own specific channel and this cannot be duplicated by traditional radio broadcasts.

Satellite radio can have a reach that dwarfs terrestrial radio stations who are limited to where you can pick up the broadcasted signal. Satellite subscriptions are sluggish while production costs can be high. Especially for talk radio on satellite with a famous host. What satellite talk radio did not realize at its inception was that filling air time with no commercials is difficult. Talking for sixty straight minutes with no commercial breaks can be taxing for the host. Hence, many talk shows now on satellite radio DO have commercials allowing the satellite network to double dip, collect monthly subscriptions from consumers and charge advertisers for commercials on their channels. How long will the subscriber put up with this? We will see. Satellite music channels, who also can have famous disc jockeys, traditionally do not have commercials with only a few words sometimes mentioned in between songs, this seems to work. I spend a lot of my life in the car and I personally enjoy satellite radio, especially the music channels, with no commercials and very deep genres of specific music that I enjoy causing me not to bristle when I have to pay for this service on a monthly basis.

The same concept of reach and frequency associated with television advertising also applies to radio advertising. Traditional terrestrial radio can have issues regarding the reach of their broadcast. Using the New York City marketplace as an example, the radio signal is so strong that it can stretch across over a seventy-five mile radius from Times Square, reaching millions of potential listeners. The greater the reach the more expensive the commercial. What if you are advertising a business or product that is only available on one side of this metropolis? The advertiser is wasting money on the commercial. While the commercial is heard by everyone tuning into the radio station, half of the listening audience has no interest in the business or product because the location is so far away.

A smarter strategy would be to control the reach. How do you limit or control the reach? Pick a radio station that has an audience on one side of the metropolis or the other. In New York City there is a Classic Rock station with a reach that covers the aforementioned entire market. However, that humongous reach comes with a huge price tag to advertise on the station. What if you are located on one side of Times Square or the other? There are Classic Rock radio stations to the west of Times Square located in Northern New Jersey. There are also Classic Rock radio stations located to the east of Times Square on Long Island. The cost associated with advertising on these radio stations is nowhere near the cost of advertising on a radio station that can be heard throughout the metropolitan area. This controls the reach and can be a successful solution when it comes to maximizing your radio advertising expenditures.

Frequency of the radio commercial can also be an effective form of advertising. Here is the difference. The consistent, constant repetition of a radio commercial can plant a seed in the back of your mind, specifically the jingle associated with the commercial. Have you ever experienced this? You are on a long car ride moving along on the highway focusing on the road. A frequent commercial comes over the air and you start singing the jingle and you do not realize what you are doing? That is effective radio advertising, the advertisement planted enough of a seed in your mind that you know the words to the jingle. The down side to over frequency is that the jingle annoys you so much that once it is played again on the radio you immediately change the station to something else.

Are there trends and future considerations that can threaten the radio industry which can ultimately effect advertising on the radio? A trend associated with the way radio is consumed is the ability to listen to your favorite radio station streamed over the Internet. Now you can be physically located out of the reach of the traditional radio signal and still have the ability to listen to your favorite radio station. I find myself doing this all of the time. There is a specific Classic Rock radio station whose signal I cannot receive from my home in New York City. I enjoy their format and mix of music that I cannot hear from radio stations located in New York City. I often stream their station on my computer, tablet or my phone. What is interesting about listening to this stream is that the commercials that are being played on the stream are different from the commercials that they play when I am in the range to hear the radio station on traditional radio. This has created, no pun intended, an additional revenue stream for this radio station. This type of radio consumption and radio advertising will only continue to grow as we move into the future.

The way that radio is consumed in our homes is also evolving with the advent of smart speakers and cable systems who broadcast music commercial free. Why listen to radio the old fashioned way through an alarm clock, stereo or transistor radio when the technology that is available at your fingertips can enhance the overall radio experience?

While radio has an immense reach when you talk about the amount of consumers who listen to the radio while driving in their cars, specifically in what is referred to as the morning and afternoon drive, when many people are on their way to and from work, ratings for radio soar through the roof. So does the cost of radio advertising. This is the equivalent of television's prime time. What can threaten the cash cow of drive time radio advertising? The driverless car! The matrimony between radio advertising and the drive time audience might have seen better days. Why? When you are driving your car you are a captive audience, you have to keep your eyes on the road, yet your ears can be tuned in to the radio. If the evolution of the driverless car becomes a reality your eyes are freed up to view a device while the car drives itself. Why only listen to the radio when you can watch something on a device? If less consumers are listening to the radio while in their cars the ratings will go down. If the ratings go down so does the cost of the radio advertisement which can threaten the entire radio industry.

Outdoor

Outdoor advertising is exactly what it means, it is outdoors, and it is outside. Outdoor advertising can be as basic and as primitive as putting flyers on cars, sticking menus in mailboxes, stapling advertisements to telephone poles and your old fashioned sign on the corner pointing in the direction of an open house, or a garage or yard sale. One form of outdoor advertising that I get a kick out of is the person in New York City not only handing out printed advertising but actually wearing what looks like a flat board, or an easel, on the front and back side of their body with their head popping through the top, they are the advertising!

Billboard advertising has always been a staple of outdoor advertising. Placement of the billboard advertisement is the key. Sure you can place the billboard ad on a super highway with cars zooming passed it exceeding the speed limit. Did the consumer actually consume the advertisement? How can you consume the advertisement when you are flying by at over seventy miles per hour? Again, another example of the intangibility of advertising. A better bang for your buck is to place your billboard advertisement, while still on the highway, strategically placed on a high traffic portion of the highway, where the traffic slows down, and you are forced to view the billboard because your car is crawling through the traffic. Another example of bang for your buck. Does the high traffic billboard cost more money than the billboard in the middle of a stretch of the highway where speed is excessive, of course it does?

Billboard advertising has also capitalized on the utilization of the technology that is at our fingertips. Lighted billboards that illuminate the sky and look like large television screens, where a message can be rotated, splits the cost of the advertisement for the sponsor and is a long way from the days where billboards were literally pieces of wallpaper pasted together to deliver the message.

Another form of billboard advertising on the highway that has evolved and is quickly becoming irrelevant are the much smaller advertisements on the side of the road that indicate at the next exit there is food, fuel or lodging. It was a smart idea to pay for a billboard that indicated that your establishment was at the next exit. Why this might be a waste of advertising resources today is the way that we search for food, fuel or lodging on our devices as we drive down the highway. Our devices alert us where the next food, fuel or lodging establishment is, how far away it is, how long will it take to reach it, eliminating the need for the billboard reminder of what is coming up at the next exit.

As a salesperson I have spent so much time in my life on the road, specifically driving from hospital to hospital. When I first started my career I actually hung a map, a paper map, not an electronic map above my desk in my office. I would plot my daily route based on where each hospital was. How do you find a hospital while drive on the highway? Look for the blue "H" on the highway. My entire sense of geography is based on where the hospitals were. If I meet someone and I say, "Where are you from", and they tell me what town. I immediately reference the nearest hospital, I know where you are from, close to hospital "X". Ask a millennial to read an old fashioned paper map, good luck, they have no idea what you are talking about!

Another form of outdoor advertising is a marquee or storefront. You have no idea of the power that is associated with a marquee or storefront. The number of potential customers that drive past your business will astound you. The more elaborate the marquee, the more expensive the marquee. However, this is money well spent, you need to raise the awareness of your business. I had a discussion once with a business owner who did not have any lights on their storefront. I said, "Why don't you light up your storefront?" Their response was, "I close my business at five in the afternoon, why would I need lights on my storefront when I am not open for business?" Very short sided.

The poster child for outdoor marquee advertisement is Times Square in New York City. Can you imagine what the electric bill is for the all of the bright lights up and down Broadway? You also find the most creative and high tech billboards on the planet in Times Square all with an astronomical cost associate with the technology. Why would you invest that much money in this form of advertising? Back to bang for your buck. The amount of people that walk through Times

Square every year is in the millions. The amount of consumers who watch the ball drop on New Year's Eve on television, globally, would blow your mind. It creates a sense of credibility and legitimacy for a company and a brand. Oh, "Look at how big we have become, we have made it to Broadway!" Brilliant Marketing!

Stadium and arena advertisements are also considered outdoor advertising. Why would a company pay millions of dollars for the right to plaster their logo and brand name all over a stadium? Bang for your buck. When the broadcasting of a football game in Texas begins the announcer does not say, "We are broadcasting from the stadium where boys rustle cows, we are broadcasting from a wireless cell phone provider stadium." The same goes for baseball where here in New York a stadium and baseball field is named after a bank associated with a city. The professional football teams in New York City share a stadium and blew a fantastic marketing opportunity when they decided to sell the naming rights to their stadium. Instead of selling the naming rights to an insurance company they should have capitalized on the opportunity to combine the two names of the teams, one associated with large men colored in blue and the other team associated with an airplane and made a deal with an airline that combines the two teams. That would have been Brilliant Marketing!

Why would you sell the naming rights to a stadium? Why not name the stadium after the team that plays in the stadium. Why not the dogs, the cats, the owls? Of course it brings brand recognition to your franchise. But that does not create a revenue stream for your franchise. What is the definition of found money? Found money is money that you just stumble upon, money that you find with little or no effort. That is what the naming rights to a stadium provide. How much found money are we talking about? The naming rights fee can exceed hundreds of millions of dollars. Using the example of a major league baseball team that sold the naming rights to their stadium for four hundred million dollars over a ten year period. That is forty million dollars a year of found money. That is a lot of found money! For that price call the stadium whatever you want. Litter the stadium everywhere with your logo all day and all night! At the end of the contract if the company that made you the benefactor of the found money does not want to renew the contract, another sponsor will be out there will to let you FIND more money. That is becoming a popular trend.

Why would a company shower you with this generosity? What if the team that occupies the stadium is a winning team, the sponsor can ride these coattails and associate their brand with the winning brand of the team. If the team is a winning team the ratings for the broadcast of this team will soar and every time an event is broadcast from that stadium the name of the stadium is mentioned in the broadcast.

This is not a new phenomenon and has been going on since the beginning of the twentieth century. One of the baseball teams in Chicago which won nothing for over one hundred years plays in a stadium that was named after a chewing gum company. Is there a down side to selling off the naming rights? What if something negative happens to the company? One of the baseball teams in Texas which used to play in a stadium that was known as the "Eighth Wonder of the World" sold the naming rights of their new stadium to an energy company that was part of a huge embezzlement scandal causing them to go out of business, placing a pall over the stadium and creating such a negative stigma that the naming rights were sold to an orange juice company. A football team in Florida with the nickname as the "fish" even though that fish is technically a mammal, originally named their stadium after the owner of the team. They sold the naming rights to a sports apparel company, who went out of business, another black eye associated with the selling of the naming rights of stadium intended to rake in the found money.

Signage or a billboard on display in a stadium or arena goes beyond the reach associated with the consumers who are sitting there watching the event and every time that they look up at the scoreboard to check the score, watch a replay, or check the time that is left in the game they are reminded with a subtle message.

This is where outdoor advertising meets television advertising. Watch any sporting event. There are advertisements all over the place. When a home run travels over the wall, there is a logo on the wall. When a football team crosses the fifty yard line they walk over a logo. When a hockey team skates across the ice they skate over a logo. When a basketball team scores a point and the ball hits the ground there is a logo on the court.

This is not a new phenomenon. Stadium advertising goes back almost one hundred years, but it was in moderation. If you ever watch a replay of a sporting event from a generation ago, sure there were billboards all over the stadium, but not to the excess that we have today. The advent of technology today has taken this form of advertising to the next level. During a baseball game they can superimpose the logo of a sponsor behind home plate. The consumers in the stadium see one advertisement while the viewers on television see a different one, which can be rotated from sponsor to sponsor. The same goes for a basketball game where behind the net one image can be portrayed and the next time down the court a different sponsor can be featured.

The point is that everything is for sale. How can we create revenue streams is the order of the day. Everything is sponsored from the pre-game show to the post-game show to the first pitch of a baseball game to the first touchdown of a football game. All in the spirit of awareness!

The model where outdoor advertising of sporting events is heading is the car racing model. Have you ever looked at the driver of a race car when they get out of their car after winning a race? They are a walking billboard. Have you ever watched car racing? Why would a sponsor paint their logo on a car that just circles around a race track, around and around for five hundred miles? Consumers watch this and what they do not realize is that every time they view the car circling the track the logo of the company is planting a seed in their mind. What I love about the post-race interviews of the winning driver is that they will, midway through the interview change the hat that they are wearing because they have multiple sponsors that they represent. Soccer, especially global soccer clubs, also have sold out. Soccer players are walking billboards for their sponsors with the logo on their uniforms actually larger than the name of the team or the name of the player on the back of their uniform.

This trend is inevitable for the major sports in this country. The revenue streams that this will create are so strong that they cannot and will not be ignored. The greed of the owners and the players will make this happen. Before you know it the baseball team from The Bronx, with the most recognized and the most valuable logo on the planet, will have their pristine pinstriped uniform littered with the logo of the golden arches of a hamburger chain!

Print

No other form of advertising since we have moved into the digital and electronic age has suffered more than print advertising, specifically newspaper and magazine advertising. Printed newspapers and magazines are dinosaurs, heading toward extinction. The number of newspapers that have closed up shop in this country is staggering. The immediacy of news, and the twenty-four seven news cycle have all contributed to this slow death.

There was a time when print advertising was king. I have had a lot of jobs in my life, one of my first but not my first job was as a paperboy. Ask a millennial what does that mean? Good luck! The occupation of paperboy has gone by the wayside and is on the pile of jobs that have been eliminated by technology along with the bank teller and toll collector. It was a great job but a tough job. What was so difficult about the job? It was a daily newspaper that had to be delivered every day. No days off! I had to work every day along with going to school and playing sports. It taught me the importance of work, forced me to learn about the importance of hard work. Back in the heyday of print advertising there were a couple of days during the week that the newspaper was exceedingly heavy. Wednesdays and Sundays. Why? Those were the days of the week when the newspaper was flooded with coupons, deals and sales. I dreaded delivering the paper on those days! Saturday was a piece of cake, the thinnest paper of the week was Saturday.

As a matter of fact I turned it into a profitable enterprise. Not only did I deliver the daily paper, there was another newspaper company in my town that had a Wednesday only publication, more of a circular that advertised local companies, filled with coupons. In addition, there was a newspaper company in my town that had a Saturday only publication, same thing, a circular that advertised different businesses filled with coupons. I incorporated all three newspapers in my paper route. I was collecting checks from three different newspaper companies. Talk about bang for your buck! I was loaded and I was in the seventh grade!

The printed magazine and the associated advertising in magazines is dying as well. There was a significant difference between advertising in a magazine versus the newspaper. The life of the newspaper advertisement was short lived. It was for today, or maybe lasted a few days and then it was discarded. It was black and white compared to color. While the newspaper industry tried to implement color advertisements into their newspapers the quality of the print was just not the same as a magazine. Magazine print ads can be flashy and impressive. Magazine advertisements can have a long life. I cannot tell you how much time in my life that I have sat in a doctor office waiting to make a sales presentation in front of the doctor. While sitting in the waiting room there is always a stack of magazines just sitting there. Are they today's edition? No! Most of the magazines that I have perused through could have been sitting there for months. Extended the life of the magazine advertisement way beyond the life of an advertisement in a daily newspaper.

Another form of print advertising that has become extinct is the phone book. The yellow pages. The phone book was the go to source to find products. Before the search engine with the funny name that sounds like giggle, the way that consumers searched for products was the phone book. The cost associated with a full page advertisement in the phone book would amaze you. Even a small advertisement on one tenth of a full page in the phone was exorbitant. Why? It was effective, it worked! Incredible bang for your buck. You had no choice if you were serious about your business you HAD to have an advertisement in the phone book.

As previously mentioned advertising is a mentality, it is a belief. The marketers who believe in the notion that advertising is a necessity are the successful marketers. The intangibility associated with advertising prevents or clouds the judgement of the business owner to believe in advertising. I understand this because believe it or not it is very difficult to measure the return on investment of advertising. I had a customer who believed in advertising. He was an extremely successful businessman. He owned a retail surgical supply store in New York City. He had his regular business phone number, the same phone number for years that his customers would use to call his business. Then he wanted to advertise in the phone book. He set up a second phone line for his business. The only way that you found this phone number was if you saw it in his advertisement in the phone book. This phone number was not promoted anywhere else. Every time that second phone line rang he recorded the amount of business that the phone call generated. He was able to track and analyze if the expenditure for the phone book advertisement was worth the cost of the advertising. He was trying to measure a tangible way to measure bang for his buck. Brilliant Marketing!

Internet

Profound is the only way to describe the impact and influence that the Internet has had on our lives. To me, profound means something that changes our lives dramatically like the light bulb or the automobile. At one time we sat around burning candles for light and road around on horses. Can you picture that today? The Internet has become the most profound innovation on our lives since the advent of television. Television changed our lives. How many consumers get up in the morning, go to work, return from work, have a meal with their family, and then sit down and watch television? A staggering number of consumers. Today the same routine is in place, get up, go to and from work, still have a meal with their family, but instead of sitting down in front of the television how many consumers are on their devices? That is profound change. Think about it this way. What is the first device that is turned on when you come home at the end of the day?

Internet advertising is a rapidly growing medium. In the 1990s traditional advertising was shaken to its core. The same way that traditional retail was shaken to its core. Was this new phenomenon (Internet) going to put the conventional methods of advertising a product out to pasture? Yes! It was not as seismic a shift as initially predicted but the game has clearly changed. It was not the gold rush that many marketers predicted. Original forms of Internet advertising focused on pop-up ads that would occupy the middle of your screen and would not let you proceed to the website that you were searching for until you viewed the ad. Banner ads that ate up the borders of your computer screen would infringe on the actual space of what you were attempting to view were in vogue. Anytime that you wanted to listen to a song or view a video you were held hostage waiting precious seconds where you could click on the bottom right hand corner to skip the ad. These are revenue generating forms of Internet advertising. All of these forms of Internet advertisement fit seamlessly into the narrative of "If the marketing gimmick did not work, they would not do it anymore!"

There are other methods of Internet advertising that do not generate any revenue and in fact can cost a fortune. Start with the homepage of the website. When this innovation burst on the scene there was a rush to create a flashy website. Pour resources into the website. You do not need the most sophisticated website that you have ever seen but you do need one that is functional, simple for viewers to navigate through and an easy pathway to possibly purchasing a product from your website. Your website does need to have a professional appearance. Your webpage is your storefront, it is your marquee, and when viewers are "Window Shopping" the same way that retail shoppers used to walk up and down Fifth avenue in New York City, your window display needs to stimulate the consumer to enter the store, albeit your website.

I understand this philosophy but what has evolved into reality is that the placement of your website is more important than the flash associated with your website. The same Real Estate rules apply to where your website resides on the information superhighway. Location! Location! Location! The beauty of the web is that your actual physical location CAN be located in an undesirable or unreachable part of town, or let's face it in a bad location which previously could have led to the extinction of your business. Now the placement of your website on a Search Engine has supplanted the notion of a physical location, location, location to a virtual location, location, location!

Search Engine Optimization (SEO) is the key to Internet advertising. Where are you located on a search engine matters more than anything else. When a keyword is entered into a device, where are you located in the standings of the search is the question, are you at the top of the results? Are you on the first page, in the middle of the pack or did the results of the search stick you at the back of the line? All of this must be considered. Initially it was hard to figure out how does a search engine operate? How does the search engine monetize the content? The search engine charges customers to have an "Optimal" position. The more popular the category that is being searched the more expensive it is to get to the top of the list of the search engine.

Although the number of consumers who access the Internet has steadily grown over the past twenty years, not every consumer has access to the Internet. My point is that if you do not have access to the Internet do I really want you as a customer today?

Chapter 9

The Life of a Salesperson

Personal Selling

The Importance Of Selling

Someone once said that, "Nothing happens until something gets sold." There is nothing to market unless it can be sold. There is no question that the most important component of the Promotional Mix is Personal Selling. Marketers who believe in this concept are leaders and forward thinkers. Marketers who do not follow suit will be left behind.

In my first book, A Salesman Walks Into A Classroom...The Art of Sales Meets the Science of Selling, a comprehensive and expanded view of Personal Selling topics are explored.

Traditional Transaction Selling Approach

The role of the salesperson is crucial to the overall success of an organization. Generating sales revenue and sustaining sales revenue were traditional roles. Current competitive trends in the industrial marketplace have rendered these roles increasingly less effective in establishing loyalty among buyers. The role that the salesperson plays in establishing long-term loyalty among buyers needs to be redefined.

Traditionally, basic selling skills taught by sales trainers are based on models developed in the 1920s by E.K. Strong, who introduced such ideas as the use of open and closed questions, the presentation of features and benefits, objection handling methods, and closing techniques. Today these foundations for effective selling can still be utilized in formal sales training programs, with one obvious difference. These foundations are rooted in aggression and persuasion. These foundations were constructed during an era where straight commission was the primary form of salesperson compensation. This philosophy has bred a perception of deception, with regards to how salespeople treat potential customers. This is the transaction mentality. Relationship selling focuses on the long-term relationship between the salesperson and the customer. The prior foundations, which were rooted in aggression and persuasion, have been replaced with foundations rooted in empathy and ethics.

Established models of successful selling focused on the transaction itself. Completing the transaction and making the sale was paramount. Transaction selling concentrates on making the sale today, and is not concerned with tomorrow's relationship with the customer. It was a short-term approach to selling. Transactional relationships represent the traditional buyer-seller relationship. The underlying assumption is that value is maximized by an adversarial stance within the relationship where the buyer plays the suppliers against one another to extract a price or concession. Today that short-term approach has been replaced with a long-term relationship. The transaction approach focused on the close, while the relationship approach concentrates on the development of a partnership between buyer and seller.

Transaction selling emphasizes the wants of the salesperson, usually rooted in the commission that the salesperson can earn on the transaction. In relationship selling, the focal points are the needs of the customer. Relationship selling involves solving problems for customers, resulting in trust, which can enhance and lengthen the relationship.

Salespeople who are customer-oriented take actions aimed at increasing long-term customer satisfaction and avoid behaviors that may lead to customer dissatisfaction. Customer-oriented salespeople must take the necessary time and effort to identify unique customer needs and wants, and match them as closely as possible to the product benefits offering of the firm.

Difference Between Relationship Selling And Relationship Marketing

Relationship selling activities focus on the needs of the customer while relationship marketing attempts to create a desire and a want in the marketplace. Relationship selling activities include the use of active listening skills, listening to the customer, to determine if the customer has a problem and a need for the salesperson's product. Relationship marketing is more concerned with getting the message out to the customer (talking) through the various forms of integrated marketing communications which include advertising, sales promotion, public relations, and publicity.

Salespeople are typically compensated based on the sales volume that is generated by their sales territory, while marketing executives are typically paid on the profitability of their product line. Relationship selling activities involve selling yourself to the customer before you sell your product. This includes presenting your personal image that can leave an indelible impression on a customer that can endure with the relationship between buyer and seller regardless of the company and product that the salesperson represents. Relationship marketing does have a long-term focus on the image that they portray to their customers, but it is more of a corporate image, not a personal one, that will generally outlast the salesperson's tenure with the organization.

Shift From Transaction Selling To Relationship Selling

Traditionally, the emphasis in sales was on closing (transaction) the sale, with little thought being given to the means by which the sale was obtained, customer expectations of the sales process, or the likelihood that any particular buyer would be a source of future business. Following completed transactions, the exchange relationship essentially ends.

Transaction marketing requires the availability of a mass market of willing, potential customers. Relationship marketing represents the opposite end of the hierarchy to transaction marketing. Thus, relationship marketing involves the establishment of an enduring, interdependent association between the buyer and seller.

Despite the importance generally ascribed to the idea of exchange, marketing research has largely neglected the relationship aspect of buyer-seller behavior while tending to study transactions as discrete events. The lack of attention to antecedent conditions and processes for buyer-seller exchange relationships is a serious omission in the development of marketing knowledge.

The archetype of discrete transaction is manifested by money on one side and an easily measured commodity on the other. Relational exchange occurs when events are guided by the context of the interaction, including past, present and (expected) future experiences, and are different from discrete transactions, which are usually short-term events that are market driven.

Summary Of The Differences Between Relationship Selling Versus Transaction Selling

The fundamental difference between transaction selling and relationship selling lies within the mindset of a short-term occurrence (transaction) versus a long-term association (relationship) between the salesperson and the customer. To persuade customers that they need a supplier's product, salespeople in this role focus on achieving short-term results for their companies by using aggressive selling techniques to persuade customers to buy products. Transaction salespeople focus on today, and live for today. What can I sell today, how much commission can I make today, who can I take advantage of today, and are not concerned with tomorrow, or their future interactions (relationships) with their customers. If I do not continue to develop a relationship with this customer beyond this transaction, so be it, I made the sale today, I earned commission today, and I completed the transaction. Transaction salespeople push (sell) the features of a product, while relationship oriented salespeople sell the benefits (solution) of a product to a customer.

Relationship selling focuses more on the development of a connection between the salesperson and the customer, and relies on the enhancement of rapport building between both parties. Relationship selling is more concerned with tomorrow than today, if you are not ready today to make a purchase, or do not have a need for my product today, again, so be it, I will be there tomorrow when you are ready.

Traditionally, transaction salespeople were paid on straight commission, meaning that if you made a sale today, you earned a commission today. If you did not complete a transaction today, you did not earn any compensation for your efforts. Sales organizations have come to the realization that the commission earned on a transaction can affect the ethical behavior of a salesperson. If the salesperson's sole method of compensation is based on the transaction completed, this can have an effect on their behavior. While there are still many salespeople who are compensated on a straight commission basis, today it has become fashionable for salespeople to be paid a comprehensive compensation plan that includes the combination of a base salary, plus commission, bonuses, and related expenses. This type of compensation plan allows the salesperson to take the commission earned on the transaction out of the equation, or at least not forcing the salesperson to make the sale today because they need to make the sale today in order to receive any compensation for their efforts. It allows the salesperson to walk away from the transaction and not be empty handed because their base salary provides them with an income that does not hinge on completing the transaction.

Transaction salespeople are self-centered and direct their efforts towards their needs, specifically their need to make the sale and earn commission. Relationship salespeople center on the needs of the customer, and act as detectives trying to uncover a need that the customer can have. If the customer has a need for a product, they have a problem. Relationship salespeople are perceived by their customers as problem solvers, compared to the pushy salesperson perception of traditional transaction oriented salespeople. Transaction salespeople stretch the truth, and try to fit square pegs into round holes. Relationship salespeople are more concerned with the integrity of the relationship, and their reputation as a professional, and fit square pegs into square holes.

Steps In The Selling Process: The Importance Of Moving Your Business Forward

To be successful in sales you have to be persistent, dedicated, and hard working. You need to be scientific in your approach, meaning you have to have a plan. You have to be robotic with your activity, every day you need to have a routine that identifies and follows steps that can lead you to success. You need to move your business forward every day, you need to accomplish something today that gets you closer to surpassing your quota.

The sales process can be defined as the steps that you need to follow starting from scratch, or locating your potential customer, to approaching the customer, making a presentation to the customer, answering any questions or objections that they have, closing the sale, and following-up with the customer after the sale. If you follow these steps, and adhere to this model, you can be successful at selling. You need to know where you are going every day, you need to know where, and what stage of the sales process your customers are in. Every customer is at a different stage of the process, you need to be able to juggle this, know when to move to the next stage, and when to start the process over again with your next customer.

The sales cycle is the amount of time it takes from the first time you identify a potential customer to the time it takes to close the sale. It is the "A to Z" of selling. You need to know where you are in the sales cycle from "A to Z". Some sales cycles are short, some are longer. The more dollars that are at stake, the more departments that get involved in the process, the more departments that get involved in the process, the more people get involved in the process. The more people that get involved in the process, the longer it takes to close the sale. The key is to shorten the sales cycle. Salespeople who are able to move their business forward every day and shorten the sales cycle are the salespeople who consistently exceed their quota, and become super-star salespeople.

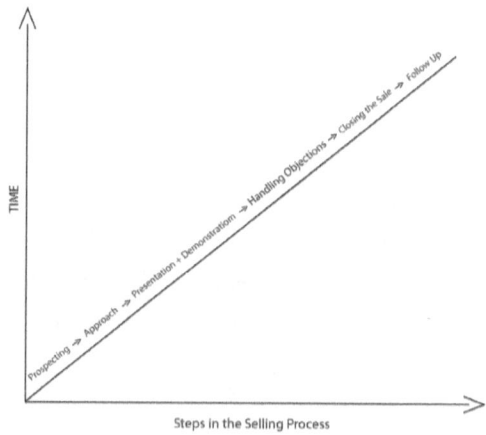

Steps in the Selling Process

Prospecting

How do you get started? Where do you go? Who do you see? Some companies put you through their sales training program, release you into the field, and hand you the keys to the company car and say, "Go ahead, go get them!" Now, this is not necessarily such a bad thing, to be cut loose into your territory where you are in charge of where you go on a daily basis. You have to have a plan. It all starts with prospecting.

There are several methods of prospecting. Which is the most effective form of prospecting? This is a trick question. The most effective method is the method that works for you. It is the method that you are most comfortable with. Make no mistake about it, you HAVE to prospect. You have to always be hunting and searching for new customers. The day that a salesperson wakes up and is comfortable with the amount of current, existing customers that they have in their territory, is the first day that the sales in your territory will slowly begin to erode away.

Prospecting is not fun, closing the sale is fun. Prospecting is painful, closing the sale alleviates the pain associated with prospecting. If you don't prospect, you will never get to close the sale. Prospecting is not fun because it is filled with rejection. Having the phone hung up on you, having a door slammed in your face, having a prospect tell you to get lost is not fun. That is why you need to find the best method of prospecting that works for you. There is a helpless sense that you are wasting valuable sales time, because you will waste time prospecting. Remember the quota clock is always ticking, and a minute wasted by unproductive prospecting is a minute that could have been spent closing a sale.

Prospecting is a mentality, it is a grind, prospecting is a necessary evil that must become part of your daily sales activity. Whatever works for you, whatever you are comfortable with will be how you establish your routine. Some salespeople prospect early in the day, to get it out of the way, some salespeople handle immediate, pressing sales and customer related issues first, and leave their prospecting for the end of the day. Some prospect earlier in the week, some wait until the end of the week. The same goes for a monthly basis, some salespeople prospect in the beginning of the month because they know that their time at the end of the month is more beneficial to be spent closing sales before the end of the month.

A method to alleviate the pain associated with prospecting is to sandwich your prospecting around solid appointments during the day, week, or month. Too much prospecting in a given time period can weigh on you psychologically. As you review your daily activity your day can be highlighted by the sales calls that did move your business forward, as opposed to a full day of prospecting that can leave you with a depressing, empty feeling that you were spinning your wheels all day and were not productive. Call reluctance can set in where you are doing too much prospecting and the rejection that you are experiencing can actually prevent you from making your next attempt at prospecting. A mentality exists where, "If I do not pick up the phone, they cannot hang up on me." Call reluctance can also exist in physical, face-to-face (door-to-door) prospecting. If you do not knock on the door they cannot slam the door in your face, or throw you out of their office or place of business. You have to fight through call reluctance, which is common and normal, but if you do not pick up the phone, or knock on that door you will never find any new customers. As you become more experienced you can handle the rejection associated with prospecting, and recognize that it is a part of the life that you have chosen as a salesperson, and you will develop a thicker skin that can help you adjust to the rejection.

Sales is a numbers game and the more prospects that you ask to purchase your product the better your chances of someone saying, "Yes, I will take it!" If you ask one hundred prospects to purchase your product, you will have a chance of making a sale, but if you ask one thousand prospects to purchase your product your chances of making a sale will increase tenfold. It is common for salespeople to loathe or dread the concept of cold calling. Here is a tip, sales managers love the idea that their salespeople are cold calling. It shows initiative and dedication to the cause. Any salesperson can get an existing customer to re-order a company's product. The over achieving salesperson consistently cold calls and brings in new business from new customers. Yes, any sale regardless of size is considered a win. A sale that is consummated as a result of a cold call is a much sweeter victory. Sales is a roller coaster ride filled with highs and lows, and the high that you will experience from a "cold call" sale is one of the true enjoyments in the life of a salesperson. You did it, you germinated, and nurtured the process, you can take full credit for it, and this will go a long way with sales management.

Approach

Prospecting is a funnel where a ton of names of potential customers are dumped into, filtered, and sanitized and a few make it through the separation process of prospects and suspects. What do you do next? How do you approach the list of customers that the funnel has spit out and dumped in your lap? You will only get one chance to make a first impression on your customer, so you do not want to waste the opportunity. How you approach the customer is vital to the process.

Approach is your initial contact with the customer. Your approach has to be accompanied by an immediate value statement that catches the attention of the customer. Your approach is a prelude to the next step in the process, presentation and demonstration, but you need to get to that step. An effective approach can inaugurate the footing of a successful presentation and demonstration. What does it mean when a customer says, "I will give you a few minutes?" Understand they are busy, they have a job to do, and you need to understand where you fit in their totem pole of importance. You are lucky if you are near the top, most times you are not. You need to respect their time, if you do not, you can ruin the opportunity. When they say I will give you a few minutes, only take a few minutes, it is up to them to send out signals that they will give you more of their valuable time. In your value statement you need to introduce yourself to them, always thank them for taking the time to meet with you, and tell them how you can help them solve their problem. An old axiom was to have an "elevator speech", a brief statement that you would say to a customer if you bumped into them on an elevator that grabs their attention and can lead you to the next step.

Selling is always confrontational, even if you are making a sales call on an existing customer, who can be a friend, they know that when you walk in the door you are attempting to sell them something. You need to break the ice, make them relax, make them feel comfortable and not confrontational. This all falls under the category of developing rapport with a customer. People buy products from people they like, and there is nothing wrong with trying to develop a relationship, or rapport with a customer.

Once rapport has been established, and you have preceded to get them to relax, you need to move to the next step in the approach process which is to prepare to get to the next step of presentation and demonstration. At this point the direction of the conversation has to shift their way. Too many salespeople do too much talking. You need to be quiet and let them explain why they have agreed to meet with you. Obviously they have a problem, which translates into a need. Let them state the problem. You are a detective on a crime scene. Gather information that helps you to decipher the problem. You are in the need discovery stage of the approach process. If you determine that the customer has a problem (need) that you can solve with your product being the solution to their problem, then you should gather as much information as possible for you to move to the next step in the sales process which is presentation and demonstration. If you determine that at this time you cannot provide a solution to their problem, thank them for their time and move on to your next prospect. This customer will respect that you did not push a product on them that will not satisfy their needs, and keep you in mind down the road when their needs might change.

Presentation And Demonstration

Preparation is the key to making a successful sales presentation and demonstration. There is no such thing as being too prepared, or overly prepared for a presentation and demonstration. The day that you leave a sample in your car, or piece of literature or brochure behind, is the day that you will need it for your presentation. Always prepare for the worst, because if you are prepared for the worst then you can handle any quirk or curveball that is thrown your way.

Expect the technology that you are using for your presentation to fail, expect your product to malfunction during your presentation, expect to have problems with the room that you are planning for your presentation, and expect your customer to cut you short on the time that they told you will be allotted for your presentation. If you are prepared for this and any other circumstances that can pop up to sabotage your presentation and demonstration you will be fine.

There are two elements that are common denominators of most sales presentations, a salesperson and a customer. Salespeople make common presentations to the same kind of customer every day. It behooves a company to make sure that a salesperson is delivering the proper message to the customer. During the sales training process it is crucial to educate your salespeople on what to say when you get in front of a customer. A common method is to develop a script, or memorized presentation, where the salesperson recites the same verbiage, in all of their presentations. Another word for this is a "canned" presentation which is a packaged and manufactured set of words that can assist a salesperson specifically when they are new to a company, product, and industry.

It is imperative to tailor and customize your presentation to your audience. Many of your presentations and demonstrations will have commonalities, but the customization of the presentation and demonstration comes from the information that you obtained during your initial approach meeting. If you give your standard, generic presentation and demonstration that includes elements of your presentation and demonstration that you give to all of your customers, it can include information that does not pertain to the current presentation. Customers can be distracted and lose interest during your presentation because you are discussing product features and benefits that are not relevant to their situation. On the flip side if your presentation and demonstration is tailored to their needs, can be an indication that you did listen to their concerns during the initial approach meeting and increase your credibility.

Show and tell has been a popular method to make a demonstration that dates all the way back to when you were in kindergarten. The most effective product demonstrations are the most realistic product demonstrations that place a product in the hands of a potential customer so they can see firsthand the features and benefits that the product can offer. If possible, place a sample of your product in the hands of the prospective customer. Let them touch and feel the product, let them sample and evaluate the product. If they try the product, and like the product, they might buy the product. During the demonstration it is paramount for you to validate the ease of use of your product. The more comfortable that they become with your product because of an effective demonstration, the better the chance of closing the sale. It is essential to get the customer involved in the demonstration process. You can verbalize features and benefits to a customer, but it can be convenient for them not to remember a word that you have said. You can exhibit the features and benefits of your product in front of your customer and they will have a better chance of retaining the information. If you solicit the participation of your customer in a "hands on" demonstration of the features and benefits of your product, the probability of the customer retaining an increased comprehension can be maximized.

Body language and room logistics are elements of the presentation and demonstration that often are overlooked. In a one on one meeting, when you walk into the room, after you look around to scan the environment, where is the best place to sit? The worst place to sit, which is often where you will end up, is directly across the desk from the customer. Face-to- face, eye-to-eye, why is this the worst place to sit? It is the worst place, but the most common place to sit, because face-to-face, and eye-to-eye, represents confrontation. If possible sit on the same side of the desk as the customer. Side by side is more of a collaborative approach, we are on the same side of the problem and not as confrontational. Getting a seat behind a customer's desk right next to them is tough, and can be a challenge, people become protective of their space, and entering or invading that space can become problematic. What if they have a separate table in their office, adjacent to their desk, ask them to sit there and when they get up from their desk to sit at the table sit next to them. This also gets them away from the work that is on their desk, their phone, computer, and any notes that are in front of them. If possible get them out of their office element, customers are chained to their desks, and welcome a reason to get to vacate their desk. Take them to a coffee shop, or out for breakfast, lunch, or dinner to get them away from the distraction of their desk. In a committee presentation or demonstration in front of a group of customers, it is important to watch where everyone sits. Never discount any participant's role in the committee, you never know who has the power and influence over the group. Usually there is a leader, or chairperson, who has the most influence. Watch where they sit, most times it is either at the end of the table or in the middle. You need to spot the body language of the group, usually the group will defer to the chairperson, so within a few minutes you need to determine who in the room is running the show, and who is just a spectator.

During your presentation and demonstration you need to gauge how it is going, and a message that is sent to you is the body language that your customer indirectly communicates to you. If a customer is leaning towards you with their arms open, it can be a signal that they are interested and are looking for help to solve their problem. If the customer has their arms crossed, they do not believe a word that you are saying. If they are staring at their watch, looking at their computer screen, checking their phone, or simply looking out the window, they are not listening to a word that you are saying. Who do you have a better chance of moving to the next step with? A customer who just sits there with no response, or a customer who interrupts every word you say with a question or objection to what you are saying? An interruption or question is great. It shows you that they are listening to what you are saying, are interested in what you are saying, you have said something that has struck a chord, spurred their interest, and compelled them to say something.

Customers can ask all kinds of questions during your presentation and demonstration. There are good questions, questions that are on point and questions that can come from left field. You need to be able to think on your feet. Thinking on your feet means that you need to be able to digest the question and give the best response that you can, on the spot. Remember, the more that you repeat your presentation and demonstration, the more comfortable that you will become. You sell the same product every day in front of the same type of customer. The questions are similar. A salesperson makes so many presentations that the salesperson should know what can hook the customer and what can drive a customer away from making the sale.

What do you do when a customer asks you a great, on point question that you cannot answer? Do you change the subject? Do you distract the audience? Do you spin the question around and respond with an answer that does not really answer the question? Understand, the customer does not know that you do not have an answer to their question, to them it is just a question, and to you it is a question that you cannot answer. If you distract the audience they might forget about the question. The best way to answer the question that you cannot answer is to acknowledge to the customer that it is a great question, and that you are not sure and you will get back to them. Write the question down in front of them. If possible pick up the phone and call your sales manager or headquarters and try to get an answer to the question on the spot. This will increase your credibility with the customer. If you cannot get an immediate response, get an answer back to the customer as soon as you can. Record that great question in the back of your mind, because it can come up again, as early as tomorrow in your next presentation or demonstration, and now you will prepared to answer the question in front of your next customer.

Handling Objections

Not everyone is going to agree with everything you say in every sales presentation that you make. If every customer said, "I'll take it!" everyone would become a salesperson. There is a humongous misconception about a customer making an objection during your sales presentation and a customer rejecting your sales presentation. Objection is not rejection and there needs to be clarification of the two. Rejection means no. Rejection means I am not interested. Rejection means this meeting is over. Rejection means, "Do not call me, I will call you!" Objections are good. Objections should be welcomed. Objections are a request for more information. Objections show interest in your sales presentation. Objections mean that the customer is interested in something that you have said in your presentation and demonstration, but they have a question that you need to clarify. Common objections include price, quality, delivery date, competitive offerings, product features, and product functionality. A shrewd technique to overcome a product objection is to encourage that the customer participates in the demonstration process.

The more presentations that you make, the more experienced that you become at anticipating where the meeting is going. You need to be able to take the temperature of the situation, to gauge the level of interest of the customer. You make the same presentation every day in front of the same type of customer. You know who is really interested and who is not. You say a lot of the same things every day, and so does the customer. If you get to the point of your presentation where objections are usually raised, it is wise to forestall the objection. Forestalling the objection means that you address the objection before the customer makes the objection. You can sense that the objection is coming, so you are better off addressing the objection before the customer makes the objection. Other tips are to handle the objections as they occur. You do not want the objections to pile up and then you are spending too much time responding to the multiple objections that are preventing you to go to the next step, closing the sale. You should always let the customer state the objection, hear them out, and do not interrupt their concerns. If it is a legitimate objection, acknowledge the objection, comprehend the objection, confirm that it is a great question they have raised and respond accordingly.

Some objections are concealed and problematic to respond to because the customer is not as forthcoming as you would like them to be. They might not be ready to make a decision, the need for your product can be disguised, or they simply need more time to evaluate, or think about their alternatives. Pushy salespeople respond to this objection, by stating that they have answered all of your questions, and push to move to the close. Problem solving salespeople understand that it takes time to make the decision to purchase a product, answer the objections the best that they can, and let the customer breathe a little bit, to give them the opportunity to make the decision on their terms, when they are ready. If you have satisfied all of the customer's concerns (objections), and you have leaped over this giant hurdle, you are now staring at the most important step in the selling process, closing the sale.

Closing The Sale

Most salespeople can be trained to get to this step. You can be trained on how to get better at prospecting, better at approaching the customer, better at presenting and demonstrating your product, and better at handling objections. Closing the sale is what separates the average salesperson from the good salesperson. It delineates the great salesperson from the good salesperson, and it becomes a line of demarcation between the great salesperson and the super-star salesperson. Hands down, closing the sale is the most significant step in the sales process. It is the most arduous step in the process, because the close is where you are asking for a commitment from the customer. You are reaching in their pocket and taking their money. Customers like their money, and are not as enthusiastic about parting with their money as you would like them to be. Without the close there is no bullion, there is no treasure, there is no gold.

From the first time that a company puts out a job advertisement or job posting, in the job description is states, "Must have a documented history of closing sales, or strong closing skills required, only top closers apply." The job description never says, "Looking for prospecting experts, or experienced sales demonstration skill required." The same goes for the interview process. Yes, it is a good idea during an interview to mention that you love to prospect, and that cold calling is something that you truly enjoy, and you will be asked to explain your interpretation of the sales process, but the sales manager will specifically ask you to describe the biggest, hardest, or most challenging sales close that you have had in your career. All of the other steps can be taught or enhanced through sales training and sales development, but closing skills are tough to teach. Closing skills are not only tough to teach, but they are tough to learn, and closing skills are tough to master. There is an innate characteristic that must be brought out in a salesperson that can make them better at closing sales.

Do you need to follow all of the steps in the sales process, in the actual order that has been depicted? The answer is no. There is an old rule of thumb, ABC, ALWAYS BE CLOSING. You should be closing the sale from the minute that you introduce yourself to the customer. The customer might be ready sooner than you think, and you do not want to talk yourself out of making a sale. You should use a trial close technique. A trial close means that you are "trying" to close the sale as you go through your presentation and demonstration. A trial close is a stab, during your presentation or demonstration, to inspire the customer to take the necessary action and make the purchase of your product.

As noted earlier, the time that you spend during the sale process to get the customer to this point can be monumental. At this point you have still not made the sale, and all of your efforts still can go down the tubes overnight. If you have invested all of this time, remember, the quota clock has been ticking during all of the steps of the sales process, and you have not had any return on the investment of your time. There becomes a time during the close to get a little heavy handed and ask the customer for the order. Are they going to move forward or not?

You need to know where you stand. There is a professional way to take this approach and also a pushy way to take this approach. If you ask an open ended question, which gives the customer the chance to elaborate and verbalize exactly where you stand in the sales process, it gives them the opportunity to voice any concerns or objections that they may still have. An example of an open ended question can be, "Are there any questions that you may have, or any details that we have not discussed that you need to have clarified before we move further?" The open ended question is soliciting a lengthy response filled with words. If you can satisfy their concerns then you can start to ask closed ended questions. Closed ended questions solicit short, one or two word responses, usually, yes or no responses. Examples of closed ended questions are, "Have we identified that you have a need for my product? Are you the sole decision maker who is making the decision to purchase this product?" The closed ended question is used as a confirmation and clarification tool.

The pushy salesperson utilizes high pressure closing tactics such as, "If you do not take advantage of this deal today, I am not sure if I can guarantee this price tomorrow, or if you do not buy this product today, I have other customers lined up who are ready and I cannot guarantee that this product will be there when you are ready to buy?"

Preparation is a consistent thread that is sprinkled throughout the steps in the sales process. Asking for the order becomes more routine if the salesperson is tactically prepared for the close. Salespeople become gun shy when they get to the close. Not asking for the order is a huge mistake, or just asking for the order only once can also be a mistake. Do not be bashful or gun shy, to get to this point in the process you have already established a relationship with this customer, and have developed a rapport with this customer, and now is the time to cash in, cross the finish line, complete the task at hand, CLOSE the sale!

You need to exude self-confidence during the close. You need to be relaxed during the close, and you need the customer to relax during the close. If you are self-confident and relaxed, this can permeate and come across to the customer that they are making the right decision. If you are rushed, unprepared, and nervous, it can come across that you are not so sure that this is a great proposal that you have put on the table. If you are prepared for the close you can minimize and avoid any surprises at the close. Surprises can include last minute requests by the customer, eleventh hour last minute proposal changes, and desperate competitive bids that can be a scare tactic. You need to be poised and professional, you need to believe in your product, and that your product is the solution to the customer's problem. This sincerity will be transmitted to the customer and they can look at you as a true problem solver.

Follow-Up

In the transaction model of selling, closing the sale was the final step in the sales process. Once you close the sale, you have made your commission and the next step is to start the process all over again and begin to prospect for your next customer. That has been changed today, where the importance of post-sale follow-up and service has become a critical element of the sales process.

What infuriates customers about salespeople? Is it the pushy, aggressive approach, the never ending hounding? All of the above. What annoys a customer the most is a salesperson who seems to be pushing and annoying them to make a purchase, then once the purchase is made, the salesperson cannot be found. The salesperson cannot be found because they are following the transaction model where they made their commission and have moved on to their next victim (customer). It gives the customer the impression that they have been duped, they have been had, and they proceed to place the salesperson on top of the pile of salespeople who run after they make the sale. Following-up with the customer means that you will be there, you will be available, and you will be around after the sale is made. A successful follow-up technique is to contact the customer within a few days of making the sale. Contact them to thank them for the business, contact them to ask them if they have any questions, any concerns, and let them know that you are around to ease them into the implementation of your product. The tip is to call them before they call you. If you intercept their call beforehand, it will show the customer that you have not run away, and that you are available and you are there to help them with the transition to your product.

Does this mean that you have to morph into more of a service technician than a salesperson, the answer is yes? Salespeople have a problem with this metamorphosis because you are not being paid to be a service technician, you are being paid to sell. This irritates salespeople because the quota clock is ticking and if you are spending too much time following-up it can distract you from starting the sales process again with a new customer. All of these follow-up techniques are designed with one goal in mind, a long-term relationship with your customer. Once you complete the process with one customer you need to start the process again with your next customer. If you build a territory populated with satisfied customers they will call you back again when they are in the market for another product. If you followed up on your promises that you made during the earlier steps in the sales process, you can bypass most of the previous steps and shorten the sales cycle. Your prospecting time is cut down, presentation and demonstration is in the rear view mirror, and closing and negotiation is not as painful the second time around. It's all about time management, the quota clock is still ticking, and you can shave off valuable time in the process if you have a satisfied customer.

When does following-up become excessive? When does following-up turn you from a salesperson into a service technician? When does following-up cut into your valuable time as a salesperson? When I made the largest sale in my life at the time, there was some expected follow-up, but come on! The medical device was over twenty-five pounds. It took up a lot of space. There were components inside the box as well. It was a huge box. One hundred units were ordered. One request that the hospital made was that they do not have the physical space in their warehouse to store the equipment when it was delivered. On the actual Purchase Order, in large bold font was a request by the customer, to split the order into four shipments of twenty-five, and stagger the delivery over a four week period. The hospital hands me the order and says, "Paul, make sure you split the order, we don't have enough space here." It was the largest order in the history of the company for this device. I arranged a conference call with everyone from the corporate office to discuss the shipment, from the Regional Sales Manager, Director of Sales, Vice-President of Sales, Vice-President of Manufacturing and the Head of Customer Service. I sent everyone a copy of the order. I say on the call, "Is everyone clear that we need to split the order, stagger the shipments." I specifically asked the Head of Customer Service and the Vice-President of Manufacturing, are they sure that they read the bold font request made by the customer? They both confirmed that they have the instructions.

What did we do? We shipped all one hundred units in one shipment. No staggering of the order! The hospital was livid. The hospital wanted to refuse the shipment because we ignored their request and they frankly had no room for one hundred huge boxes. As a salesperson you are the face of the franchise. You are the person who they see. The customer does not see or interact with the corporate office, they see you the salesperson who convinced them to make the purchase. In their eyes I was the fool who could not read the instructions not the people behind the scene who made the error.

What did I do? Remember commission gets paid on shipment. If the shipment is refused and sent back to the manufacturer the order could be in jeopardy and your commission can be flushed down the toilet. I went out and rented a truck, you know the kind of truck when you are moving your house. I show up at the loading dock of the hospital. The one hundred boxes were massive, creating issues on the loading dock. I left twenty-five units of the equipment on the loading dock (first shipment of twenty-five) and put the other seventy-five units on the truck. I took the truck home and parked it in my driveway. Every week for the next month I would show up and make my weekly delivery of equipment to the hospital. I took pictures of me loading and unloading the truck, with my hand truck, and the backdrop of the hospital's marquee and loading dock and sent them to all of the aforementioned corporate stakeholders. That ate up too much of my valuable selling time but sometimes as a salesperson you literally have no choice.

Closing a million dollar capital equipment deal on a ten plus hospital account comes with a boatload of follow-up. From the first day of walking into the flagship hospital to the final follow-up on the last implementation of the equipment at the last hospital took close to twenty-four months. Once the equipment was shipped to each hospital the follow-up began. I am not even referring to the training of the staff of a few thousand nurses who would be using the equipment. The assembly of the equipment and the training of the staff had to be staggered over time. The first domino was the main campus of the chain and the subsequent smaller hospitals followed suit. The last hospital was the co-flagship account that was not ready for the implementation until the end of the project. The equipment arrives at the hospital and sits on a pallet for almost a month. I receive a call from the higher ups at the hospital SCREAMING at me because the equipment was still in its boxes three plus weeks after the delivery. I follow-up with the warehouse and the biomedical engineering department who have to inspect, check and sticker every piece of new equipment that comes into the hospital to insure that it is safe to use on a patient. There were one hundred devices in boxes. There were several components to each device also in their own box. Have you ever opened something that comes in a box, that comes in another box, and that comes in another box? Same situation. Too much corrugated paper! The staff looked at the mountain of "Corrugation" and said, "Not today!" The assembly of each piece of equipment took at least fifteen minutes, not counting the time associated with the programming of each device to meet the specific drug library of the hospital that needed to be downloaded manually to each device. One hundred devices. A lot of work! A lot of man hours! I had no choice. I had to stop selling and start assembling equipment. It probably took more than a week of valuable selling time that I never got back to insure that the customer was satisfied. Too much follow-up!

Chapter 10

Incentive and Image

Sales Promotion

Again, Sales Promotion does not mean that you get promoted into sales management. Sales Promotion from a Promotional Mix standpoint can be defined by one word, incentive. What is the incentive to purchase the product today? Not tomorrow or next week, today! What can I do to get you to take action and make a purchase today?

Like so many elements of our lives that have been transformed from paper to electronic formats, where devices are dominating our lives, Sales Promotion is not exempt from this. A traditional method of Sales Promotion were coupons. When consumers would scour their local newspaper and cut out a paper coupon that they could redeem at a retailer and save five cents on a pound of coffee. Was this an effective form of Sales Promotion? Yes! Did it work? Yes! What was appealing about this form of Sales Promotion was that the redemption of the paper coupon meant that the consumer DID see the advertisement and took their time to cut it out and bring it with them to the store. The trend today is to honor competitive coupons, meaning that you did not spend any resources on the coupon yet have to honor your competitor's coupon just to stay competitive!

I have always asked this question in class. Has anyone ever worked at a supermarket where customers would come in with a stack of coupons and present them at checkout to save a few pennies on their purchases? It was an overwhelming yes. Have you ever been stuck on a line at the supermarket where the customer in front of you hands over an outrageous number of coupons holding up the line? Of course you have!

Many forms of promotion are hard to track and trace. How do you know if your promotional dollars were well spent? By having the ability to track the amount of coupons that were redeemed was an excellent way to justify the promotional expense. A lot of promotion is intangible, did the consumer watch the television commercial? Did the consumer hear the radio advertisement? Did the consumer see the billboard on the highway? It is difficult to put your finger on the effectiveness of the promotion. Typically the only way to measure the effectiveness of promotion was to answer the question, "Did the promotion help to increase the overall sales of the product?"

The on-line promo code has replaced the paper coupon. The ability to track the effectiveness of the promotion, whatever the form, is paramount. Part of research is observation research. Observation research entails gaining an understanding of the environment that surrounds you. I am a proponent of observation research. I love to observe impressive marketing, whether it is a television commercial, radio advertisement, or the way a salesperson approaches me as a customer. What is interesting about utilizing a Promotional Code, "Promo Code", is that you can flood the market with a radio commercial spread over many different radio formats. As a salesperson you live in the car. So much of your life is spent driving from customer to customer. Depending on the day or my mental state of mind I will surf around the radio dial from every genre including sports talk radio, political opinion shows and classic rock music. Depending on the time of year advertisers bombard you with the same radio advertisement spread across the different genres.

Whether it's a commercial for chocolate berries for Valentine's Day, flowers for Mother's Day, or just a commercial telling me that I should buy someone's pillow, the prevalence of reminder advertising is overwhelming.

Where is the brilliant marketing? Each commercial on each radio station has a different promo code. The brilliance lies within the ability to trace where the order came from. Did more orders come in from the classic rock station or the sports talk radio station? This data can assist the marketer and justify the expense associated with the promotional expense. This was difficult to track in the past when radio promotion was a shot in the dark. Yes, there is a ratings system put in place, but that is not an exact science and there was no other tangible way, other than an overall increase in sales, to measure the effectiveness of the promotion.

Marketers love to push the envelope and cross the line of deception with their customers. Maybe marketers do not cross the line but they get as close to the line as possible without doing something unethical or illegal, it may just not be nice.

Superb marketing allows the marketer to take advantage of the customer without the customer realizing what is going on. An example of this are rebates. If I am running a company, I am playing the rebate game all day. Let's say that the customer knows what the established price for a product is, let's say one hundred dollars. The customer needs the product, the customer will eventually buy the product, but the customer needs to be nudged a little bit to pull the trigger, reach into their pocket and fork over the one hundred dollars. This brings us back to the true definition of Sales Promotion, incentive. What is the incentive to buy the product now! A rebate can be the incentive. Whether the customer is physically in the store or virtually online, they notice a sign, or banner ad that lists the aforementioned one hundred dollar product for seventy-five dollars, a twenty-five percent discount. This immediately catches the eye of the customer, and they say to themselves, "Wow, I was eventually going to buy this widget, and I can get it for twenty-five percent off?" Sounds like a good deal and they proceed to complete the transaction. They go to the check out, again whether virtually or physically, only to find out that the product is actually one hundred dollars, not seventy-five. There is a manufacturer's rebate that has to be filled out and mailed in to receive the twenty-five dollars off. Sure some customers do not complete the transaction because of the rebate but many customers do complete the transaction and spend the one hundred dollars to procure the product.

Here is the beautiful, deceptive marketing. I would love to know what the percentage of rebates that never get redeemed is. Why do they not get redeemed? The customer never sends in the completed rebate form, the customer forgets about the rebate. The manufacturer takes their sweet time to send the customer the funds. Think about that. The manufacturer has your money. Multiply how many transactions are completed because of the rebate, and the manufacturer just sits on that cash and does not pay it out on a timely basis. I love this one, the rebate is mailed to the customer in a blank, non-descript envelope. It used to be a paper check now it can come in the form of a gift card. The point is that it looks like a piece of junk mail. What does the average person do when they look at the mail that they receive on a daily basis? They place the mail in three piles, bills, checks sent to you, and junk mail. The junk mail gets tossed immediately. I wonder what the percentage of rebates that get tossed away because the customer thinks its junk mail. What happens is that over time the customer forgets about the rebate, never redeems the rebate and in the end pays one hundred dollars for the product. Outstanding marketing, using the illusion of the rebate as an effective form of Sales Promotion!

Gift cards are another excellent form of sales promotion where the company can benefit over the customer. When you purchase a gift card the company receives a timely payment off of your credit card. The same way that the rebate is now in your corner so is the redemption of the gift card. If the gift card gets lost or never redeemed they get your money. If you leave your gift card in your wallet a percentage is deducted off of the total amount of the gift card. How do they get away with that? What about this. How many times have you redeemed a gift card for a purchase that is exactly what the amount of the gift card is? Many times you spend more money than the gift card is actually worth. Brilliant Marketing!

Rewards programs have become a popular form of Sales Promotion. The root of this type of Sales Promotion started with the concept of a frequent flyer program offered by an airline. Has this concept been beaten to death and copied by other industries anywhere from hotels to sandwich shops? Yes! What is misleading is that you have to spend so much money and time being a loyal customer to accrue the reward.

I remember an episode from one of the most successful television sitcoms in history. The show was about life in New York City in the 1990s. No, is was not the "friendly" show it was the show about "nothing". The female character became obsessed with the reward program for a local sandwich shop.

The sandwich shop would give the customer a card that they would punch a hole in every time you bought a sandwich. Once you accumulated ten holes in your card you would receive a free sandwich. The customer did not even like the sandwiches but became obsessed with the notion of getting the free sandwich!

Sampling

I believe in the, if you try something, and you like something, you might buy something philosophy of marketing. Where do you see sampling as a form of Sales Promotion? Manufacturers will employ Brand Ambassadors who stand at a display in a store and offer you a sample of the product. This has become so popular that customers actually will travel to a local retail outlet to get the free samples of products. Does this work? Of course it does, like anything in marketing if it did not work they would not continue to do it. I remember getting my son a job on his winter break from college. He needed a job and did not care what he had to do. I got him a job as a Brand Ambassador for a popular brand of chocolate that was giving out samples at supermarkets across the country. I said, "Just take the job, you need to do something while home on break." He said, "Chocolate, you want me to sell chocolate?" There is an inside joke here. One of the most popular cartoon television shows of his generation involved a character who lived under the sea. There was an episode where they were selling chocolate. If you do not know which show I am referring to, ask a millennial they will tell you. Millennials cannot tell you who their local congressperson is, or cannot spot Peru on a map but they can quote, verbatim, this episode from this show. Every day he sold out his quota of chocolate.

Sometimes your style of marketing and selling is dictated by your company and your industry. I grew up in the medical device industry. Two components of the sales process in the medical device industry that are unavoidable are the length of the sales process of the sales cycle and the notion that nothing will be purchased until the customer tries and evaluates the product. For Free! It is not a test drive at a car dealership! Some marketer is going to walk into a hospital one day with the cure for cancer in their bag. What an incredible innovation! What an incredible day! The reaction from the hospital should be, "Thank you, we have been waiting for this for some time now." Instead, the two initial reactions will be, "How much is it and we have to try it first!" That is a pathetic but accurate response. What's to try? The innovation has been trialed and proven as a successful product. Medical journals have published the results of clinical trials. Flagship accounts across the country have implemented the innovation. What's to try? With a mountain of evidence to support your case you are still going to have to give samples and conduct a trial before the customer will ever think about purchasing your product.

What is amazing to me is that the practice of sampling does not automatically lead to an increase in sales. I am giving you free product, all you have to do is try it and if you like it, purchase it. Yet there is still the resistance to change and customers are creatures of habit. Even a free sample does not necessarily correlate to an increase in sales.

A robust sample campaign can become an integral piece of your marketing strategy. Where does this cross the line of ethical versus unethical behavior? Is the only reason why the doctor is prescribing your product is because the doctor receives free samples? What if the sampled product is not the correct solution for the customer? Can the amount of samples influence the prescriber to prescribe a medication that might not be the best choice for the patient?

When does the sampling become excessive and counterproductive? Can and do customers take advantage of your sampling generosity? Of course they do! Especially when you are selling commodity products where there is not much of a difference between product offerings. Customers get samples from you, they get samples from your most expensive competitor, and they get samples from your cheapest competitor. Samples, Samples, Samples! Before you know it the customer is not purchasing anything because of the deluge of samples!

I had the number one prescriber of surgical stockings in the country in my territory. This doctor wrote so many prescriptions that he wrote them with two hands. He was the Chief of Vascular Surgery at major teaching hospitals in New York City and was world renowned as a vascular surgeon. Obviously this surgeon was so busy that he had no time to talk to me as a salesperson. One of the first times that I met with him he said to me, "Take care of my staff and I will take care of you!" What did that mean? He had a staff of more than a dozen nurses, medical assistants, office staff and his wife as well. Nurses are on their feet all day. An occupational hazard of a career where you stand on your feet all day is that over time you can develop a vascular condition that can affect the circulation in your legs. This condition can worsen over time where conditions can progress from tired legs to venous insufficiency. Ask any nurse, "Do you have tired legs?" It is a loaded question. The common response is, "Of course I have tired legs, I am a nurse and I am on my feet all day!"

The star product for this company was their surgical stockings. The gold standard, it was the market share leader. It had incredible brand recognition and brand loyalty. When you have this type of competitive advantage you can charge a premium for your product. This brand of surgical stockings was not only the best on the market but the most expensive as well. One pair can cost well over one hundred dollars, and that was a half a generation ago.

What did he mean by taking care of his staff? The first Wednesday of every month I had a standing appointment with his office where I would not only bring lunch for the staff I would walk in with a shopping bag filled with samples for the staff. I would take orders from each individual nurse. Mary was a size medium, Jane was a small, Susie was a large etc. It became such a ritual that over time I knew exactly which size and style sample each staff member needed. The nurses would wear their surgical stockings and show the patients that they used the product as well, prompting the customer to purchase the product. This went on for years, I supplied the samples, the surgeon continued to lead the country in prescriptions. That is what he meant by taking care of his staff and I will take care of you. I love samples.

All of the sales representatives had a sample budget, yet some of my colleagues did not take advantage of this. I saw this as a Sales Promotion tool that could help me develop relationships with my customers. I would place my monthly sample order. Then whatever was left over in the regional sample budget my regional sales manager would ship to me. It was a typical budget situation. If a company allocates resources in a budget, and that budget is not exhausted, then the company will take that budgeted resource, in this case samples, away from you. There were times when I would receive crates of samples and almost needed a fork lift to maneuver the samples from my basement, to my garage and to my attic. The most common sample that I would give out were another star product, a pair of surgical socks. Yes, they were just socks, but they were just not any regular pair of socks. They were medical grade surgical stockings that cost around twenty dollars a pair. Those are expensive socks. Another illustration of the power of samples was detailed in the buying center section. The largest sale in my life hinged upon my ability to provide a surgeon with free samples of socks. Yes, a several hundred thousand dollar capital equipment sale was saved by my ability to provide the surgeon with samples of socks. Go figure!

At one point I had so many samples in my possession that I could not give them away fast enough. Not only to customers, but to family, friends and neighbors. I left the company over twenty years ago. I had so many samples that I actually went twenty-eight years myself without having to spend a penny on socks! Yes, they were socks, but every year I sold close to one million dollars of surgical stockings and expensive socks in my territory.

The parent company was in the skin care industry with extremely successful global brands of over the counter consumer products that were predominantly distributed in pharmacy chains. They had a strategy of flooding the market with samples as well.

They wanted us to expand our net of potential customers beyond the vascular surgeon to dermatologists, plastic surgeons and primary care physicians who might have patients that needed surgical stockings, but also treated patients who suffered from skin conditions. I said that I needed a fork lift to maneuver the amount of samples of socks, this was worse. An eighteen wheeler would pull up to my house and drop off thousands of skin cream samples. So many samples that I had to rent storage space. A great star product and customers loved the samples and it did open doors for me to sell more surgical stockings. Another excellent example of how Sales Promotion can help you market your products.

Back in the day, pharmaceutical sales people were overloaded with samples to give to the prescribing doctors in their territory. It worked. The more samples that were given, the more prescriptions that were written. There was no documentation. Everything was on paper. A salesperson would arrive at a doctor's office and unload a boatload of samples and leave. How many samples did you leave behind? Did you get to make a sales presentation to the doctor? Who knew? You could put anything down on a paper report. Nobody was required to sign for the samples. If you don't think that there was a nurse in every doctor's office in this country who knew how to sign a doctor's name you are fooling yourself. That includes nurses signing the doctor's name on a prescription pad. My how things have changed!

The current climate that we live in has turned the sampling process on its ear. It is a collaboration of two factors, the technology that is at our fingertips and the prescription drug epidemic that has hit this country. The days of the paper prescription that the doctor wrote out at their desk and handed to the patient who had to physically deliver that paper prescription to the pharmacist are over. Electronic prescriptions are the norm and delivering the medication to your door, like everything else that we can purchase today, is growing as we speak. Today every prescription that a doctor writes is tracked and monitored. Today every sample that a doctor signs for is tracked and monitored. How is this accomplished? Pharmaceutical reps are given tablets to use when they make a detail sales call at a doctor's office. It is the same thing as when a package lands on your doorstep and you have to sign for that package. Your signature creates a time stamp of when you accepted delivery of that package. It is the same thing for samples at a doctor's office. The doctor signs the tablet and boom, a record of the sample transaction is recorded.

Prescription medication needs to be monitored more closely. Technology IS helping with the prescription medication epidemic by not only monitoring how many prescriptions the doctor is writing but how many free samples is the doctor receiving. If a doctor starts writing an inordinate amount of prescriptions for a specific drug, or is signing for an inordinate amount of free samples, it can trigger a red flag in the electronic prescription system. What is the end result of this? Doctors are averse to writing prescriptions and are averse to signing for samples. This has thrown a monkey wrench in the Sales Promotion process known as sampling. The tablet software is so sophisticated that it can monitor an imperfection in the actual signature. Another red flag that goes up with the question, is the actual doctor signing for the samples or is a nurse signing the doctor's name to receive the samples? Many doctor's offices are being bought up by local hospitals. Hospitals do not want any part of an audit regarding the abuse of prescription medication and have implemented "No Sample" policies where marketers are not even allowed to visit doctor offices, let alone leave them samples of their product. This has forced marketers in this industry to look at different avenues of marketing their product moving away from the popular Sales Promotion practice of sampling.

Doctors do not have time to sign for samples today. Think of the last time you went to the doctor. How much time did you spend waiting for the doctor as opposed to how much time the doctor spent with you the patient? The same goes for marketers, the amount of face time with the doctor has dwindled as well. Believe me doctors are not thrilled about this either. Doctors want the samples, doctors need the samples, and patients want the samples and ask the doctor for the samples. If a patient realizes that their doctor cannot provide them with samples they might look towards the competitive doctor across town who does give you quality time with them and does give the patient samples. It takes you back to the day when you walked into the bank and left with a lollipop, if your bank stopped giving out lollipops you would take your business elsewhere.

Here is an interesting scenario. I was promoting a line of respiratory drugs for a global leader in the pharmaceutical industry. They executed a brilliant sample campaign. They had three drugs, one a star, one a question mark and one a dog. The dog was difficult to get the attention of the doctor, that is why it was a dog. Getting the doctor's attention for the question mark was a challenge because it was a new drug that faced serious market share competition from two star competitors. How did they increase the awareness of the dog and the question mark? A sample crusade that involved the star product. Marketers were given samples of the star product tied to the samples of the dog and the question mark. Doctor's loved the star samples and this opened the door for a conversation regarding the previous cash cow now dog and the unproven question mark. What was an interesting development was that the samples of the star product were not as available as they were back in the day when you were bombarded with samples. What this meant was that some sales calls were made with only samples of the dog and question mark. What a difference! They loved you and would see you and would sign for the samples when you had samples of the star product, and it was just not the same conversation as to when you had samples of all three medications.

With the massive cutbacks in the promotion of medication some companies have taken an outside the box approach. Samples are becoming scant. Here is an example. Market leaders of star products have decided to eliminate their sampling programs. A pharmaceutical company with a question mark medication heading towards becoming a star had decided to engage in an aggressive sampling initiative. What are the results? The lack of samples for the star products has opened the door for this next generation medication. Not only has it opened the door for this medication it has opened the door for other medical device products that the company is attempting to market to their doctors.

Something to ponder is tying in your position in the BCG matrix with your sampling philosophy. If you have star and cash cow products do you really need to sample these products? If you have question marks and dogs should you be more belligerent with your sampling strategy? Should you tie your stars and cash cow samples to your question marks and dogs? Some medical device companies with stars and cash cow products actually charge the hospital for the samples during a trial. How bold is that? They also limit the time of the trial or new product evaluation. If the hospital cannot make a decision after a two week trial then they pull the device from the hospital and move on to the next potential opportunity. You have that luxury of a "Take it or leave it" mentality when you market great products. When you have question marks or dogs it is hard to justify charging the hospital for the free samples given during the product evaluation. In this scenario you are also inclined to stretch the length of the trial because you have to. You do not have the best product and you are at the mercy of the customers to give them free samples and extended time to make a decision on which product they are looking for. This lengthens the sales cycle and will frustrate the marketers of inferior products. I was in that situation where we clearly had an inferior product. I am not saying that I had to beg a hospital to start a free trial, but yes, I had to beg them to try my product. Not only did I have to beg them but I had to give them a ridiculous amount of free samples with an open ended time frame of how long they needed to trial the product. I had no choice. If I said, "You can trial the product, but you have to pay for the samples used during the trial, and you have two weeks to make a decision." Their response would have been, "Get lost!"

Public Relations And Publicity

Public Relations and Publicity are not the same, but they are certainly related. The easiest way to separate the two is to understand that one you pay for and one is free. Public Relations is a function of the marketing department. Hence, a cost is associated with this function.

Typically, Publicity is free. The fundamental difference between Public Relations and Publicity is control. Who is in control of the message you (Public Relations) or the media (Publicity)?

There are many Public Relations strategies that can manipulate the message. Is a career in Public Relations a good job? Let me rephrase the question. Can a career in Public Relations be a good job? Yes, of course it can be. Photo opportunities are a blast. Handing out a big check is cool. Public Relations promotes the positive image of a company, product or brand. Image is everything.

Until the nightmare. Until the disaster. Can you hide in Public Relations? Until the disaster. It is all about damage control. It is about limiting the collateral damage and spinning the message. How do you confront the situation? One strategy is to get out in front of the story, admit the guilt, say that you are sorry, promise that it will never happen again and announce and implement a program that will insure that safeguards are in place.

The other strategy is to stay silent immediately after the incident. Gather your information, start an investigation, get your story straight and hope that something knocks you off of the front page of the newspaper or the lead of the evening news.

News conferences and press releases have optimal times when information is released. Is this a Public Relations trick or ploy? Of course it is! If you have bad news to report, is there an optimal time to announce it? The same goes for good news. Today we live in a twenty-four seven news cycle which means instantaneous coverage. There was a time when the news of the day had to wait until the evening news or the next day's newspaper. Those days are over and have gone by the wayside forever. Technology changed that forever. You used to need an eye witness. The eye witness has been replaced by the selfie, or if you will, a camera inside of a phone.

The traditional time to release bad news was a Friday afternoon. Why? Late Friday into early Saturday was a slow time for news to break. Consumers abandon their work lives on Friday to focus on quality time with their family. Holiday weekends are even better, more elapsed time. By the time Monday morning rolls around hopefully something else has occurred that bumped your bad news to page thirty-eight of the newspaper.

The role of a publicist is to marry Public Relations and Publicity. The publicist is the broker between the two forms of the Promotional Mix. I love the famous people who before they were famous would do anything to get noticed. Once they have cashed in they shun the publicity. Until they run out of their cash and now need the publicist to jumpstart their career.

There was a time when there was a sentiment in marketing that there is no such thing as bad publicity. It is all about awareness. Negative awareness is still awareness. I don't know about that anymore.

The power of publicity today can build you up and tear you down before you know it. We love to build up an individual, tear them down, and after a time of penance give them a shot at redemption. Vicious is a good word. Relentless is another. Making the argument that bad publicity is just bad for business!

Social Media

Today's Promotional Mix has added a new component, Social Media. I have been teaching Marketing 101 for the past half a generation, from the commencement of the Internet explosion. I have been reluctant to add Social Media into my traditional Promotional Mix lectures for one reason. Today's popular social media outlet might be in vogue today but can be extinct by tomorrow. Do I incorporate Social Media into my lectures as an additional Promotional Mix outlet, yes, and moving forward I have and will add Social Media as a major component of the Promotional Mix. Here is what tipped the scale adding Social Media to the Promotional Mix. Traditional promotion involving a famous sponsor endorsing a product was in the format of a television or radio commercial, or a picture of the celebrity on a billboard or in a magazine with the endorser pledging their confidence in the product. Once endorsers were paid to tout their preference of a product via a handheld device, Social Media began to make the leap. Social Media is not a fad, Social Media has changed the way we communicate as a society, and will only grow in importance and continue to dominate our lives! Hence, many of the contemporary marketing textbooks have replaced the term "Promotional Mix" with the idiom "Integrated Marketing Communications."

Just look at how Social Media has evolved in the last decade. Especially demographically. It started with a space that was yours, which was crushed by the book with a face. At one time the book with the face was popular with millennials and baby boomers had no idea what it was. Today millennials, while still using the book with the face find it more hip to utilize instant grams, chats that snap and birds that tweet while baby boomers are still learning how to navigate the book with the face. Apps used to mean food that you eat before your dinner and the tube was a reference to watching television and had nothing to do with broadcasting yourself! Social Media reviews of your product are crucial to the success of your product. How do you trust reviews? Consumers tend to voice their negative opinion via Social Media more than they take the time out of their day to say something positive on Social Media about their product experience.

Who knows what the next platform will be? You know you have made it in Social Media when your logo is displayed on a company's marketing material asking you to follow them on the various social media outlets. Evolving is the key to Social Media survival. How does your platform evolve into something that is still relevant catching the eye of the follower? More tangible evidence regarding the effectiveness of Social Media needs to be established and concerns regarding not only the fact that not all consumers have access to the Internet and while they might spend time on the Internet they are not all consumers of Social Media.

SECTION 4

Where Oh Where Do I Get My Products?

This section details the change in how products are obtained elevating the importance of distribution

Chapter 11

How Place Has Morphed Into Distribution

Channels Of Distribution

Traditional Distribution Channel

Manufacturer

Wholesaler

Distributor

Retailer

End User

This is the model of the traditional distribution channel. Contemporary distribution channels have become so complex that it can be confusing. The traditional channel was more vertical while the contemporary channel is filled with the circumvention of distribution alternatives.

Today's Distribution Channel

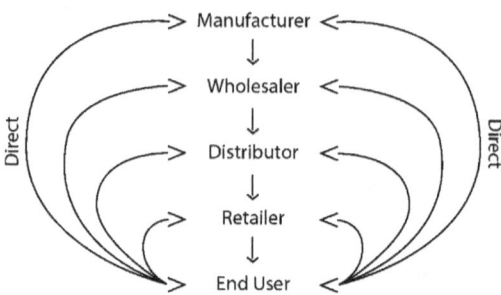

Manufacturer

It always starts with the manufacturer. The manufacturer produces the product. The manufacturer controls the product. Without the manufacturer there is no need for the other channel members. If you had a choice of which channel member to work for it is the manufacturer for the aforementioned reasons. There was a time when the strategy of the manufacturer was to produce the product. That is it. Sell it to next channel member. Once the product left the loading dock of the manufacturer it was the responsibility of the next vertical channel member. The manufacturer actually sold the product to the wholesaler who continued the distribution channel. The manufacturer then went back to what made them successful, manufacturing!

Wholesaler / Distributor

The term wholesaler and distributor are interchangeable. They are both in the middle of the channel. They move boxes. That was their traditional role. Typically a regional wholesaler, who purchased the product from the manufacturer, then sold and shipped the product to a local distributor. The distributor would continue the channel by selling the product to the retailer.

Retailer

The retailer would purchase the product from the distributor and sell the product to the ultimate end user and complete the distribution process.

End User

There are many factors contributing to the overhaul of the traditional distribution channel. What has ignited this change is that the end user today does not purchase products the way that products were purchased a generation ago. This is detailed under the category of "Levels of Distribution Intensity".

Channel members were viewed as partners interdependently linked in the distribution process. Every partner made money. The pie was split between the partners. The manufacturer grabbed the largest piece of the pie because they had to manufacture the product, the next biggest piece of the pie went to the retailer because they had to inventory the product, and the wholesaler and distributor partners were compensated for their movement of the box from one channel member to another.

This model thrived for decades. What happened? What turned the traditional distribution channel on its ear opening the door for the more multifaceted contemporary channel? Direct Distribution. Once it became apparent that the customer does not have to get off their backside to purchase a product, this sent the traditional channel spiraling out of control.

All bets were off. The once partnership between channel members, where each partner had a distinct and defined role, became a battle of survival of the fittest. Examples abound! Today manufacturers are in the retail business. Sneaker manufacturers have retail outlets in malls everywhere. Retailers are now manufacturing products that they sell in their stores. Even the wholesalers/distributors are in the game, with the planets largest on-line distributor becoming one of the most powerful company's in the world.

Today it is imperative to employ a dual distribution or multi-channel distribution strategy where multiple channels are utilized, hence the crisscrossing of distribution channels. It is painless to make that decision today a half a generation into the Internet age. This was not the case a half a generation ago. When the concept of on-line purchasing of products was first introduced in the 1990s there was a lot of trepidation, cynicism and skepticism about this concept. Many retailers viewed this as a fad, something that will fade away soon. Boy were they wrong!

Here is an example of how the traditional distribution was compromised by the use of the Internet. One of my first medical device sales jobs was for a company that was founded in the 1950s. It was a family run business based in Ohio. Forty years later they had built up a network of five thousand retailers. The product was sold to surgical supply stores, a retailer where you could purchase needed medical products when you were ill, or recently returned home from the hospital such as a wheelchair, cane or any other type of durable medical equipment.

By the early 1990s the company was sold to a massive global conglomerate making the family millions of dollars. The new direction of the company was to implement a multi-channel distribution strategy that included not only the existing five thousand retailers, but chains of pharmacies and the sale of products on the company's website.

This ruffled a lot of feathers! This decision did not sit well with the retailers. I made a sales call to one of my largest customers. This retailer was one of the first customers of the company dating back to the 1950s. Do you know how when you have an account with a company they assign you an account number? Usually it is some long number like 123456789. This retailer's account number was five. Five? Yes, they were the fifth customer of the Ohio company, for over forty years.

The owner of the retailer was still around, in his nineties. When he saw me walk into his store he immediately let me have it. "I have been a loyal customer of your company for over forty years. My account number is five! This is how you treat me after all of these years!" He was one thousand percent correct. Without that distribution partner and the other five thousand retailers across the country that company would never had made it out of Ohio. When you are a small, family owned business in Ohio, how do you reach customers from Miami to Seattle? By creating a distribution network where everyone gets to eat a piece of the pie.

Everyone is stealing pie from one another!

Distribution And Technology

Supply Chain Management

Supply Chain Management, or how you manage the movement of your product through the distribution channel must be a major component of your distribution strategy. The supply chain is more in depth than the traditional distribution channel. It involves logistics, the coordination of the movement of stuff from one point in the channel to another. It is a partnership between all channel members, where the overall success of the distribution of the product falls on the shoulders of all channel members. Channel members are not just vendors they are partners. Why not utilized the technology at your fingertips to help resolve this issue?

Just-In-Time (JIT)

JIT means having low levels of inventory on hand, the lowest amount possible, with more frequent deliveries. It involves scheduling when components need to be delivered to a manufacturing facility, only the components that are needed today and not a stockpile of inventory.

In this era of stock price management where the price of the company's stock is the most important stakeholder, JIT fits like a glove. The traditional strategy was to load up the warehouse to the rafters with finished goods (products) then sell them off as orders came in. That ties up cash. Why not lower your finished goods inventory to only what is demanded by the market? The cash previously utilized for finished goods now sits in the bank as cash. Cash on hand looks better on a balance sheet than inventory, hence a stronger stock price.

Salespeople can have issues with a JIT strategy. Most sales people are paid their commission when a product is shipped from their company to the customer. If there is not enough inventory on hand because of the JIT program, an order can be shipped incomplete or possibly canceled because there was not enough inventory on the shelf creating a back order where the customer does not receive their product when they place an order. It can cause a customer to look to your competitor who can fill the order with their competitive alternative. No shipment no commission.

I understand the concept of JIT but here is where it can go awry. The price of a high ticket piece of equipment can be expensive to manufacture and place on the shelf in finished goods. I do understand that there can be a lead time that is necessary to manufacture capital equipment. I also understand that there is a shelf life associated with the life of a product. It does not make sense to load up the warehouse with equipment that has a software component that constantly needs to be upgraded. What about products that do not have a shelf life, products that can sit on a shelf and not become obsolete. They might begin to collect some dust but there is nothing wrong with the product, they are just waiting to be sold. What about products like this that have a consistent history of being sold? Cash Cow products with no shelf life.

Hospitals purchase scissors every day. Believe it or not the variations in hospital scissors run the gamut from short scissors to long ones, to thick scissors and thin ones, scissors that are curved to the left, and scissors that are curved to the right. There is one scissor that is a standard regular size that is used in every hospital in the country. This used to infuriate me. The medical device company that made adhesive strips and baby powder famous also manufactured this scissor. No shelf life. Every day hospitals in this country would place orders for this Cash Cow. There was a documented history of how many units were sold last week, last month, the same month last year, five years ago and beyond. This product would consistently go on back order. All it did was open the door for a competitor who made the exact same product to fill the order and displace you as the vendor of choice. Why? Unacceptable! This occurred because of the JIT and stock price protection mentality. That used to burn me up. Commission lost because we could not ship the order.

A warehouse is a black hole for a company. That space is expensive when you factor in rent, heat, electricity, insurance, general maintenance and other ancillary expenses such as a security system. While a necessary expense for a business, you have to have inventory, it is a black hole because it does not generate any revenue for your business. As a medical device salesperson you spend a lot of time in a hospital's warehouse, checking on shipments that have been delivered, are they accurate, did they get what they ordered, another necessary follow up in the sales process. I remember a hospital that had a massive warehouse on the first floor of the hospital towards the rear end of the building. I did not have a reason to visit the hospital for months. On my next sales call I noticed that some construction that was going on in the warehouse. It looked like they were shrinking the warehouse space. I inquired. I was told that the space was being converted. Converted? To what?

A hospital has many departments. Two departments that generate revenue for a hospital are the Operating Room (OR) and the Emergency Department (ED). When you have a surgical procedure in the OR the hospital generates revenue. When you visit the ED the cash register rings. The warehouse does not have a cash register, when you stay overnight in the hospital the revenue generated by your visit is capped and often costs the hospital money. Not good business!

Traditional Hospital Floor Plan

| Warehouse | Operating Room (OR) |
| | Emergency Department (ED) |

The black hole space (warehouse) was being converted into more OR and ED space turning that space into a revenue stream. Brilliant Marketing! What happened to the products that occupied the space that was converted? JIT. Utilizing bar code technology the hospital replaced the warehouse space with rolling carts filled with supplies from medication to adhesive strips almost like a vending machine. The cart gets wheeled up to a floor to a specific nursing unit. When nurses needs a supply they come over to the cart, swipe an ID card, enter the product that they are looking for, and the product is dispensed. At the end of the shift the cart is rolled down to the loading dock and is sent back to the distributor where the stock is replenished. Just as one cart is wheeled onto the truck a new fully stocked cart rolls off the truck and is rolled up to the nursing floor. No need for a warehouse. The warehouse is on wheels, wheels on the cart and wheels on the truck that go back and forth from the hospital to the distribution center. Sounds nice? Sounds efficient? It can be. Of course there is a cost associated with JIT. If an adhesive strip costs a dollar through traditional distribution, including the cost associated with the onsite warehouse, tack on another three to five percent for the JIT convenience fee. The adhesive strip now costs the hospital one dollar and three to five cents. Do the math. Does the new revenue stream associated with the additional OR's and ED's outweigh the cost associated with the convenience of JIT? It can.

Hospital Floor Plan

Utilizing Just In Time

JIT

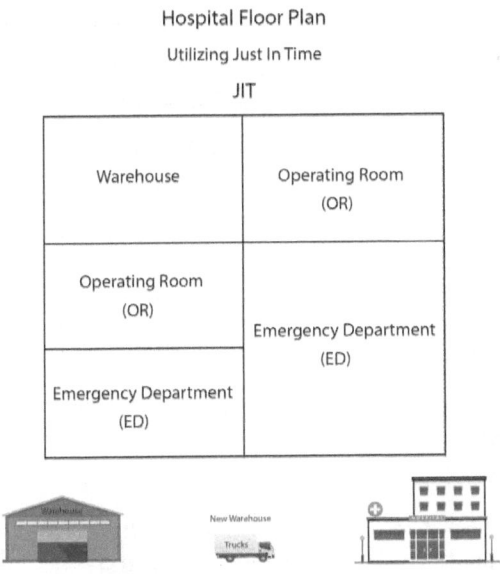

There is a downside associated with this strategy. What if something happens to the truck? Traffic issues, weather issues, or remoteness of the hospital all have to be considered. What if a hospital's medication supply is drained by an outbreak or an epidemic and there is no medication onsite? We are not talking about a fast food chain that cannot have their French fries delivered, it can be a life or death scenario.

Electronic Data Interchange (EDI)

I remember in grammar school there was a contest. Whichever class collected the most labels of a product with a bar code on it won the contest. Somehow the labels were submitted to a charity to raise money for a cause. An incentive given to the students was that if you submitted one hundred labels you would get a week off from all homework assignments. No homework for a week? I was all for that. All of my classmates scoured their homes for labels with barcodes. I was very enterprising. I looked at this as a business opportunity. I asked my mother to drive me to the supermarket. I purchased one hundred cans of the Cash Cow brand of soup in a can. All flavors and varieties. I cut off all one hundred labels, won the contest and was released from my homework responsibilities for a week. Money well spent. What did I do with all of the soup? I figured out that if I removed the label I had no idea what kind of soup was in the can. I devised a coding system with a magic marker and I labeled each can of soup. Needless to say it took a long time to consume one hundred cans of soup. That was my first experience with a bar code. For all I knew the bar code on a product was used to raise money for a charity. Clearly there has to be another purpose for placing a bar code on a product. But who knew in 1976?

Bar codes are placed on everything from cans of vegetables to boxes of cereal to bananas. How and where do you put a bar code on a banana? On a sticker. What is the purpose of the bar code? EDI. Facilitating the transaction is one purpose. So is identifying the price of product in the aisle as well as replacing the labor associated with placing a sticker with the price on every single item in the store. Remember the days when you would walk up and down the aisle of a store with an employee with a sticker gun that would place a small sticker on the item? What happened if the price changed, someone would have to put a new sticker on top of the old sticker. Extremely labor intensive. Today the price change is made on a computer and within a couple of clicks all of the inventory has the updated price within seconds. EDI is efficient. EDI is expensive yet it will reduce labor costs.

EDI goes way beyond the sticker on the banana. In essence EDI can best be defined as computers talking to computers. No paper. No conversation. No human interaction. This is the world that we live in today. The main purpose of the bar code is to ring up the purchase at the cash register. Today's cash register goes way beyond ringing up the price. Today's cash register is a computer. A computer that tracks every keystroke including the scanning of the bar code. When the shift changes the cash register closes down. A report is sent from the cash register at the retail outlet to the warehouse. Every item that was scanned during that shift gets replenished and is shipped to the retail outlet. Computer talking to computer. Think about a chain of pharmacies. How many items are literally sold in each of these outlets? Thousands of units thousands of products. How do you manage your inventory? EDI is the solution.

Technology is eliminating so many jobs. Going to the bank is an example. Before technology, when you walked into a bank there were people, bank tellers behind the window, maybe ten windows with ten bank tellers behind the glass. The bank today is a ghost town. Bank tellers have been replaced by ATM's. Yes, there may be ten windows but only two people behind the window and eight machines. The job of a salesperson is one of the last occupations to be effected by the computer. There is still value in the notion of a salesperson making a physical sales call on a customer to make a presentation. Until EDI. Salespeople do not like EDI. Salespeople despise EDI. Why? EDI is replacing the need for a salesperson. EDI takes the "Salesmanship" out of the equation. Let me explain. Before EDI the purchasing decisions were made by the interaction between the "Buyer" making the product decisions for the chain and the salesperson representing the manufacturer who wants to get their product on the shelves of all of the stores in the chain.

During the presentation the salesperson recommends that the chain purchase twenty units to be placed on the shelves of all of the retail outlets in the chain. Why twenty? The salesperson makes more commission if twenty units are purchased compared to fifteen. The salesmanship of the salesperson dictates the quantity. If you are a good salesperson you might be able to persuade the buyer to purchase twenty units per store. No rhyme or reason, why twenty, except for the commission earned on the transaction.

As mentioned earlier EDI tracks every keystroke and every item that is scanned at the checkout line. EDI generates reports that provide historical sales data. The buyer can now look at the EDI reports to help manage their inventory. The EDI report states that on our best day ten units were sold, on our worst day two units were sold, on an average day six units were sold. So why are you proposing twenty units? Yes, you need some safety stock, so you never run out of inventory. Utilizing the combination of inventory management software programs such as JIT and EDI the inventory that was depleted from the retail store today can be replenished overnight. SO WHAT? The so what is why do you need twenty units on the shelf? You don't. The buyer chops the order from twenty units to fifteen units, reducing their inventory by twenty-five percent. An electronic Purchase Order is cut and emailed to the manufacturer (computer talking to computer). No need for the physical interaction between the buyer and the salesperson. Less inventory means less commission for the salesperson. Less physical interaction between the buyer and the salesperson means that you don't need as many salespeople eliminating jobs. Salespeople hate EDI!

Levels Of Distribution Intensity

The growth of importance of the fourth "P" Place in the Marketing Mix spawned the metamorphosis into the term "Distribution". This cannot better be explained than the shift in the Levels of Distribution Intensity. Traditional marketing theory focused on the product itself. Manufacture a superior product and the market will come to you. What does the market will come to you mean? The superiority of your product compared to competitive alternatives and substitutes will attract the market to your product like a magnet. "Place" or where you physically procured the product was irrelevant. Procuring the product was relevant. It was a sound strategy. It worked. The market was willing to hunt and search for your product. That was part of the strategy. To create the desire to obtain the product. The hunt and search was part of the process. That was before the "commoditization" of everything. That was before the myriad of competitive offerings, substitutes and alternatives. Everything used to be exclusively distributed.

Yes, there was a time, and I remember it well, when you would pack up the kids, throw them in the back of the station wagon, with the wood grain on the sides (ask a millennial what that means), and take a family road trip in the pursuit of a purchase. Spending the entire day on the journey. Wasting the whole day on the trek. Back then that was spending "Quality" time with your family. Forget that today. Consumers just simply do not have the time. Between job commitments, second job commitments, driving to and from youth sports practices and games, dancing school rehearsals, piano lessons and every other activity that parents, and even grandparents, today are compelled to enroll their children in, who has the time? Time has not changed. There are still twenty-four hours in a day, seven days in a week, sixty minutes in an hour, yet we just do not have enough time. Fitting neatly like a glove into the notion of Intensive Distribution.

For whatever the reason, more distribution outlets, lack of time, and the ease associated with purchasing a product off of a device, everything is being pushed down the continuum of "Distribution Intensity." Products that used to be exclusively distributed are now selectively distributed, and products that used to be selectively distributed are now intensively distributed. Can you purchase that five thousand dollar watch today without ever visiting the previously exclusive jewelry store? Go right ahead. Can you purchase that expensive car without ever taking it for a test drive? Sure you can. Would you not want to kick the tires first? Technology is pushing everything down the channel. More intensive and less exclusive. Get used to it, the horse IS out of the barn!

Distribution

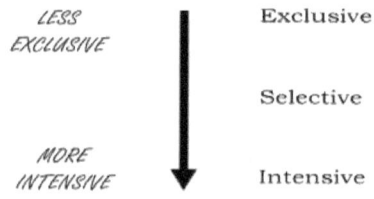

Exclusive Distribution

I got it. Create the profound and ground breaking innovation, the market will seek you out. If the product is so unique and so ground breaking the market will seek YOU out. The core of exclusive distribution is one or two retail outlets in a geographical market. Price does factor into exclusivity. Expensive watches and expensive cars are examples products that are exclusively distributed. There are tons of jewelry stores in a given market but not all of them sell expensive watches, the same goes for expensive cars. You can drive down any main strip of town and find car dealerships, but not expensive car dealerships. There might be one or two in a given geographical market but there are not a dime a dozen. The manufacturers like to and want to retain some sort of exclusivity. The theory behind the exclusive distribution for expensive products is that if you are willing to pay a premium price you are willing to spend the time to hunt and search.

Selective Distribution

Selective distribution employs the strategy of more than two but less than ten retail outlets in a geographical market. Consumer electronics fall into this category. You can name on less than two hands the type of retailer who distributes consumer electronics such as televisions, electronics retailers, department stores, and warehouse chains. The product is not everywhere (Intensive Distribution) but the hunting and searching (Exclusive Distribution) is not necessary.

Intensive Distribution

Intensive distribution means as many retail outlets as possible. Consumers do not want to hunt and search for a product. They want to turn the corner and find the product. Soda is intensively distributed. Walk down any main street in this country and where can you find the product? In supermarkets, pharmacies, convenience stores, delicatessens, vending machines and every alliteration of a restaurant possible from pizza, to burgers to egg rolls. You stumble into soda. If you cannot find soda something is wrong with you. That's the essence of Intensive Distribution.

The evolution of the convenience store changed distribution forever. There was a time, and there still are places where things close down for the evening. What put the popular convenience store chain on the map was their availability to remain open from a number after six but before twelve. Back in the day that was the availability of products from seven in the morning until eleven at night. Intensive distribution blew that concept out of the water. I remember back in the day that you needed to rush to the store to purchase a product because the store was closing. In the early mid 1980s the concept of the twenty-four seven store started to gain steam. During that time the legal age to purchase alcoholic beverages was eighteen. I was right on the cusp of that demographic. An "All Night News Stand" opened up, never closing its doors, twenty-four seven three sixty-five. There was no question that they sold more beer off hours than the traditional hours. It was a revelation! It was convenient! You could purchase beer on demand whenever you were thirsty. Brilliant Marketing!

An excellent example of this shift is a store that started out as a local distributor of consumer electronics, starting out selling televisions. Over time they started selling appliances such as washing machines. Today they not only still sell televisions and washing machines they started hawking a line of mattresses. What's next? Laundry detergent and linens for their washing machines and mattresses? Oh my how things have changed. Intensive distribution at its best. I believe in intensive distribution. More products, on more shelves, in more stores, in as many markets as possible.

Push Versus Pull Strategy

Remember marketing costs money. How do you as a marketer utilize this resource? Do you spend your money on Personal Selling or Advertising? It is an interesting debate. Do you push or do you pull? What does that mean? Personal Selling pushes while Advertising pulls. It has a lot to do with the distribution channel. A push strategy relies on Personal Selling to push the product down the distribution channel while Advertising pulls the product from the bottom of the distribution channel up by stimulating demand by the ultimate end user.

The best example of each strategy is what has happened in the pharmaceutical industry. Traditionally, "Big Pharma" relied on the push strategy. Legions of sales people were hired at every step of the distribution channel where the manufacturer sold the product to the distributor/wholesaler, who sold it to the retailer, who sold it to the end user. Additional sales people were hired to "Detail" the physician completing the continuum of channel members to insure the sale of the product. The Push strategy while effective, is costly. How costly? The average "Big Pharma" salesperson can earn more than six figures when you add up the compensation package including expenses and benefits. Multiply that by ten and there's a quick million bucks. Multiply that by one hundred sales people and now you are talking about ten million bucks.

Government legislation has forced the pharmaceutical industry to rethink their promotional strategy. Labor is the most significant cost to an organization. This regulation has forced the pharmaceutical industry to downsize their massive salesforces. However, the brand still needs to be promoted. Many manufacturers have implemented "Pull" strategies that direct the resources that were once utilized for "Push" strategies. How do they do this? Advertising that is aimed directly at the patient or in this case the end user. Raising awareness for the medication through successful advertising campaigns where the patient walks into the doctor's office and requests a prescription of a drug that they became aware of through a television commercial, radio advertisement, or brochure found in the doctor's office while waiting to see the doctor.

Push versus Pull Strategy

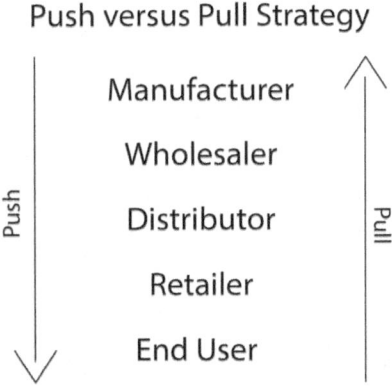

Chapter 12

What Happened to The Five And Dime?

Retail Marketing

Retail is dead, or is it? I pass a local funeral parlor in my neighborhood going to work and coming home. Embedded in their facade is a statement, "Life has not ended but merely changed." Can this be applied to the current retail landscape? Absolutely!

A Life In Retail

I need to qualify my opinion on this topic with some relevant real world retail marketing examples. My grandfather was a tailor by trade. By the late 1940s early 1950s he began to hone his craft and opened his own manufacturing factory. My family was thrust into the garment industry in the heart of the garment district, New York City. We were in the women's coat business and manufactured everything from rain coats to fur coats. I started working in the factory at a very early pre-adolescent age lasting through high school and learned everything from how to turn the inside liner of a coat, to make a button hole, sew a button on, press a garment, move it through the assembly line, and have it ready to be shipped out to the distribution channel member. I will never forget the deadlines that my family and factory had to meet by shipping out an order of coats to waiting channel participants. At the height of production the factory would manufacture over one hundred and twenty thousand units per year, sometimes three to four thousand units in a week. That is a lot of needle and thread, a lot of buttons, a lot of ironing and pressing and a lot of blood and sweat by everyone at that factory. It was the family business. It was a big family, my grandparents took care of everyone. We made wine in the basement of the factory. How much wine? Barrels and barrels. Enough wine for the entire year. My grandmother would make dinner for my grandfather every night and not just cook for him, but the next day's lunch at the factory was Grandma Lucy's dinner from the night before.

Here is where I learned about the beginning of the channel of distribution and the significance of the retailer in the process. If that given retailer did not place the order for the coats to be manufactured, what would we have done all day in that factory? You can only make so much wine!

When I started college, I needed a part-time job. A friend had said go to the mall they are hiring. I will never forget this. I was standing outside of the store where I was about to apply for a job, I looked up at the store marquis and I said, "I am never going to work here." Why? I was an eighteen year old college student/athlete who spent their life on a football/baseball field with my spare time in the family factory. It was a women's clothing store. Why would I work there? The manager hired me on the spot. This was 1983 so understand the political correctness environment of a generation ago. She said, "We need a man in the store", her quote not mine! There were twenty-two female employees and the manager wanted a man to complete tasks that the other employees were uncomfortable with. What kind of tasks? Everything from unloading boxes from the truck, to emptying the boxes and placing the merchandise on the retail floor. Disposing of the boxes, moving display units around the store, standing on a ladder to hang merchandise, change overhead light bulbs and chase shoplifters out of the store.

This store was part of a major retail chain that had over one thousand stores in malls all over the country. By the time I left I was promoted to store management, often dealt with corporate buyers who would visit the store, and worked in multiple store locations in malls across the region. It was a great experience to learn the strategy of a major player in the retail marketplace.

When I graduated from college I was not sure what I wanted to do. I had an athletic background, my father was a high school football coach, and we had connections everywhere. I went into the sporting goods business opening up a retail sporting goods store that catered to the institutional customer such as leagues, schools, and teams, specifically team uniforms, and other related sporting goods. It was as Mom and Pop Main Street retail as you could get. I took over a Main Street retail business that thrived on Main Street for decades until the invasion of Big Box, Chain Store retailers. That Main Street is still there today a shell of what it once was back in the day of Mom and Pop!

My first job with a national company was with a manufacturer of medical devices. Half of the product line was sold to the hospital and half of the product line was distributed through retail surgical supply stores. I covered the eastern geography of New York City which included Brooklyn, Queens and Long Island. Within my assigned territory I had over one hundred and fifty retail outlets. Most of these outlets were Mom and Pop family run businesses. This was right before the explosion of pharmacy chains delving into the surgical supply market and the selling of products online. What was sad about having conversations with the long time Mom and Pop business owner was that they knew the end was near. They knew that this current generation of the Mom and Pop management would be the last generation of Mom and Pop management even though the business had been in the family for decades.

All of this was accomplished by my early to mid-twenties.

By my mid to late twenties I started my career teaching at the university level. One of the first institutions that hired me was at a community college in New York that offered a Marketing/Retail/Fashion major for their students. The college had an articulation agreement with the most prestigious fashion university, not only on New York, but one of the most famous in the world. Our students had the ability to start at the community college and transfer into their program. The community college was located adjacent to one of the largest mall complexes in the country. The college hosted a conference and there were top retail executives from all of the major players in the retail industry in attendance. The topic of the conference was what impact would the Internet have on retail? I sat in the back as a quiet observer. I was shocked at the discussion. Understand this was the mid-1990s and this concept of shopping, without shopping as we knew it, was new to everyone. To be fair this was a novel concept to all. What was shocking was that the room was almost divided in half. Half of the executives dismissed the Internet as a fad, something that will dissipate over time, and they did not see the Internet as a threat at all. The other half of the room was shaking in their boots with the notion that the customer does not have to physically walk into the store to purchase a product. The boot shakers recognized this seismic paradigm shift and got in on the ground floor of dual or multi-channel distribution. The fad believers were left behind and it took years for them to catch up with the trend.

Where are we today more than twenty-five years later? It is easy to make a judgment today when all of this has shaken out through the laundry. What do we know? The Internet is not going anywhere and has had a profound effect on not only the way we shop but the way we communicate and search for information.

For many years my retail marketing lectures focused on trends in retail which include all of the aforementioned trends. Here is another trend just hitting the retail landscape today. The mall was thriving.

223

Even with the convenience of shopping online there was a market for customers who still "enjoyed" the "in store" shopping experience.

Hurdles in the transition from retail to etail (on-line) include the tangibility factor of the product. Some products are more of a proverbial fit for on-line purchasing, some are not. Books and music are a natural fit for on-line the same way that shoes or a mattress still have a solid retail presence. You have to try the shoe on or sit on the mattress to experience the tangibility of the product.

The mall has been able to stave off the onslaught of on-line purchases for the first half generation of the Internet age, but is starting to succumb to the wave. The issue is space, and what to do with it. Especially the space occupied by the "Anchor" stores. Most malls are horizontal with "Anchor" stores, major retailers, located at each end of the mall. Here is the first domino to fall in the potential demise of the mall as we know it. The mall may be where Main Street retail was twenty-five years ago. The rent in the Anchor store is staggering and stifling. The amount of square footage in the Anchor store is excessive. The problem is that subdividing the Anchor store can be problematic. Do you really need all of this square footage? If less consumers are trekking to the mall less square footage is needed. The smaller spaces connecting the anchor stores are one issue but what about all of the open space in the anchor store? What can it be converted to? A hotel? Apartments? Something else? Could you picture living in an apartment that is part of the mall? How much shopping can you do?

When I started working in the mall more than thirty years ago the atmosphere at the mall was so different than it is today. This mall opened during the golden era of mall construction in this country, the early 1970s, so this story is an excellent caricature of the life of the mall as we know it. It was horizontal in structure with two Anchor stores at the end. The novelty was unique. You could park your car once and shop in what in so many words was a climate controlled

Main Street of shopping connected by two major retailers. What a concept!

The mall was new, the mall was shiny, but the mall was expensive. More expensive than traditional main street retail. The novelty did last for a few years but by the time I got there the mall needed a facelift. The mall was occupied almost exclusively with tenants selling everything from clothing to shoes to jewelry. Mostly tangible products. There was maybe one or two places to get something to eat or perform a service such as going to the bank while at the mall.

The script needed to be flipped! Once that mentality sank in to Marketers running the malls, they never looked back. Services not products? Interesting thought. Or how about this, services and products? A match made in heaven. Once the concept of going to the mall changed from just buying a pair of jeans and a pair of shoes to an experience other than purchasing a product the mall exploded in popularity. The mall needed a transformation from shopping to an experience beyond shopping.

Think of what you can do at the mall that has nothing to do with purchasing a product. You can go to the doctor, go to the salon, get a massage in a reclining chair, see a movie, play video games for hours, and of course eat!

The "Food Court" concept at the mall was genius. Back in the day the only people purchasing food at the mall were the mall employees and consumers who were shopping. A very limited selection of food choices. A marketer had an idea to devote some space in the mall, strategically placed in the center of the mall, to attract the most traffic to a smorgasbord of food choices that could please every taste of the consumer.

Here is the proof of the genius. Corporate workers who work in office parks located adjacent to malls often get in their car during their lunch hour and drive to the mall for lunch. The food court has something for everyone, once lunch is finished take a stroll and run an errand while at the mall. Brilliant Marketing!

The mall became an event. It became a magnet for traffic. It is all about traffic. At one time the traffic was directed towards Main Street and then towards the mall and now to a website. The mall as an event attracted all kinds of traffic demographically. It attracted the pre-teen and teenage demographic as a place to go on the weekend. This attracted their parents to the mall who had to drop them off and pick them up. Why not do some shopping while waiting for the kids? The demographic group that caught my eye is interesting. I worked at the mall all kinds of hours. I would open the store, close the store, days, nights, and weekends. That was the schedule. In the morning the mall would open early but the actual stores were not required to be open until 10AM. I would notice people just randomly walking around the mall. All of the stores were closed? Why would you travel to the mall and walk around when you cannot shop? The answer was they were there for the exercise. They were walkers not weirdos, randomly walking past stores that were closed. Why walk at the mall in the morning for exercise? The mall is climate controlled, in the summer it is cool in there, and in the winter the mall can be toasty. It is a safe space to walk, with flat ground and no curbs to step off of and get injured, and no taxi cab drivers to worry about while you cross the street! While you are done with your walk maybe you sit and have a cup of coffee in the food court or stop on your way out to purchase that last minute item that you forgot about. My point is that this traffic is being generated off hours. Why are they walking in the morning? Nobody is in the mall. It is an easy stroll. Getting this concept of maximizing every possible revenue stream is not only the key to success in Retail Marketing but every aspect of Marketing.

There are two driving forces behind the push or shift to on-line purchasing. The first one is that the consumer prefers it. If the consumer did not prefer on-line versus in store, retail would be thriving. The second one is that manufacturer's makes more profit on the on-line transaction. The expense of brick and mortar retail crushes the expense associated with selling a product on-line.

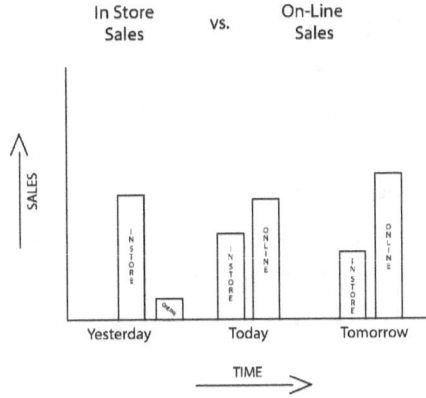

The Death Of Mom And Pop

My early experience in the sporting goods business is a perfect example of how "Mom and Pop" businesses at one time ruled the day. I purchased an established retail sporting goods store located on a popular "Main Street" retail destination. The niche that I decided to pursue was the team uniform business. I contacted every team, league and school in the area making them aware that I could solve their uniform problems. All sports and all teams. Uniforms were uniforms regardless of the sport. I grew up in this community. I was a customer in this store going back to my days of tee ball baseball and pee wee football. I still reside in the same community and I can walk to the store from my house. The store was part of the fabric of the local sports community for decades. Now I was in charge.

I contacted the little league where I played baseball. I played on championship teams there. My brother and sister played there, my cousins played there, my classmates and friends played there, and my other brother who this book is dedicated to also ran on those fields when he was a little boy. My kids played there. It taught me the life lessons of winning and losing.

Although I played on championship teams and was a big part of those winning teams the big deal was making the All-Star team. All of my friends made the team. I was not selected. It crushed me. To this day I remember the day that the team was selected. You received a phone call at home. The phone at my house never rang. Before the next game the coach pulled me to the side, outside the dugout up the third base line away from the other players. He knew I was upset about not making the team. He knew I was a good player but explained why I was not selected. He was upset too. He encouraged me to work hard and become a better player. I listened. By the time the group of selected All-Stars completed high school only one of the little league All-Stars had a better career as a player than I did!

I scheduled a meeting at the same little league more than a decade later to make my presentation to the Board of Directors about their uniform and equipment needs for the upcoming season. The last time that I was in that clubhouse I was a boy, now I was walking in as a man, a businessman. I walk in and who is at the meeting? My old coach. Of course he remembered me. What I did not know was that he followed how I did not only on the baseball but football field through high school. At the end of the presentation he stood up and pointed his finger at the group of board of directors and said, "We are going with Paul, he is one of our own."

They became my largest account. Once the season began and all of the players in the league had their uniforms, business started to slow down. The phone rang one day and they needed end of the season All-Star uniforms. All-Star uniforms for the team that I never made? I remember sitting on my sewing machine, sewing the initials of the little league on the front of the uniform, royal blue shirts with maize gold letters, saying to myself, "What is better? Making money on the uniform or donning the uniform as an All-Star player?" Money is nice, and money makes the world go around, forego the bullion, putting on that uniform would have been sweet. Twenty years later the phone rang at my house notifying us that my son was selected to the All-Star team that I never made and it was a big thrill. Starting the game in the same royal blue and maize gold uniform that I never had the opportunity to wear but was given the opportunity to market. I love karma! Nothing is more Mom and Pop than that!

The sporting goods business is as seasonal as it gets with highs and lows. After the holidays and early winter are a slow time. I remember sitting at the counter of the store on a cold, dreary February afternoon. Nothing going on. Football season was over and we were a few weeks away from when baseball and softball teams started to think about ordering their uniforms for the upcoming season. It was late in the afternoon when a nun walked into the store. That's right a nun in a sporting goods store. I looked at her. She looked very familiar. She looked like Sister Joseph, the Principal when I was in the first grade in 1971. She was tough! She was mean! This was back in the day when the nuns would walk around a classroom with a ruler in their hand. Remember the ruler with the thin slice of metal inserted in the top that helped you draw a straight line? Nuns used that side of the ruler to crack down on your fingers when you misbehaved during class. Nuns used to walk by you in class and pull the parts of your hair that were below your ear and near your shirt collar scolding you that your hair is too long. Picture doing those things in a classroom today!

I said, "Sister Joseph? Is that you?" She peered through her glasses and said, "Yes, it is me." I told her that I was a student of hers where she used to be the Principal. She looks at me puts her hands almost together and says, "I need a football?" She had no idea what a football was. I could have put a baseball, basketball, soccer ball or even a volleyball in her hands she did not know the difference. I said, "Sister Joseph, WHY do YOU need a football?" She said, "One of the parents knows THIS guy who is coming to the school tomorrow, he plays football." His name is Phil Simms. She had no idea who he was. I did!

I said, "Phil Simms is coming to your school tomorrow?" She said, "Yes, and I want to give him a football." Again having no idea who he was. This was February 1988 one year after Phil Simms led the New York Giants to the Super Bowl championship and he was the Most Valuable Player in the game setting records that made him a hero for all Giant fans. He was the biggest star in New York sports and I was a big fan. I said, "Phil Simms is coming to your school tomorrow, give me a minute I have to go in the back to get you a football." It was the end of the season, I was thinking about the upcoming spring baseball and softball seasons, I did not need any footballs until next season. I had a handful of footballs in the back of the store. I brought all of them up to the front of the store put them in a bag and said, "Sister Joseph take all of these footballs with you as a donation to the school." She said, "Do you want to meet him?" Again, not knowing who he is and what he meant to Giant fans, and I said, "Of course I do!" She said, "Come to the school tomorrow morning." I get there, walk into the Principal's office and who is sitting there behind her desk, Phil Simms. I will never forget this. My heart was pounding through my chest. He gets up from behind the desk, extends his hand to me and says, "Hi, I am Phil Simms, (no kidding), and I just wanted to THANK YOU for donating the footballs to the school." Thank Me? Thank You for the memories! They were leftover footballs!

He then proceeded to walk from class to class telling the students about the importance of doing well in school, staying out of trouble and other words of wisdom. Instead of gathering all of the students in one assembly hall and getting the visit over with so he could leave, he took the time out of his day to make his visit more personable. I never forgot that. Famous people are great when the bright lights are on and a camera is rolling during a photo opportunity. There were no cameras there, no media present, no public relations opportunity just a role model giving something back to the community.

I took a picture with him. I put the picture right in the middle of the store where every customer could see it. Months later I was looking at the picture and I remember saying to myself that it would be great if I could get him to autograph the picture. How was I going to do this? It was the start of football training camp. Phil had not yet reported to training camp while going through a contract negotiation. I mailed the picture to the team with a note for Phil recanting his visit to the school. The day that I mailed the picture he signed his contract and reported to camp. I remember thinking that I will never get that picture back, he reported to training camp and had a lot more important things to worry about than signing my picture. Within a couple of days the signed picture was sent back to me. I knew he signed it because he had signed one of the footballs that I brought to the school and he wanted me to keep one, the signatures were an exact match. Great man! A highlight of my days in the sporting goods business. Nothing gets more Mom and Pop than that!

Mom and Pop are fielding daggers from every direction from multiple traditional distribution channel members. Where and how is the end user killing Mom and Pop and Main Street? What the chain can offer, and when I say chain I mean everything from the pharmacy chain to hardware chain and everything in between, that the Mom and Pop corner pharmacy, to the generationally run hardware store, cannot are typically two solutions. Price and selection. What are two things that are a guarantee when you walk into the chain superstore? Have you ever looked at the price of a product at the chain? Especially if you know the manufacturer's suggested retail price? Have you ever said that's a good price and purchase the item? Why such a good deal? When the Mom and Pop pharmacy calls up the manufacturer and says I want to purchase some adhesive strips, they might purchase a case of ten boxes of the product because they do not have the space to store more inventory and one case fits their needs for today. When the chain pharmacy calls up to order adhesive strips they do not purchase one case, they purchase ten thousand cases to be distributed to thousands of retail outlets. Do you see the difference between the one case price and the ten thousand case price? When the Mom and Pop hardware store calls up the manufacturer to purchase a box of ten hammers that they want to sell in their store they get the ten hammer price. When the hardware chain calls up they purchase ten thousand hammers at once!

All you need are a few of the major chains, each with a few thousand retailers and they become your distribution partner. They do the distribution for you.

The second issue is selection. Mom and Pop have a limited amount of floor selling space and an inadequate amount of stock room space. What is the impact that this can have on selection? Mom and Pop can offer a scant offering of choices, the cheap one and the expensive one. The chain has miles of selling and stock room space which affords the customer not only an enticing price but an attractive selection. The selection available in the chain guarantees the customer that they will find something that they are looking for. I think back to the sporting goods days my floor space was so diminutive that maybe I could place no more than ten baseball gloves and ten baseball bats on display. Today I walk into the chain sporting goods retailer and they have hundreds of gloves and bats on display!

If the end user is killing Mom and Pop from the bottom up, what goes unnoticed is how the manufacturer, the start of the distribution channel is also dealing Mom and Pop a death blow from the top down. There was a time when there were twenty thousand independent, Mom and Pop pharmacies spread across every Main Street corner in every community in this country. There are approximately one hundred pharmacy chains in the country. There has been some consolidation and merging of local, regional and national chains, but let us use the one hundred chain number for this example. As a manufacturer I do not want twenty thousand small independent accounts that I have to sell to, service and collect money from. Today's manufacturer wants fewer larger accounts to sell to, service and collect money from. The manufacturer does not need as many salespeople, they need fewer customer service employees and even less accountants. It is more efficient to manage one hundred large customers than it is to manage twenty thousand miniscule accounts. The manufacturer does not care about Mom and Pop, they cater and bow to the chains, and if Mom and Pop went away they would not shed a tear.

The thread of hope and one of the only lifeline that Mom and Pop has is the service that they can provide. Mom and Pop loses the price battle, they cannot compete. Mom and Pop loses the selection battle, they do not have the space to house the massive inventory that the chain can offer. I even think of this myself. I am very handy. I can fix many things around the house ranging from painting to plumbing to basic electrical work. When I can figure out the issue myself I head over to the massive chain hardware and home improvement store. You know the one that advertises that their employees in the paint department are former professional painters, and their employees in the plumbing department are former plumbers. Yea Right! Try to get someone in these departments to help you. Good Luck! What I think is pathetic is that sometimes I will travel to the chain store, price out the items and get back in the car and literally drive less than one minute to the competitive home improvement store to compare prices. There goes a few hours of my life that I will never get back. However, if there is a household chore or repair that I cannot figure out on my own I will travel to the Mom and Pop plumbing supply store or local lumber yard to get the personalized service and attention needed to complete the project. Once the service component is eliminated as an advantage for patronizing the Mom and Pop establishment the acceleration of the death of Mom and Pop will commence.

If you really think about it, all you need is one or two customers to make a million bucks. How is that possible? Well if your customer has thousands of retail outlets all you need is them to say I will take it! When the chain says that they will take it they do not mean for this one retail outlet they mean for the entire chain. Think of the chain pharmacy with five thousand retail outlets. They become your partner, they do the distribution for you. How about getting two chains of pharmacies to distribute your product now you are looking at potentially ten thousand distribution outlets. Now you are talking about distribution.

Why do customers shop at the chain versus mom and pop? Consumers are cheap. Price is always a factor. A consumer will shop at the chain just to save a few bucks on a year's worth of toilet tissue rather than shop at the mom and pop retailer who can solve your toilet tissue needs today!

Roles in the traditional distribution channel have also been combined. There was a time that you were the manufacturer and someone else was the distributor and another partner was the retailer. This has gone out the window. Sneaker manufacturers who were in the business of manufacturing sneakers now sell their sneakers in their retail outlets. Retailers who were in the business of retailing a manufacturer's product now are in the manufacturing business themselves not only retailing the product but manufacturing it as well. What about the middle intermediary in the traditional distribution channel. The box mover. The wholesaler and distributor in between the manufacturer and the retailer. How has that changed? The box mover with the name associated with a race of female warriors is now one of the largest companies on the planet!

I am all for mass distribution with more products on more shelves in more stores in more markets, but once in a while it crosses over the line. There was a time when you sold this and I sold that and we did not cross paths. You sold coffee and I sold gasoline and that was it. How many products can you purchase in a gas station today that have nothing to do with gas? How about purchasing music or gifts in a coffee shop? This one bothered me recently. I was walking through a chain that sold office supplies, think of a store that sells paperclips and albeit staples. Walking down the aisle I noticed a line of surgical scrub tops and bottoms. As a medical device salesperson, you accumulate a wardrobe of scrub attire that is used almost as an occasional work "uniform." I stopped at the display and started to shake my head. How is this an office supply? A paper clip or staple is an office supply, but a scrub top? I guess technically it can be classified as a "uniform" which can be worn to work. The point is that there are no more boundaries, no more lines of delineation between products, it is survival of the fittest.

Go back twenty plus years when everything was sold in stores and this concept of on-line purchasing was a notion. This craze has reached the level where there was a time when the consumer posed the question, "What can you buy on-line?" This question has been replaced with, "What can't you buy on-line?" Think about that! Then the trend started to shift with the in store purchase transferring to the on-line purchase. It was easy to measure where the sale was made. Either in the store or on-line. One of the most important numbers that a company must have on their radar is the mix of in store sales versus on-line sales. Where was the sale consummated? A conclusion that can be drawn now that we are a half a generation into this phenomenon is that this must be looked at as a hybrid sale. Half of the credit should go as an on-line sale and half of the credit should be as an in store sale. Consumers are doing their shopping, their comparisons on-line and then purchasing the product in the store.

Here is a great example. I was in the need of a hand truck to bring samples and demonstration equipment into a hospital. The hand truck that I had was damaged so it was time for a new one. I did not have the time to the visit both home improvement chains, I needed it that day, so ordering it on-line was not an issue. I remember saying to myself that I dreaded the notion of spending time walking around looking for a hand truck. Then an idea popped into my head. Why not check the websites of each chain to see what they had. I did, I actually went to both websites and cut my shopping time to seconds instead of an hour. Have you ever gone to a website and used the store locator feature? I did. I entered my zip code and the address and phone number of the local chain popped up. I called the phone number, gave them the item number and said I am on my way. The hand truck was waiting for me at the customer service cash register and I was in and out of the chain home improvement store in record time. It was the shortest time anyone has ever spent in the history of shopping at the chain! Who gets credit for the sale? The store or the website? It is an interesting debate. The shopping was done on-line but the transaction was completed in the store. This type of transaction can fall through the cracks and needs to be identified as a legitimate channel of distribution sandwiched in between the traditional in store purchase and fashionable on-line transaction.

All distribution options must be explored. Dual distribution channels or Multi- distribution channels must become part of the distribution landscape. What this has done to the vertical distribution channel is morph the vertical arrows down the traditional distribution channel to arrows that point in multiple directions.

All of this commotion regarding distribution has led to the elevation of the fourth "P" Place/Distribution. When you factor in the impact that global distribution, which has more complex distribution channels than domestic channels, it makes sense to recognize the power of distribution.

The answer to eliminating all of the stress associated with distribution is to follow the cliché of, "If you want something done you should do it yourself". Direct distribution or using a direct channel where you are the manufacturer and the conduit to the end user is a viable option.

Circumventing the traditional distribution channel became an option. A manufacturing hub for furniture in this country was the Carolinas. About thirty years ago the word got out that if you contacted a furniture manufacturer in the Carolinas with a model number of a furniture set, whether it was living room furniture, bedroom furniture or whatever room in your house that you wanted to furnish, the manufacturer would deliver the product DIRECTLY to your house. The price was so low that it made you think about going to the store and just call the manufacturer on the phone and place your furniture order direct from the manufacturer. This took off like wild fire. This became an enterprise. Entrepreneurs from New York City would rent their own trucks, drive to the Carolinas, fill their trucks with furniture, drive back to New York City and set up shop in the parking lot of a gas station on a weekend and peddle the furniture. This went on for years. Brilliant Marketing!

Non-Store Retailing

Another trend that bucks the traditional retail establishment is "Non-Store Retailing". My interpretation of non-store retailing is purchasing a product any way other than the traditional means of walking into a store and purchasing a product. This goes way beyond the trend of purchasing a product on-line off of a device. Non-store retailing is not a new phenomenon, it has just been elevated to new heights. Forever, one of the largest department store retailers would send out their paper catalog encouraging customers to buy products while sitting on their couch and ordering the product over the phone. Many retailers followed suit and the paper catalog business thrived for decades. It was an early form of non-store retailing.

There are so many examples of where a marketing idea was laughed at and became a humongous success. Some marketers bristled at the idea of a television network where the entire programming of the network was based on displaying and peddling products. You could shop from home, while watching television. Who would watch this type of television programming? Would you watch it as a television show? As a matter of fact consumers did. This network and a competitive one that was launched a few years later actually generating a rating, enough of a rating that these networks remained on television for a couple of decades!

This led to an expansion of the network to an entire program that was a commercial for a specific product. It was as simple as delivering "Information" about a product in the form of a "Commercial", hence the concept of the "Infomercial". Are infomercials effective? It brings us back to "If it did not work, they would not do it anymore". Someone even wrote a book on how to market your product utilizing infomercials. Millions of dollars of products have been sold through this channel. Everything from household cleaning products that make you say "Wow", to food products that help you "Chop" your vegetables with a "Slap", to exercise equipment that helps you "Master" your "Thighs" to self-help motivational videos that turned one entrepreneur into a billionaire.

I get a kick out of "Brilliant Marketing" and I love a few of the infomercial tricks. I love the counter that tells you how many items have been sold during this television show. I also love the counter that goes down in descending order alerting you how many items are left. There is always the belief to get the consumer to act now. It is the fundamental premise of Sales Promotion. Hurry up place your order! If you ever believe that it is a limited time offer, or that this is how many units have been sold, or that this is how many items that are left in stock, I have some swamp land in that I want to sell you! Brilliant Marketing!

The rule of thumb for a television commercial is thirty seconds. The infomercial model is a thirty minute model. When is prime time for infomercials? Off hours, the middle of the night, late nights and early mornings on the weekends? Why? This is the only time slot where you can justify the cost associated with the thirty minute commercial compared to the thirty second commercial. Of course it is all about "Bang for Your Buck". If you wanted to buy thirty minutes of prime time network television commercial time you could, which maximizes the reach, but it would come with an exorbitant price tag.

The vending machine business has exploded. Is the vending machine business a good business? Where can you make money by plugging in a machine, fill it with products, leave and return at your leisure to restock the inventory and collect your cash? Not a bad concept. When I think of the classic vending machine I think of vending machines that dispensed two kinds of products, tobacco and music. The old fashioned cigarette machine and juke box. Does anyone remember the diner "Juke Box"? You know the one that was at the individual table where you put some change in and you had to flip through the song selections with a dial on the side, playing your selection at you table? Explain that concept to a millennial! They have no idea what you are talking about.

I also get a kick out of some of the products that you can get out of a vending machine today, much more of a selection that goes beyond dispensing cigarettes and music.

The captive audience is the segment of non-store retailing that is growing like a weed. Why? The profit margin associated with the advent of the captive audience is off of the charts. The MSRP (Manufacturer's Suggested Retail Price) goes out the window because with a captive audience your pricing strategy can be MSRP Plus! MSRP Plus means that you can add a premium on top of the MSRP because you can. The consumer is a "Captive" consumer and has nowhere else to go. If you do not want to purchase the product, too bad, you are stuck and are at the mercy of the non-store retail channel.

Let's start with the airport. Our lives changed forever after September 11th, 2001. Forget about making a purchase on the plane itself. If you are nervous about your flight and think that an adult beverage will calm your nerves, you will pay anything for a shot that can calm you down. Traveling through an airport is now an event. There was a time when you could pull up to the curb at an airport terminal, jump out of the car, show your boarding pass, and be on the plane in a matter of minutes. Unless you are flying on a private plane, that practice has gone by the wayside. Now you have to arrive, sometimes hours, before your plane departs. How do you pass the time? Once you are cleared by security you have to wait for your plane to board, cannot walk out of the terminal, hence, you are captive.

The airport is capitalizing on your captivity. Many airports have gone through renovations, specifically to the areas of captivity. There was a time when the notion of "Airport Food" was reserved for last minute, last resort, consumption of food only because some food, albeit airport food, was a better option than no food at all. Oh has that changed! Have you taken a look at the food offerings in an airport lately? Of course you are surrounded by a myriad of food court fast food choices but it is the sit down restaurants that are popping up occupying space in airport terminals. Even high end restaurants such as steakhouses, which were never found within the confines of an airport.

The entire retail shopping experience has changed as well. Taking a stroll through an airport terminal is like taking a stroll through a mall today. The next time that you are walking through an airport close your eyes and forget that you are waiting for your flight and realize that you are walking through the mall waiting to board your plane.

What about the stadium, arena or theme park? Think of the profit margin associated with the price of a hot dog, adult beverage, bottle of water, or souvenir to commemorate your family activity. Try telling your kid that they cannot have that overpriced bottle of water as you wait on line at the theme park, or they cannot have that tee shirt being sold at the teeny bopper concert. They have got you and they know it! Captive audience at its best!

SECTION 5

The World Is A Smaller Place

This section illustrates the reasons why a domestic marketing strategy needs to be replaced by a global marketing vision

Chapter 13

The Importance of Developing
a Global Vision

Global Marketing

It is important today to develop a global marketing vision. A global strategy must be put in place today for the long term health of the organization. This was not the case in the past where a domestic strategy dominated the corporate landscape. Why a domestic strategy? It made sense. The formula for success included two main ingredients. A customer and their ability to pay for a product. The domestic market is an immense market with over three hundred million consumers, stretching three thousand miles in one direction and two thousand miles in the other direction. The domestic market also can afford your product with a robust per capita income. You need to have a strong presence in your backyard. The domestic backyard is a big one. All of your profit goals can be satisfied by serving the domestic market. That was the former direction.

Why should you have a global focus? Corporate America has made the shift and so should you. There was a time when the domestic approach ruled the day. If you looked at a company's mix of domestic sales versus global sales the percentage of domestic sales dwarfed the global sales. Global business was viewed as extra revenue, the cherry on the top of the cake. Today the mix of domestic versus global sales is swinging in the opposite direction. Every year that domestic dominance of the mix between domestic sales versus global sales has eroded as companies are progressing through these stages. Many companies today sell more of their product outside the United States than inside the United States. Here are a couple of examples. There is nothing more American than soda, specifically cola. There is more cola sold outside the United States than within the United States. The same is true for another famous American brand, adhesive strips. There are more adhesive strips sold globally than domestically.

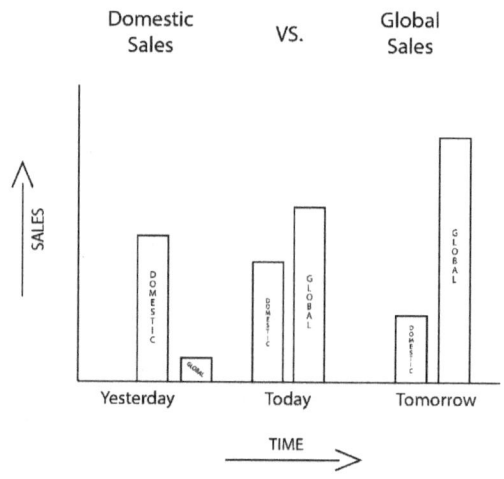

More proof of the need to be more global and less domestic is the academic focus on globalization. I tell my students all of the time "International" and "Foreign" is the old terminology, today use the word "Global" it makes you sound like you learned something in college. When I was an undergraduate student in the early 1980s "International Business" was a topic skimmed over in business courses, with only a few pages in business textbooks dedicated to how to conduct business outside of the domestic market. By the time I attended graduate school in the mid-1990s there were entire courses focusing on globalization. Today you can major in global business at any university in this country. That makes sense to me, why is that a smart decision? The companies are thinking that way and are looking for candidates with a global business background.

There is a progression of the growth of a product and a company. The same way that a product goes through a life cycle, so does a company. None of this happens overnight. Everything starts locally. A company is founded somewhere domestically. It made sense to develop a presence locally, in your backyard or home market. Let's use New York as the example. Over time things start to go well and you expand to the north and south and before you know it you are now a regional company. Business continues to expand and before you know it you are developing markets up and down the eastern seaboard. Eventually you develop markets from coast to coast and now you are a national company with business spread across the continental United States. The next phase is to start to export your product outside and now you are a global company with a domestic headquarters and customers outside of the United States.

That was the model. Can you start a global company in your basement, garage or attic? Yes, how? By utilizing the technology at your fingertips. Here is the misnomer. The true definition of a global company is having customers in more than one country. Utilizing the Internet and forming a partnership with a global distribution partner can make you a million bucks working out of your basement, garage or your attic! Your shipping partner can deliver a box anywhere on the planet as long as they have a physical address. Is it a good day in the life of your business when you have to move out of your basement, garage or attic? Of course it is, it means you are selling so much of your product that you need more space.

You wake up one day and realize that there is a tremendous amount of potential for business outside of the United States and the company evolves into a Multinational Corporation (MNC). Up until this point all operations were domestic. Once another physical operations unit pops up in another country, the company has become an MNC. The true definition of an MNC is significant operations in more than one country. Significant operations can be in the form of a factory, warehouse, distribution center, sales office or any physical structure located outside of the domestic market. Taking the next step is to become a Transnational company. Trans means across. Transnational means across nations. Some mammoth companies are already there, eventually most of the MNC's will become Transnational. Transnational means that you have significant operations that blanket the globe.

Every product starts as an idea, every company starts as an idea. Something is triggered in an entrepreneur's mind that spurs the desire to convert the idea into a product or a company. The success stories abound about an idea that was in somebody's head potentially forged in their basement, garage or their attic. It was local, it was the back yard. Everything starts locally. How do you start locally and become global? It is the essence of today's marketplace where you need to be more global and less domestic. Domestic means home. The traditional strategy focused on the domestic market. This made sense. The domestic market is a huge market. The domestic market, the backyard, was fruitful and bountiful.

I am not intimating that the soil has dried up here in the domestic market. I think I learned this somewhere in grammar school. Part of the history of agricultural success in the domestic market was that the soil here was so rich that you could plant your crops and not have the restrictions of space where the same crop dried up the soil over time, and there was so much soil that you could rotate your crops and not saturate the market. This was a tremendous competitive advantage because competing markets were just not as vast as the domestic geography, giving the domestic market a leg up on their competition.

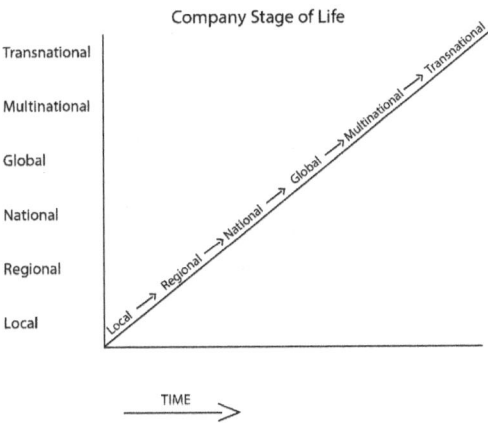

Company Stage of Life

Local

Everything has to start somewhere. The easiest and most economical and cost efficient model for success is to focus on your local market, your backyard. You have an encouraging story to tell, "We came up with an idea for a product, and we are local, your neighbor, located right in OUR backyard." This strategy made sense for so many reasons. You are right there, you speak the local language, you know how business is done locally, and you have mutual business connections with your local customers. It made sense.

Regional

Your product and your company starts to achieve some local achievement. A natural reaction is to expand to more of a regional market. Instead of focusing on a local market here in New York City, you want to cast your net to the next two largest regional markets, Philadelphia to the south and Boston to the north. You wake up and boom you are now a regional company with customers spread across the Northeast.

National

Before you know it you are coast to coast with your product, and now the question is which domestic markets are the right fit for the product. Chopping up the domestic market on a national basis can be complex and problematic. Do you focus on the top fifty markets domestically, or do you drill down where the domestic market can literally be carved into several hundred markets? This all fits into the overall Marketing Mix, where marketers are challenged daily by decisions like this.

Global

I can run into you in ten years and I say, "What are you up to? How is business?" Your response can be, "I am the CEO of a global company." This might impress me. Here is the delineation between the national company and the global company. A national company has customers only in their domestic backyard. Once a company starts to export their product in a box and ships it outside of the domestic market, BOOM, the company has made the progression into the global marketplace. The true definition of a global company is a company that has customers in more than one country.

You can be a CEO of a global company working out of your basement, garage or attic. Remember the true definition of the global company, and if you export your innovation via a box delivered by a global shipping partner, you are technically a global company, even living out of your parent's basement, garage or attic!

Multi-National Corporation

This is the most essential ingredient in the continuum of the progression from local to transnational. Why? The Multi-National stage of life is THE stage of life that the majority of companies are going through. If the company is not at the Multi-National stage, they want to be at the Multi National stage of life as a company. What confirms this are my observations of how Multi-National Corporations, or MNC's, if you will, are depicted on cable business news broadcasts. The term they use all the time is MNC this, and MNC that. How does this impact the MNC's, how are MNC's going to react to this, etc.?

Is the day that you have to move out of your basement, garage or attic a good day for your company? Of course it is! Why are you moving out? You are moving out because you have outgrown the basement, garage or attic. You start putting enough widgets in boxes and ship them out of the domestic market you wake up one day and say, "Hey, we are putting a lot of widgets into boxes and shipping them to this global market. Maybe we should go down there and figure out why?" You get to this global market and you realize that you are only scratching the surface of this opportunity, and make the decision to expand with significant operations in the new global market. The company just became an MNC.

The most beneficial experience of having me as your marketing professor are my lectures. The most difficult experience of me being your marketing professor are my exams. I say this to the students at the being of the course. They looked at me with bewilderment and ask for me to give them an example. True or false, all global companies are Multi-National Corporations? Let me ask it the other way, all Multi-National Corporations are global companies? Now that I have you confused you let me explain. All global companies are not Multi-National Corporations. They are not because the global company is headquartered in one domestic country but can have customers outside of the domestic market. All Multi-National Corporations ARE global companies. Why? Today you might be a Multi-National Corporation, but yesterday you were a global company.

Transnational Corporation

The final stage in the progression in the life of a company is a Transnational Corporation. The Multi-National stage is important to understand today because that is the stage that many companies are in right now. Where are they going down the road? What is the future of the Multi National Corporation? To become a Transnational Corporation. The mega oil, automobile, software, and social media companies, along with other industries, have Transnational players already in this space.

I attended a national sales meeting for the global leader in the healthcare industry a half a generation ago. One of the presenters had some fancy global title, Vice-President of Global Business Development, or something like that. His presentation was on what is the global vision for the company as we headed into the new millennium. Behind him was a flat map of the planet. As he started his slide presentation he identified, with a big red star, where the domestic headquarters was located, and referred to this as home. As he panned the globe he explained where on each continent the company had significant operations. A red dot began to appear on the map as he went from continent to continent. By the end of his presentation there were over one hundred and fifty red dots that blanketed the globe. That's Transnational! Across every market and every corner of the green earth!

The tipping point, and many companies have blown past the tipping point, is if greater than fifty percent of your sales are now global and less than fifty percent of your sales are domestic. Once this is achieved there is no turning back with the ultimate goal of becoming the Transnational Corporation.

It is very elementary to remember the neoteric vision regarding globalization. You need to be more global and less domestic. It is that simple! Get it in your head, more global and less domestic. Why?

This is the vision and direction of the prominent, lucrative, forward thinking companies who you want to align your vision and direction with.

Reasons For Globalization

Technology

Why has this changed? There are several reasons for the metamorphic shift in strategy. Technology is the driving force behind the increase in globalization. The world is a smaller place today. What does that mean? The globe is shrinking? No, the physical geography has not changed but the way we communicate globally has. It goes beyond just the Internet and when you include all of the toys at our disposal today including smart phones, tablets, laptops, videoconferencing, software and other devices it is clear that the technology today has enhanced communication and shrunk the globe. There was a time when you made a long distance phone call and the recipient on the other end sounded like they were far away. Forget about an international phone call. Today with smartphone technology the recipient of the long distance call sounds like they are around the corner!

A reason for the domestic focus was risk. The domestic market was safe. Everything was in the backyard, albeit a massive backyard. If you were experiencing an issue, it was a backyard issue. If you had a global issue it was not as easy to resolve. Global markets were risky. Fifty years ago if you put a million dollars of your product on a ship that sailed to the Far East you had no idea where your product was, did it get there, when did it get there, did it reach the proper market? All factors driving the risk of globalization through the roof. Technology has alleviated the risk. Think of the tracking technology that we have today. You ship out a box from your loading dock and are wondering where it is. Your distribution partner provides you with a tracking number and you can literally follow your product on its journey from your loading dock to the distribution channel member.

Trade Agreements

Globally, trade agreements, where countries agree to reduce barriers to trade, have been enacted with one goal in mind. To make it easier to trade between two countries. Specifically tariffs, or taxes imposed on imported products, have been lowered fostering an environment of global trade. While I understand the concept of trade agreements there are issues facing the United States market. Opening up the border for trade between the United States and Mexico, while on paper sounds enticing, has had a dramatic effect on manufacturing jobs in this country. Labor is the number one cost for a company. In a sluggish economy, companies look to cut costs wherever they can. By shifting manufacturing from the United States to Mexico can do wonders for a company's bottom line. Mexico is such an attractive trade partner because it is literally in the backyard of the domestic market. Not every company has shifted their manufacturing plants to Mexico but it has been a slow drip that after twenty years has placed a drain on the United States manufacturing base.

China is another manufacturing partner. The difference between China and Mexico is that while Mexico is in the backyard, China is still half way around the world. I think I learned this in the sixth grade. You need to have a favorable balance of trade, meaning if an economy exports more than it imports you have a favorable balance of trade. This is not the case with China where the United States has a negative trade balance with China surpassing five hundred billion dollars. That is a staggering figure and something has to change to reduce that deficit and create more of a fair trading marketplace.

Emerging Markets

There are two types of markets, established markets and emerging markets. An established market is where a company has a footprint in the marketplace. An emerging market is a market, for whatever reason, sometimes political, that needs to be penetrated. The United States is an established market, Western Europe is an established market. China and India are a couple of emerging markets.

Here is the issue with the emerging market. As mentioned earlier the formula for success includes having a customer and they must have the ability to pay for the product. There are multiple emerging markets globally, with huge populations. However many of these customers are located in third world countries and the per capita income of the average consumer is very low and they cannot afford the product. China has over one billion people, so does India. That is over two billion consumers in one corner of the world, almost one third of the entire global population.

The question is not should you go global, the question is where should you go global. Marketers must match the demand for their product with the associated emerging market. Blue jeans are a famous American product. For whatever reason the demand for American blue jeans in Russia is through the roof. Why? American blue jeans in Russia are a status symbol. While the demand is higher in Russia compared to the global demand, this has elevated the price of blue jeans, pricing out many of the everyday consumers. I am not saying that there is no demand for American blue jeans in South America, but the demand is higher in Russia, hence having a global strategy focusing on the emerging market of Russia makes sense.

One domestic industry that no question has to be more global and less domestic is the tobacco industry. The government prohibits the promotion of cigarettes in this country. Should Big Tobacco just fold up their tent and go home? No, they need to employ an aggressive global marketing campaign. Where is there a market for cigarettes globally? How about every market outside of the United States. Do consumers smoke cigarettes in Europe, The Middle East, South America and Asia? Yes to all. The difference between the blue jean analogies compared to the cigarette analogy is that cigarettes are an affordable product globally.

Where is the last frontier of emerging global markets? The continent of Africa. I would not run over there today. Africa has serious infrastructure issues that have begun to be resolved, and can take decades to complete. Think of your global marketing opportunities like a kitchen stove. Certain markets are on the front burner such as China and India and certain markets are placed on the back burner such as Africa and will be penetrated after the low hanging fruit is picked.

Need For Growth

The domestic market has become saturated, and I am not advocating abandoning the domestic market. This is where your bread is buttered, the domestic market keeps the lights on. Every company needs to grow. There is "Good Growth" and there is "Flat Growth". If the arrow of growth starts to flatten out this can become problematic and lead to issues including the stock price of a company beginning to plummet. How does a company avoid this flat growth? Enact a global marketing strategy that can be the fuel that leads to solid, "Good Growth". The global marketplace not only provides the opportunity for growth, it can be extremely profitable growth.

Good Growth vs. Flat Growth

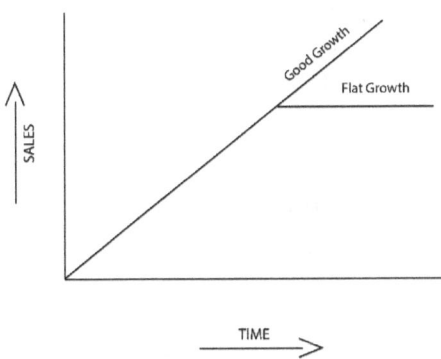

These are not the only reasons for globalization just a few. If you summarize the reasons for globalization, because of technology the world is a smaller place, trade agreements make it easier to trade between countries, there are emerging markets that need to be penetrated and you have to grow. It makes sense to me to be more global and less domestic with your marketing strategy.

Standardization versus Adaptation

An issue that must be resolved when making the decision to go global is what to do with your product. Do you keep your product the same or do you make changes to match the preferences of the local global market?

Standardization means that no changes are made to the product. Everything is the same from the product design, to the packaging, to the promotional message delivered to the consumer. Standardization is a successful strategy. When you are driving down the highway and you are hungry and you see a sign for the Golden Arches of a popular burger chain you know exactly what types of fries that they serve. They are the same whether you are in Texas, California, Florida or North Dakota. As opposed to a sign on the highway that says, "Joe's burgers and fries next exit." Who is Joe? Who knows what kind of fries you are going to get! Standardization is what built the success for that product. Everyone gets the same product. Another signal of standardization is when you open up a package and there are multiple languages either on the packaging or on the instructions. That means that that product can be delivered anywhere with no changes made to the product at all.

Adaptation means that some slight modifications have been made to the product to meet the local preferences of the consumer. How do you know what modification need to be made? That's what marketers get paid to do. Here is the problem, the modification can be so subtle that you do not recognize the need for the adaptation. How is beer served domestically? As cold as possible. How is beer served in Europe? Not the same way that it is served here, closer to room temperature than as cold as possible. What if the domestic beer tastes great when it is as cold as possible and you sell millions of dollars of product domestically? The marketer makes the decision to go global and employ a standardization strategy. Only to find out that the product is a dog in Europe because of the temperature of the product. Temperature? How are you supposed to know that!

The mistakes happen when the marketer decides to keep everything the same when they should have tweaked the product offering, and when they tweak the product instead of just leaving it alone. Think globally but act locally!

Cultural Differences

While a positive picture for global marketing has been painted, there are some roadblocks, issues and concerns that must be addressed. Why and when does globalization fail? The biggest culprit are the cultural differences between the domestic market and the new found global market. There are tastes, preferences and local customs that must be identified when attempting to penetrate the global market. Language, or the translation of language from English to the foreign global language can often cause disconnect between the interpretation of what a product is in the domestic market compared to how the product maybe perceived in the global market.

The key to a smooth, seamless transition into the global marketplace is to recognize the potential cultural differences and engage into a relationship with a local individual or organization who can explain the cultural differences to the domestic marketer. A joint venture is the solution.

Globalization is a commitment. Do you really want to be a global player or just a bit player in the global marketplace? It is all about risk. What type of risk do you want to take? The domestic market is safe, the global market is precarious. The best example is you are standing in front of a body of water. Do you dip your toes in the shallow end, slowing wading into the water, or do you dive into the deep end of the water? There is a continuum of risk that illustrates a company's commitment to globalization.

Exporting

Exporting your product is the safest way to enter the global marketplace. It is the shallow end of the pool, dipping your toes in the global water. It is the most nimble of globalization alternatives and the shifting of a global market strategy can easily be achieved. Simply put your product in a box and ship it from the domestic market to the global market utilizing a global distribution partner. The global distribution partner can deliver that box anywhere on the planet. Where is the risk? What is the worst scenario? Your box gets lost? That is why there are tracking numbers and insurance.

Licensing

Licensing is a legal agreement where the owner of a patent, trademark or any other form of intellectual property allows another firm to "borrow" their idea for a fee. The advantage is that there is minimal risk with the licensing agreement, you are simply handing off your intellectual property to someone else who has all of the day to day responsibilities of marketing the product.

Contract Manufacturing

As mentioned earlier I grew up in the garment business. Working in a factory. We were the manufacturer of women's coats. We would receive contracts from retailers to manufacture their line of coats. That is exactly the same thing as Contract Manufacturing when you consider the global market. The only difference was that our factory was a domestic factory, where today it is a popular decision to find a manufacturer abroad who can be your partner. The advantage of Contract Manufacturing is that you do not have to make the investment or commitment that is required with Direct Foreign Investment.

Joint Venture

Establishing a Joint Venture with a global distribution partner is an effective way to avoid the pitfalls and mistakes associated with the penetration of the new market. The risk associated with forming a Joint Venture is moderate but essential. A Joint Venture comes in many formats. It can be a loose affiliation with an agent in the global market where they are paid a commission on all sales into the new market, a consulting agreement between the two parties, or even the most serious relationship where the global partner is hired as a direct, full time employee of the previously domestic and now gone global company.

The importance of the Joint Venture cannot be underestimated. Remember the domestic company is new to the global market. The domestic partner is a foreigner in the new global market place. The newly formed Joint Venture partner is not a foreigner, as a matter of fact the Joint Venture partner is looked at as a domestic partner in the eyes of the global customer. The Joint Venture partner is the tour guide, it is their country, they know the customs, they know who to see, they know how products are distributed, and they know the lay of the land.

Direct Foreign Investment

Now you are talking risk. Direct Foreign Investment is the most serious commitment in the globalization continuum. The deepest end of the pool, with no flotation device. Direct Foreign Investment involves the construction of a factory or other significant operations with a long-term plan to remain in that global market. Once this commitment is made it is problematic to change your mind and shift to another global market.

Commitment to Globalization

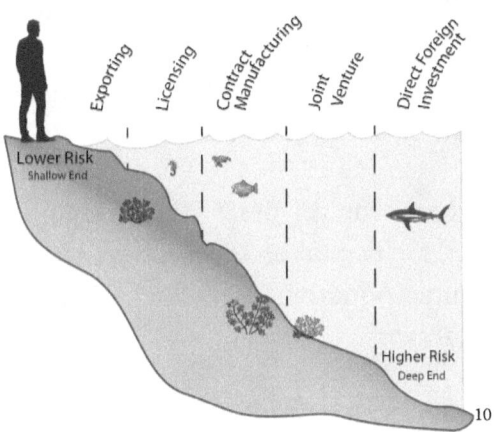

T.C. Chen

I have an incredible anecdote to share with you that ties in both technology and cultural differences with regards to globalization. When I made the decision to shift the direction of my career from

---

[10] Lamb, C., Hair, J., & McDaniel, C. (2006). Essentials of Marketing. 5th Edition, p. 96.

selling to teaching I needed to build a teaching resume. I would go anywhere to teach, and I did not have a concern about compensation, it was all about building the resume. It was the summer time in the late 1990s. I was off for the summer. The phone rang. On the other end a woman said, "Is this Professor Barchitta? I said yes it is. Who is this?" She introduced herself as the exchange program coordinator for a university in the North East. She said, "Would you like to go and teach Marketing in Taiwan?" I was silent, the first thing I said to myself was where Taiwan is? I knew it was in Asia. The second thing that I said to myself was, why would I go and teach in Taiwan? Then she told me how much they would pay me to go to Taiwan to teach, and I said, "When do I leave?" I was on a plane within a week! It was a fifteen day teaching assignment, but it was something that would look great on a resume.

In preparing for the assignment I asked a few questions, "I do not speak Chinese." Their response was, "That is why we want you, we want you to teach American business in English, forcing the students to understand and comprehend English, we do not want a professor teaching American business in Chinese."

I then asked, "Where would I live?" Their response was, "You will be living in Taipei, the capital of Taiwan, you are from New York, it is like living in Times Square in New York City, you can walk from your hotel to the university."

I had the typical American attitude as it applies to globalization. I was born and raised in New York, I have walked around Times Square my whole life. If you can make it here you can make it anywhere.

The first issue was the flight, more than twenty plus hours on an airplane, awful! I am traveling alone. I finally get there and had the worst case of jet lag in history that lasted for the entire trip. Not only is Asia half way around the world it is an exact twelve hour time difference, so midnight Eastern Standard Time is noon in Asia, my body never made the time zone adjustment. I am not feeling great. I make it through the airport towards my hotel and I realize that nobody speaks English, no one! I just assumed everybody spoke English! None of the street signs were in English, none of the marquees where in English. If you get lost in New York City at least you can look up at a street sign to see where you are and where you have to go. "I am on thirty-fourth street and second avenue and I have to go to forty-eighth street and fifth avenue." You can easily navigate that. Not if you cannot read the street signs!

Language and the translation of language is a major issue when making the transition into a new global market. I speak English, I assumed that everyone speaks English. What I did not realize until I arrived in Taiwan that literally a handful of people speak and understand English. Communicating with the locals became an issue. Another example of American arrogance.

The food? Are you kidding? Another example of American arrogance when going global. New York City has impeccable Asian food. I love beef with broccoli, egg rolls, wonton soup and of course fortune cookies. I just assumed that if Asian food was great in New York, of course it had to be great in Asia. Big mistake! To say that initially the food was pathetic is being polite. I could not read a menu, everything was in Chinese.

I walked into a restaurant and was handed a menu. I could not read a word off of the menu but there were pictures next to the words. I eat fish. I eat seafood. How bad could it be? Taiwan is an island off of the coast of mainland China, the fish must be fresh. I pointed to the picture of a fish on the menu, the waiter said, "Feesh", and he motioned with his hand to follow him to the front of the restaurant. He pointed to a large fish tank, and said again, "Feesh". I nodded my head, he scoops out the ugliest fish that I had ever seen in my life, stabs it and puts it on a platter. That was my dinner that night. Not exactly lobster Fra Diavolo!

As you can see my first few days did not go well, I felt awful, could not speak to anyone, could not read anything, and the food was an abomination. I remember going back to my hotel room, looking in the mirror, and wondering, "Why did I make the wonderful decision to teach Marketing in Taiwan?"

The next day all of this changed. It was the first day of classes. I was teaching one Marketing 101 course and one Management 101 course to around thirty graduate school students. Many of them had careers in business. One third of the room spoke no English at all, one third of the room spoke a few words of English, and one third of the room spoke enough English that we could conduct a conversation. Finally someone to talk to!

There was a student in the back of the room, who was older than me, I was in my early thirties and he was pushing forty. Every time that I made a point during class he would raise his hand with a question, "Can you explain that Professor?" By the time I was finished explaining my point his hand was raised again with another question.

What I did not know until after the first day of classes was that this student, Tai Chi Chen, who wanted to be called T.C., was a very successful businessman in Taiwan. His family was in the import/export business. His family made a fortune in the bowling alley business in Taiwan. Can you imagine that, the bowling business, it sounds so 1970s! Why the barrage of questions? I was the first American businessman that T.C. had ever met. He wanted to know everything about American business. He wanted to pick my brain all day to tell him how business is done in America.

He must have liked what he heard the first day and approached me after class and asked me if he could he take me to dinner. I said to myself, "Dinner, maybe he knows a good place to go to?" T.C. pulls up in his car, let me set the scene, Taipei is the capital city of Taiwan, like many majors cities in Asia it is filled with people. People everywhere, too many people on the streets. People either walked where they had to go, peddled a bicycle, drove a scooter or navigated the tiny streets in a very tiny car. Not T.C. Chen, he pulls up in the biggest European sports car, which starts with a "B" and ends with a "W". Jet black, it looked like a limousine. I remember saying to myself, "This guy is loaded, I am hanging out with him!"

Here is the point, once I made the friend on the other side, everything about the experience started to change for the better, T.C knew where to eat, and knew where not to eat. T.C. knew where to go and where not to go. It was as if I had my own private tour guide. That is the key to solving the issue of cultural differences when you decide to go global. Hang out with the locals, it is their country, it is their market, they can pave the way towards success.

T.C. was obsessed with golf. He belonged to multiple country clubs in Taiwan. Most of my time outside of the classroom for the remainder of the trip was spent with him. He continued to pump me for information about American business whether we were in class or on the golf course. It was an insult to him for me to reach into my pocket and pay for anything, he looked at it as the information that I was providing to him was worth every penny.

T.C. scheduled a tee time to play golf on a certain day, I said, "I can play but I have to be back to my hotel room by seven PM because I have to call my family." Yes, I had a cell phone, but forget about service half way around the world twenty years ago. Yes, I had email access but the translation of the emails never went through so for the most part the only communication that I had back home was the land line phone in my hotel. I could not call every day, but had a schedule set up to call a certain time every couple of days. Remember the twelve hour time zone change.

You know how it is when you play golf, the scenery is beautiful, the weather is beautiful, you are having fun and the time can slip by.

We were having such a good time that I forgot that I had to make the phone call back home. I realized this after dinner while we were riding in T.C.'s car that I missed the call. He saw the sadness in my face and I explained the situation to him. He said, do not worry we will call New York right now from my car. He pushed a button and a mounted car phone popped up. Ask a millennial what that is! I said, "There is no way that a phone call from that car phone is going to go through half way around the world!" T.C. said, "We have excellent cellular phone technology in Taiwan." He was right! He dialed the phone once, the call went through, I spoke with my family, and all was right with the world. The point of this circles back to the most important reason for globalization, technology. Once I was able to speak with my family it did not seem as if I was literally half way around the world, it felt like I was around the block!

T.C. was so obsessed with golf that it became his passion. He wanted everyone to play golf. He realized a gap in the desire for someone to play golf and their ability to play golf. He wanted to help people become comfortable playing golf. He wanted to train people to play golf. T.C. invented a golf training club and soft golf ball used to teach people how to hit a golf ball. The club head was bigger, almost looking like the head of a small tennis racket at the end of a golf club. The ball was made of a unique material that you have never seen. There was nothing like it on the market in the United States. T.C. wanted me to open the market in the United States for these products. For whatever reason, I passed on the opportunity, life got in the way and T.C. Chen's great golf invention never made it to the American market.

Marketing Conclusions

Wow, what a lot of information, a lot of insight, all over the map. That was a big purpose of the book, to open your mind and expose you to how massive the umbrella of what marketing is. I hope that I accomplished that. I said that I am on a crusade. It goes back to the one word definition of Marketing: AWARENESS. A goal was to emphasize the importance of awareness and then chronicle and document how many components of marketing are somehow tied to awareness. The term "Mix" was also peppered all over this book with the goal of emphasizing how important it is for marketers to figure out the right mix when making marketing decisions. Those are just two of the takeaways that I hope you may now have, and a better understanding of what BRILLIANT MARKETING is all about!

At the beginning and at the end of every sales presentation that I make, the first thing and the last thing that I do is thank the customer for taking the time out of their busy day to meet with me. That is what I am saying to you as well. A sincere thanks for taking the time out of your day and your life to read this book!

About Barchitta Consulting Inc.

Barchitta Consulting Inc. is a management consulting firm that specializes in assisting corporations maximize their sales and marketing objectives. They can customize a training curriculum to meet the needs of your sales department. Seminar topics include:

-Motivational Speaking

-Sales Training

-Managing Customer Relationships

-Understanding the Sales Process

-Shortening the Sales Cycle

-Why Customers Buy

-Time Management

Visit them on the web at: www.barchittaconsulting.com

Elsevier
ESCVS Abstracts • Sept 1996
ISSN 0967–2109

Cardiovascular Surgery

Official Journal of The International Society for Cardiovascular Surgery

45th International Congress
of the European Society
for Cardiovascular Surgery

September 15–18, 1996

Venice, Italy

Abstracts

bosis, secondary to venous intimal hyperplasia, generally occurs by the third month. Symptomatic "steal" was encountered in four patients, with one responding to graft narrowing and one requiring graft excision. For these ESRD patients in whom an autogenous fistula is not possible, PTFE conduits are a suitable vascular access site.

V6-7
Tapered Brachial Semi-loop for Ischemic Shunt Complications
P.M. KASPRZAK and H. RENNER, Regensburg, Germany

In twelve patients with hand and finger ischemia due to steal with standard brachial AV-fistula, a high brachial semi-loop with tapered PTFE graft was implanted in order to avoid steal and maintain shunt.

Eleven patients were diabetics and all suffered because of a high peripheral resistance. They were seven women and five men in a mean age of 65.2 years. No patient included showed an oversized vascular anastomosis or a high flow situation in which a banding operation would have been indicated.

The proximal anastomosis was carried out with subclavian/axillary artery and the distal one with already arterialized basilic vein proximally to the elbow. A 4–7 or 5–7 tapered PTFE graft was used. It was possible to reduce or avoid steal symptoms and maintain vascular access-side in 11 patients, due to more proximal anastomosis (non-sclerotic artery of greater diameter) and reduced inflow. In three patients already necrotic fingers had to be amputated, but no major amputation was indicated. During follow-up graft thrombectomy was carried out in four patients due to reocclusion. One patient developed anastomotic aneurysm and another one infected. In one additional patient a redo-operation was carried out after 14 months due to restenosis. Primary patency totalled 58% after three years.

Tapered brachial semi-loop in patients suffering from a high peripheral vascular resistance and distal ischemia after brachial shunt can prevent or diminish vascular complications due to steal and maintain vascular access.

V6-8
Effective Thromboembolic Prophylaxis with Gradient Sequential Compression Pump for Total Hip/Knee Replacement
F.A. ARIOSTA, N.E. HAYEK, C.M. BOHRMAN, D.A. DRUCKER, A. KOPATSIS, P.J. DINEEN, M.A. FIORILLO, A.C. CERNAIANU and R.K. SPENCE, New York, USA

This study assessed the efficacy of a noninvasive gradient sequential compression pump in eliminating/reducing new thromboembolic events (DVT and PE) in 165 adult patients undergoing elective total knee and hip replacement, over a 12 month period. Group I (79 patients) were treated with the JOBST System 2500. Group II (86) were treated with the Kendall compression stocking. All patients received coumadin pre- (10 mg) and postoperatively.

Table 1. Overall characteristics

Variable	Group I (n = 79)	Group II (n = 86)	Significance
Age (years)	69 ± 12	68 ± 10	0.540
Length of stay (days)	4.6 ± 1.5	5.4 ± 2.9	0.038
New thromboembolic events	0	8 (9.3%)	0.015

There was a statistically significant difference between the groups with regard to the length of stay ($4.6 ± 1.5$ vs. $5.4 ± 2.9$ days, $p < 0.05$). The same trend applied when patients were subdivided by the category for age 40–59 and age 60–70. In age category > 70, there was no statistically significant difference in age, length of stay and length of surgery (Table 2).

Table 2. Characteristics by age group

Age group	Age	Length of stay	Length of surgery	New thrombo-embolic events
40–59				
Group I (n = 9)	49 ± 6	5.4 ± 1.7	133 ± 44*	0
Group II (n = 10)	51 ± 5	6.2 ± 6.4	230 ± 126	1 (10%)
60–70				
Group I (n = 29)	67 ± 3	4.4 ± 1.5*	143 ± 61*	0
Group II (n = 38)	66 ± 4	5.3 ± 1.9	187 ± 111	1 (2.6%)
> 70				
Group I (n = 39)	78 ± 6	4.6 ± 1.6	153 ± 74	0
Group II (n = 37)	77 ± 3	5.1 ± 2.2	160 ± 72	6 (16.2%)

*Statistically significant, $p < 0.05$.

Group II had 8 new cases of DVT (7 hip and 1 knee) documented by duplex scanning (zero vs. 9.3%). The overall incidence was 4.8%. The majority of new DVT (6 of 8) was in patients over the age of 70.

The use of the Jobst sequential compression pump as an adjuvant in prevention of new thromboembolic events post total knee/hip replacement has made a significant impact in the outcome by completely eliminating the development of new DVT or PE.

Final Report

Retrospective Data Collection and Analysis on the Incidence of DVT and
PE in Patients Undergoing Total Knee/Hip Replacement Treated with
Anticoagulation and the JOBST System 2500

Purpose

This study assessed the efficacy of the JOBST System 2500 gradient sequential
compression pump in eliminating/reducing new thromboembolic events (deep
vein thrombosis and pulmonary embolism) in patients undergoing major elective
orthopedic surgery.

Methods

This is a retrospective chart review of 165 consecutive adult patients undergoing
elective knee or hip replacement over a 12 month period at Staten Island
University Hospital, Staten Island, NY.

Results

The overall characteristics are described in Table 1. Seventy-nine patients
(Group I) were treated with postoperative anticoagulation and the JOBST
System 2500. Eighty-six patients (Group II) were treated with anticoagulation
(Cumadin) and the Kendall compression stocking. All patients receive 10 mg
Cumadin preoperatively. The mean age for the entire group was 68.9 ± 10.6
years (34-90 years range). The length of stay for the entire group was 5.0 ± 2.3
days (1-24 days range). The length of surgery was 164 ± 86 minutes (75-576
minutes range).

There was a statistical significant difference between the groups with regard to
the length of stay (4.6 ± 1.5 vs. 5.4 ± 2.9 days, $p < 0.05$), and the length of surgery
(146 ± 65 vs. 180 ± 99 min). There was no statistical significant difference
between the two groups with regard to age (69.4 ± 11 vs. 68.4 ± 10, $p > .05$) and the
hospital length of stay. The same trend applied for when patients in the two
groups were subdivided by age category. At least for age category 1 (40-59)
years) and age category 2 (60-70). In age category 3 (>70), there was no
statistical significant difference in age, length of stay, and length of surgery.
(Table 2)

Group I treated with the JOBST System had no new thromboembolic event observed postoperatively. Group II (no JOBST System used) presented with 8 new cases of DVT all documented by duplex scanning. The incidence of new DVT for Group I was zero vs. 9.3% for Group II. The overall incidence was 4.8%. The incidence of new thrombolic events was highly statistically significant (chi-square test). The majority of new DVT (6 of 8) were present in patients over the age of 70.

Conclusion

In our series, the use of the JOBST System 2500 as an adjuvant in prevention of new thromboembolic events post total knee/hip replacement has made a statistical significant impact in the outcome by eliminating completely the development of new DVT or PE.

Table 1. Overall Characteristics

Variable	Group I (n=79)	Group II (n=86)	Significance
Age (years)	69±12	68±10	0.540
Length of Stay (days)	4.6±1.5	5.4±2.9	0.038
Length of Surgery (min)	146±65	180±99	0.010
New Thromboembolic Events	0	8(9.3%)	0.015

Table 2. Characteristics By Age Group

Age Group	Age	Length of Stay	Length of Surgery	New Thromboembolic Events
40-59				
Group I (n=9)	49±8	5.4±1.7	133±44*	0
Group II (n=10)	51±5	6.2±6.4	230±126	1 (10%)
60-70				
Group I (n=29)	67±3	4.4±1.5*	143±61*	0
Group II (n=38)	66±4	5.3±1.9	167±111	1(2.6%)
>70				
Group I (n=39)	78±6	4.6±1.6	153±74	0
Group II (n=37)	77±3	5.1±2.2	160±72	6 (16.2%)

*Statistical Significant, $p < 0.05$

Endnotes

....

PAGE 3

Dominici, G., (2009). From Marketing Mix to E-Marketing Mix: A Literature Overview and Classification. International Journal of Business and Management, 4(9) p.17-24.

PAGE 4

McCarthy, E.J. (1960). Basic Marketing: A Managerial Approach. Irwin Publishing.

PAGE 21

Top 30 Designated Market Areas (DMAs) listed by the 2018-19 Nielsen ranks.

https://en.wikipedia.org/wiki/List_of_television_stations_in_ North_America_by_media_market

PAGE 27

Robertson, T., (1967). The process of innovation and the diffusion of innovation. Journal of Marketing. 31(1) p.14-19.

PAGE 47

Ariosta, F., et al, (1996). Effective Thromboembolic Prophylaxis with Gradient Sequential Compression Pump for Total Hip/Knee Replacement. Cardiovascular Surgery.

PAGE 64

Reference of Sunshine Act

https://www.google.com/url?sa=t&rct=j&q=&esrc=s&source=web&cd=15&cad=rja&uact=8&ved=2ahUKEwjG16GJ1KneAhUxn-AKHcR7B4oQFjAOegQIABAC&url=https%3A%2F%2Fwww.pharma.us.novartis.com%2Fsites%2Fwww.pharma.us.novartis.com%2Ffiles%2Fsunshine-faq.pdf&usg=AOvVaw1aigXIth3pdbBtsVENWfmq

PAGE 79

Windrum, P., & Birchenhall, C., (1998). Is Product Life Cycle Theory a special case? Dominant designs and the emergence of market niches. Structural Change and Economic Dynamics, 9(1) p.109-134.

PAGE 89

Day, G., (1977). The product portfolio approach to marketing strategy formulation has gained wide acceptance among managers of diversified companies. Journal of Marketing. 41(2) p,29-38.

PAGE 95

Boone, L., & Kurtz, D., (1995). Contemporary Marketing. 8 p.403.

PAGE 261

Lamb, C., Hair, J., & McDaniel, C. (2006). Essentials of Marketing. 5th Edition, p. 96.

www.ingramcontent.com/pod-product-compliance
Lightning Source LLC
Chambersburg PA
CBHW020731180526
45163CB00001B/194